PETER ABAILARD

PETER ABAILARD

by

J. G. SIKES, M.A.

With a Preface

by

THE REVEREND
A. NAIRNE, D.D.

NEW YORK
RUSSELL & RUSSELL · INC
1965

FIRST PUBLISHED IN 1932
REISSUED, 1965, BY RUSSELL & RUSSELL, INC.
BY ARRANGEMENT WITH CAMBRIDGE UNIVERSITY PRESS
L. C. CATALOG CARD NO: 65-19691
PRINTED IN THE UNITED STATES OF AMERICA

21736

CONTENTS

Preface BY DR NAIRNE   *page* vij

Author's Note   ix

Introduction   xi

Abbreviations   xvii

Chapter
  I. Abailard's career to the Council of Sens   1

 II. Faith and Reason   31

> I. Preliminaries—Abailard as an apologist—his intel-
> lectualism—Bernard's voluntarist idea of faith—Abailard's
> definition of faith—his theory of inspiration—his attitude
> towards the Bible and the Fathers.
>
> II. His use of dialectic—the changed emphasis of the
> *Introductio*—validity of logic—influence of earlier writers
> —"faith for which human reason gives proof has no
> merit"—restrictions upon the use of logic—his attack
> on Cornificius—summary.

III. His use of pre-Christian writers   61

> His object in quoting these writers—the Old Testament—
> propriety of reading the classics—the trinities in Hermes
> and Plato—the World-Soul—comparison with Bernard
> Sylvester—Virgil—How did these thinkers attain to
> Christian truth?—their moral perfection—Natural Law—
> comparison with Aquinas.

IV. The *Sic et Non*   76

> A description of the book's contents—its method—how
> contradictions may be harmonized—the use of dialectic—
> Abailard's aim—not the basis of a positive theological
> system—sources of the method.

 V. Abailard's logical theories   88

Chapter

VI. Abailard's doctrine of God and of
Creation   *page* 113

I. Proofs of God's existence—the *Summum Bonum*—
divine omnipotence—God cannot do otherwise than he
does—divine immutability—God's providence and prescience—contemporary criticism of Abailard's views—
summary.

II. Abailard's account of the six days of creation.

VII. The Trinity and the Person of Christ   145

I. General remarks—Roscelin—Gilbert Porrée—identity
and dissimilarity—the divine properties and attributes—
the copper seal—the eternal Generation—the Double
Procession—general estimate.

II. Christology—comparison with St Bernard—the Word
made flesh—the Incarnation—Christ unable to sin—his
suffering and volition.

VIII. His ethical theories, and the doctrine of
the Atonement   179

I. Views of St Augustine, Anselm, and Bernard on wrongdoing and Original Sin—sin as contempt for God, not evil
will—sin and ignorance—venial sins—punishment—
earlier views of confession—Abailard on confession—the
doctrine of the Keys.

II. Original Sin—*poena peccati* not *culpa*—necessity of grace.

III. The Atonement—earlier views—exemplarism—
Christ as the Mediator between man and God—number
and doctrine of the sacraments.

IX. The Council of Sens and after   219

Conclusion   248

Appendix

I. The chronology of Abailard's writings   258

II. The Aristotelian translations known to
Abailard   272

Short Bibliography   276

Index   278

PREFACE

BY DR NAIRNE

AMONG the cross-currents in which we are drawn hither and thither to-day a fresh interest in the Middle Ages is one. Perhaps the new science, which shifts the mind of man from the centre of thought and restores the dominance of a mysterious environment, is in part the cause. Anyhow, so it is. We tend to fancy ourselves neo-mediaevalists. But we tend to fancy and are too easily mistaken in our sympathy. The mind of the Middle Ages was after all so different from our own. Athens and the Rome of Cicero are of nearer kin. We are still men of the Renascence, but disturbed by the influx of a new renascence. Here is the opportunity of Mr Sikes' book on Abailard, for which he asks this preface. The request is welcome as a pledge of friendship which I very affectionately value: it does not mean that I have the least competence to form a critical estimate of his work. Still, every one who spends his days with books can recognize scholarship even in an alien craft, and the signs of scholarship are visible on all these pages. The full documentation of every statement, with frequent quotation from originals, brings a sense of security, and the reader finds that he is in touch with bygone times, and is being weaned from fanciful mediaevalism. It is also evident that Mr Sikes knows all the latest opinions and discoveries about Abailard: the real Abailard is "documented" unmistakably. That does not make his person and character clear, but it does lift him away from the haze of romance and of hasty orientation in the scheme of philosophy. Plainly quietly and with firm line the story of Abailard's life is told. The episodic part of his relation with Héloise falls into right perspective: the continuous bond of intellect faith and goodness develops by careful delineation. Nothing creates more confidence in Mr Sikes' trustworthiness than his refusal at the end to round off Abailard's character. He discusses it but confesses that contemporary judgements are lacking for complete modern definition. His own and most valuable point of certainty is that "he was a great ethical thinker, and his preoccupation with ethics is basic to his doctrinal views". That is the outcome of the careful, and again, judiciously documented study of his written works. No one need read this book who will not concentrate attention on those, not easy, chapters. But with attention the plainest man may follow their argument. They are part and parcel of a narrative which, just because of its unfanciful restraint, sets Abailard among the great and small men of his time not as actor on a stage but as realized flesh and blood and intellect, lovable, growing in goodness, pioneer but neither solitary nor rebel, confident in logic and his own supremacy therein but more certain still of the catholic faith.

One enlargement might have been welcome, a whole chapter on Abailard and Mediaeval Latin Verse. But Mr Sikes is an artist and his plan is complete in itself. He has, I think, done what is so difficult for a young author, for a dilettante impossible, he has put his picture into the paper.

ALEXANDER NAIRNE

AUTHOR'S NOTE

SEVEN years ago, while studying St Bernard under the direction of Dr Coulton, I looked for some biography of Abailard which would incorporate the recent work of modern scholarship. No single volume was available except the writings of Deutsch. Excellent though these are, much research and criticism has been done since their appearance. Dr Geyer has edited the *Logica 'Ingredientibus'*, which gives a fuller account of Abailard's logical theories, while only last year Ruf and Grabmann published a new fragment of his *Apologia* to St Bernard. Abailard's theological writings, however, still await an editor, and it is to be hoped that in more settled conditions the appearance of a critical text will be possible. But in the meantime there seemed to be room for a new study of Abailard's life and thought. In preparing this I have attempted to trace wherever it seemed possible the sources of his ideas, and to compare these with those of his contemporaries, especially with the theological standpoint of St Bernard.

My debt to contemporary scholars will, I hope, be apparent from my references. Every student of the twelfth century must owe much to the careful work of Dr Grabmann in Germany and of Dr Poole and Dr Webb in England. Dr Badcock of this college has been ungrudging in his advice and criticism, and I wish to thank him for his pains. Dr Jenkins and Professor Whitney have kindly read the typescript, and I have profited greatly from their suggestions. An unknown reader for the Cambridge Press has afforded me much useful help. I wish to thank the authorities at the British Museum Reading Room and of the Chapter Library, Canterbury, for according me many privileges. My best thanks are due to Dr Nairne for his encouragement and for consenting to introduce the book, and to my father for his aid in the preparation of the book and in the correction of the proofs. I owe a great debt to the Syndics of the University Press for undertaking the publication of the work, and to their staff for their great skill in executing it. It remains to add the usual—but necessary—disclaimer that the author is solely responsible for the statements that his book contains, but if he has made Abailard and his thought clearer to his readers, he hopes that the kindness of those scholars who have helped him will be repaid.

J. G. S.

CANTERBURY
December 5th, 1931

INTRODUCTION

BEFORE we can understand the thought of Peter Abailard, we must have some knowledge of the character of mediaeval Scholasticism and of its history prior to the opening of our author's career. Unfortunately, like so many other similar terms, Scholasticism is difficult to define and, although many attempts have been made, for one reason or another they have proved unsatisfactory.

The tenets held by mediaeval philosophers were so different that it appears best to us to define Scholasticism—at least in so far as its mediaeval form is concerned—by its aims and method rather than by the theories held by its chief exponents. The aim of the mediaeval scholastic may be said to have been three-fold.[1] He sought to defend the traditional doctrines of the church against heretics, both when they taught doctrines hostile to the Creeds, as did Roscelin, and when, like the Averroists of the thirteenth century, they held theories—such as those of the eternity of matter—which were inconsistent with ecclesiastical dogma. The establishment of a system of theology, which was to be both articulated and unified, was the second aim which the scholastic sought to realize. To accomplish this, he found it necessary to harmonize those statements in the pages of authority which seemed to contradict one another. Lastly, the scholastic sought to build up a system of philosophy which could stand by itself and could support the theological system which he aimed at establishing. Thus, each single doctrine was to be bound inseparably to the others, since all were to be welded into one whole, while, in addition, philosophy was to sustain the dogmatic teaching of the church.

The method employed by the scholastic was that of logic. Inherited from the schools of Greece and Rome, logic was an instrument well fitted to the needs of the mediaeval thinker;

1 Cf. Grabmann, I. p. 39.

the ascension from syllogism to syllogism corresponded to the legal hierarchy of feudalism, the social system under which he lived. The mediaeval scholar did not set out to discover new worlds. For him knowledge was buried in the pages of authoritative writers, whence it had to be quarried by industrious research. Rarely did the philosopher of the Middle Ages attempt experimental science. Knowledge was deductive, entailing a close study of texts and the classification of their contents. Dialectic required a minute investigation into the use of words; its office was that of disengaging falsehood from the truth. Hence, it enabled the scholastic to unravel the meaning of his texts as well as to disprove the erroneous conclusions drawn from them by his opponents. From this description of his aims the chief problem which confronted the scholastic will be apparent. It was not, as many writers once thought, the question of the nature of universals. Whether in theology or in metaphysics, the main problem which every thinker had to face was that of the proper relationship which ought to exist between reason and faith. On the assumption that human reason could discuss the problems of theology—and this was not granted by the opponents of Scholasticism—had logic the right to override the conclusions of authority, or must it be content with the task of explaining the teaching of Revelation? And so, any account of the opinions held by a mediaeval scholastic must be prefaced by a description of the answer which he gave to this particular problem.

To assign a date for the beginning of Scholasticism is impossible. Its method is traceable in the writings of the early Fathers, although the development of theology as a science through the aid of Aristotelian logic and philosophy was peculiar to the West. The period, however, up to and including the age of the Carolingians was one of preparation. Every mediaeval writer quoted St Augustine, to whom he went for authoritative discussions of many important theological and philosophical points and for his knowledge of classical thought. Indeed, to a large extent the attention of the mediaeval theologian was directed to the task of elaborating the theology of Augustine, checking or emending it by the light of Aristotelian thought. The various books of Boethius, too, were regarded with the greatest respect. Writing at a time when the old world seemed to be passing away before the onslaughts of the barbarians, Boethius summed up much of the learning of Greece and Rome. His *de Consolatione Philosophiae* was a great storehouse of Platonic and Stoic thought, while it was upon his translations that the mediaeval logician up to the middle of the twelfth century depended for his knowledge of large portions of the Aristotelian *Organon*. And through his version of Porphyry's *Introductions* the Middle Ages inherited the old and much vexed problem of the nature of universals. But it must not be supposed that scholars then knew their classics only at second-hand. Cicero and Virgil were constantly read, and were regarded as the transmitters of Greek learning to the West:

> Ab his sectae multiformes Athenis materiam
> Nactae non liquore totam irrigarunt Graeciam,
> Quae redundans infinite fluxit in Hesperiam,
>
> Non tamen sine ductore vel tuto remigio,
> Quia navem gubernantes Maro atque Cicero
> Centum nautas asciverunt quemque studio.[1]

In the West little philosophical literature was produced between the fifth century and the Carolingian renaissance. Europe was in the throes of the barbarian invasions, and conditions were too unsettled to allow scholarship to flourish. The establishment of a more stable government under Charles the Great, the gradual pushing back of heathen races farther from the centre of civilization, the active interest of the emperor himself, all made possible a revival of scholarship. To a large extent, this renaissance was mainly literary. A great number of classical and patristic manuscripts were transcribed and their contents sifted, thus providing material for the more original thinkers of later times. Biblical exe-

1 *Die Cambridger Lieder*, ed. Karl Strecker, Berlin, 1926, Anhang, p. 113.

gesis, as may be seen by reference to the works of Rhabanus, chiefly took the form of collections of explanatory statements drawn from earlier commentators. The *de Divisione Naturae* is the sole great philosophical book produced during the Carolingian period. Theological activity, however, was stimulated by the rise of the Adoptionist heresy in Spain where Elipandus of Toledo and Felix of Urgel distinguished between Christ, the Second Person of the Trinity, and the Son of David, who was adopted by God. This renewed interest was further increased when, at Constantinople, the patriarch Photius denied the Double Procession of the Holy Spirit and taught other doctrines which were inconsistent with those of the Western church. Thus, the theological differences between Rome and Constantinople began, giving rise to many pamphlets *contra Graecos* written by Latin theologians with a view to healing the schism. The revival of theological speculation also produced the first Eucharistic controversy in which Paschasius Radbertus, Ratramnus, and Rhabanus Maurus were involved.

A change came as the eleventh century succeeded the tenth, the Century of Iron. The activities of Carolingian scholars in educative work, in the collection of manuscripts, and in the study of patristic texts were beginning to bear fruit, and we can notice the results of a greater attention which was being paid to dialectic. Berengar, once a student at Chartres—a city which, under the influence of Fulbert, was fast becoming one of the chief centres of literary scholarship in France— originated the second Eucharistic controversy. In his *de Sacra Coena* he claimed that "to take refuge in dialectic was to take refuge in reason", the two being identical.[1] Such great reliance upon human reasoning did not escape criticism. Summoned to refute the heretical opinions of Berengar, Lanfranc only made use of logic because his opponent had already done so. For his own part, he would have preferred

---

1 Maximi plane cordis est, per omnia ad dialecticam confugere, quia confugere ad eam ad rationem est confugere. Ed. Vischer, Berlin, 1834, p. 101.

to base his reply on quotations from the Fathers alone.[1]
Lanfranc, however, cannot be called a great theologian; he
was far more a lawyer, and his writings are those of a man
who had been trained in the legal schools of northern Italy.

Anselm, first of Bec and then of Canterbury, a man whose
knowledge of human and divine matters was said to be so
deep,[2] demands more than a slight notice. Steeped in the
thought of St Augustine, he reproduced the opinions of that
Father, not indeed by actually citing passages from his books,
but by making his thought the basis of whatever he wrote
himself. Like St Augustine, Anselm founded his theology
upon the data of religious experience. Though the *Monologium* is a philosophical treatise, dealing with the very
foundation of theology, the existence of God, it is in spirit
largely a book of meditation. "Have leisure for God," he
says elsewhere[3]—and the statement is indicative of his whole
outlook—"rest awhile in him. Enter into the chamber of
your mind, banish all save God and those things which will
aid you in your search for him, and, closing the doors, seek
him." Despite their metaphysical profundity, his writings
are not those of a lecturer expounding the dogmas of the
faith in an academic fashion. Anselm does indeed give reasons
for his beliefs, basing them upon analogies drawn from the
order of nature; but he argues only because he wishes to
strengthen the faith of his fellow-monks and to defend what
he had himself written against the criticism of an opponent
like Gaunilo.[4] Except for his *de Fide Trinitatis*, directed
against the errors of Roscelin, and his *de Processu Sancti
Spiritus*, written against the Greeks, his books were not controversial in character. His aim was to help and teach the
monks of Bec and Canterbury, men whose acceptance of

1 Et quidem de mysterio fidei auditurus, ac responsurus quae ad rem de-
beant pertinere, mallem audire et respondere sacras auctoritates, quam dia-
lecticas rationes. *De Corpore et Sanguine Domini*, 7, PL. 150, col. 416 D.

2 Cf. William of Malmesbury, *Gesta Prontif.* ed. Hamilton, RS. p. 122.

3 Vaca aliquando Deo, et requiesce aliquantulum in eo. Intra in cubiculum
mentis tuae; exclude omnia praeter Deum, et quae te juvent ad quaerendum
eum, et, clauso ostio, quaere eum. *Proslogion*, 1. col. 225 BC.

4 Cf. his *Liber Apologeticus*, coll. 247–60.

orthodoxy was never questioned, rather than to dispute with the heretic.

Anselm's chief importance in the development of Scholasticism was his insistence upon the meaning of the statement, *Credo ut intelligam*. This phrase, borrowed from the Septuagint Isaiah, was for him the watchword of all theological investigation. The beliefs of the Creeds were, he maintained, to be unhesitatingly accepted before any attempt could be made to understand their meaning. The teaching of the church provided the material upon which man's reason could work. Since the truth of authority was never to be called into question, the dogmas of the church necessarily limited the activity of the scholastic theologian. If he tried to shew how of necessity God must exist and how his nature must be triune, it was only because he first accepted the doctrine of God's existence and the Christian dogma of the Trinity, and wished, either for himself or for others, to discover some means of rationalizing and strengthening this belief. To proceed from dogmas which we already hold is the office of our understanding. Human reason has not the power either to found new theologies or to criticize the traditional doctrines of the church. Dialectic may not be regarded as supplying men with a criterion for the truth of ecclesiastical doctrine; logic may only be used to amplify the statements of canonical authority which have already been accepted. In all this, Anselm was delimiting the sphere of human reason in precisely the same way as did Aquinas when he declared that, once the doctrine of the Trinity has been posited, reason can shew the reasonableness of the dogma by the aid of suitable proofs.[1] Logic cannot, however, prove that the dogma is either true or false. The attitude which Anselm adopted towards the problem of reason and faith was followed by the majority of later theologians. One of our own problems will be to see how far Abailard imitated the example set by his predecessor.

---

1 ...se habet ratio quae inducitur ad manifestationem Trinitatis, quae scilicet, Trinitate posita, congruunt hujusmodi rationes. *Summa Theol.* I. quaest. 32, art. 1. ad 2.

ABBREVIATIONS

ALKG.	*Archiv für Literatur- und Kirchengeschichte des Mittel-alters,* 1885–1900.
BGPM.	*Beiträge zur Geschichte der Philosophie des Mittelalters,* Münster, 1891 ff.
CQR.	*Church Quarterly Review.*
CSEL.	*Corpus Scriptorum Ecclesiasticorum Latinorum.*
Deutsch.	Deutsch, *Peter Abälard,* Leipzig, 1883.
EHR.	*English Historical Review.*
Grabmann.	Grabmann, *Die Geschichte der scholastischen Methode,* Freiburg, 1909, 1911.
JTS.	*Journal of Theological Studies.*
MGH.SS.	*Monumenta Germaniae Historica, Scriptores.*
PG.	Migne, *Patrologia, Series Graeca.*
PL.	Migne, *Patrologia, Series Latina.*
RS.	Rolls Series.

Chapter i

ABAILARD'S CAREER TO THE COUNCIL OF SENS

I

IT was at the little village of Palais or Le Pallet, lying a few miles to the east of Nantes,[1] that Peter Abailard[2] was born in the year 1079. His father, Berengar by name, was a knight who held a small fee of the duke of Brittany; his mother was called Lucia. Berengar had had some smattering of letters before he had become a knight; and he was anxious that his sons should also be given some education prior to their being instructed in the use of arms. Either his Breton blood or the inherited genius of his family endowed Abailard with a grand aptitude for study as well as with a certain fickleness of character.[3] From Otto of Freising we know that Brittany produced men who made sharp-witted clergy, but who were nevertheless little suited for other professions.[4] Abailard himself seems to have been a typical Breton in this respect, for, although he could as the eldest son look forward to succeeding to his father's fief, he grew so fond of learning that he abandoned, as he says,[5] the halls of Mars for the lap

1 *Hist. Calam.* 1, coll. 113–14.

2 I have adopted what appears to be the most accurate spelling of the name (see Poole, *Illustrations*, p. 116 note). The more common form, Abelard, is inadmissible. The name is scanned by contemporary poets as a word of five syllables, cf. John of Salisbury, *Entheticus*, line 57, PL. 199, col. 966 B. The contemporary chroniclers vary in their spelling; Otto of Freising has Abailardus; Richard of Poitou, Baalardus. Judging from the reproduction of the Munich MS. of the *Sic et Non* (cf. PL. 178, col. 1337), Abaielardus may have been the earliest form, though a Heidelberg MS. (Cod. 359. 8, folio 14 v., early thirteenth century) has Abailardus.

3 *Hist. Calam.* 1, coll. 114–15.

4 Est enim praedicta terra (*scil.* Brittannia) clericorum acuta ingenia et artibus applicata habentium, sed ad alia negotia paene stolidorum ferax. *Gesta Fred.* 1. 48, ed. de Simson, p. 68.

5 *Hist. Calam.* 1, col. 115 A.

of Minerva and became a wanderer in search of knowledge, "an imitator of the Peripatetics".

He appears to have gone first to study with Roscelin, the famous Nominalist logician, who seems to have made his peace with the church after his condemnation for tri-theism at the council of Soissons (1092) and to have held a teaching post at Loches near Vannes.[1] In the *Historia Calamitatum* Abailard does not mention his pupilage under Roscelin, perhaps because he did not wish to be in any way connected with a heretic whose views he not only discarded but later attacked. When his own theological views came to be questioned, he certainly would not have wished it to be thought that Roscelin was responsible for the suspected heterodoxy of his own writings upon the doctrine of the Trinity. But Otto of Freising definitely declares that Roscelin had been Abailard's master, and his assertion is borne out by Abailard's reference elsewhere to his *magister Roz*, obviously a shortened form of the name of the distinguished logician.[2] Roscelin too claims that Abailard had been his pupil at Loches.[3]

It may also have been during his youth that Abailard attended the lectures of Thierry of Chartres upon the Quadrivium, but of this again we have no evidence in the *Historia Calamitatum*; our only information comes from an anonymous writer who reports that Abailard attempted to learn mathematics from a certain Tirricus, and that in his attempt he was entirely unsuccessful.[4] Now from his *Dialectica* we know that Abailard was indeed ignorant of mathematics, although he had attended lectures upon that science.[5] Further, the presence of Thierry at Soissons suggests that the two men were in some way connected. And the evidence at our disposal goes to prove that the otherwise unknown Tirricus may safely be identified with Thierry of Chartres. Yet if we

1 Poole, *op. cit.* p. 117; F. Picavet, *Roscelin, philosophe et théologien*, Paris, 1911, p. 55.
2 *Dialectica*, p. 471; cf. Otto of Freising, *op. cit.* p. 69.
3 *Ep.* xv. PL. 178, col. 360 c.
4 See B. Pez, *Thesaurus anecdot.* III. p. xxii; Poole, *op. cit.* pp. 314–17.
5 *Dialectica*, p. 182.

may accept the statement of our anonymous writer concerning Abailard's ignorance of the Quadrivium, we must
yet reject his account of the origin of Abailard's name. Our
writer tells us that the name was a sobriquet originating from
a joke made by Thierry at the expense of Abailard; *Quis canis
plenus nisi lardum bajare consuevit?* It has been shewn, however, that as the name Abailardus was also borne by a
son of Humphrey the Norman,[1] we must conclude that,
whatever its meaning, the name cannot have originated in
the way that the anonymous writer suggests.

Next, Abailard journeyed on to Paris, where he joined the
classes of William of Champeaux, then archdeacon of Paris
and the most famous teacher of logic in all France. As he
soon incurred the anger of his new master, it is from this
time that Abailard dates the beginning of his subsequent misfortunes. Elated by his success and presuming more upon
his intellectual capabilities than his years warranted, he was
anxious to set up a school of his own, and he proudly chose
the city of Melun, then a royal residence, as its site.[2] He must
have made a great mark in the schools of Paris for, much to
the annoyance of William, pupils came to him at Melun, but
it was only through some powerful men in the district, who
were jealous of the archdeacon, that Abailard was able to
succeed in his project. The attention which his lectures
attracted induced him to move his school to Corbeil, his
intention being to come nearer Paris and thus be in a better
position to attack his former master and his former
fellow-students.[3] But his residence at Corbeil was curtailed
by an illness which necessitated his return to Brittany, much
to the great regret of those who studied dialectic, and in
Brittany he remained for some years.

The chronology of Abailard's movements up to this period
is very obscure. His stay at Loches, however, cannot have
taken place before 1092, the year when Roscelin was con-

1 Robert de Monte, *Chronica, sub anno* 1129, MGH.SS. VI. p. 489; Poole,
op. cit. p. 316.
2 *Hist. Calam.* 2, col. 116 B.   3 *Ibid.* col. 117.

demned at Soissons, and must have been a year or so later, since Roscelin visited England after the council had dissolved. Picavet considers that Roscelin taught at Loches at the time when he read the *Cur Deus Homo?* of Anselm of Canterbury, a treatise the first book of which was written about 1094 and the second about 1098.[1] It is not necessary to conclude that either of these two dates fixes the period when Abailard studied under Roscelin; there is no evidence to suggest that his departure from Loches coincided with any retirement thence on the part of Roscelin. Still, I should not myself be inclined to date his entry into the school much after 1094, for Abailard would then have been fifteen, the natural age for him to study those subjects, such as the elements of logic, which Roscelin undoubtedly taught. We cannot say when he attended the lectures of William of Champeaux or when he set up for himself at Melun and Corbeil, but we can prove that these events certainly took place before 1108, and, if we allow that his stay in Brittany caused by his illness lasted for two or three years, as he appears to suggest, his departure from Corbeil must have occurred before 1106. Our evidence for this is that when Abailard returned to Paris, he found that William had taken vows. Now we know that in 1108 William brought some canons from St Rufus de Valentia to Paris, giving them a priory which had formerly belonged to Black Monks and thus founding the Augustinian canonry of St Victor which was soon to become so famous. Further, we are told that William made his own profession shortly after the foundation of the new house.[2] Abailard sarcastically maintains that ambition was the chief motive which led William to forsake the world; he wished to acquire the reputation of sanctity in the hope that he would one day be appointed to a bishopric.[3]

1 Picavet, *op. cit.* p. 55. Eadmer (*Vita Anselmi*, 4, 43, PL. 158, col. 100 A) says that the *Cur Deus Homo?* was begun in England and finished before the council of Bari (October 1st, 1098).

2 E. Michaud, *Guillaume de Champeaux et les Écoles de Paris*, Paris, 1867, p. 243; du Boulay, *Hist. Univ. Paris*, II. p. 24.

3 *Hist. Calam.* 2, coll. 118-19.

It is amply clear, however, that such strictures were due to the hostility of Abailard towards his former master.

When he returned to Paris, Abailard attended the lectures which William gave on rhetoric, but the old differences between the two men soon reappeared, and their relations grew even more strained when Abailard compelled William to discard his original theory of the nature of universals. At first, William had held the Platonic ultra-Realist view that universals exist both prior to and independently of their particulars, like the Ideas of Plato, and that all differences within a single species or genus were caused by the presence of accidental forms. As the result of Abailard's criticism he was now forced to adopt the theory that things differ through indifference, that is, through their own essence as well as through the presence of accidents.[1] Abailard won so great a victory that William was deserted even by his most loyal pupils, while the man who had succeeded the archdeacon in the schools of Paris, gave up his position to Abailard in order to become one of Abailard's students. But, in spite of his retirement at St Victor, William was still influential in the academic world. Within a few days he was able to eject Abailard and to reinstate his own successor in the chair which he had just resigned. The position of William, however, was none too secure; as his pupils doubted the real sincerity of his monastic conversion, he deemed it wise to move himself and his school farther from Paris. Profiting by his rival's action, Abailard returned to the city and, since another, presumably the master who had been reinstated by William, was teaching in his own lecture-hall, he placed his "camp" outside Paris on Mont Ste Geneviève. Whether he actually taught inside the monastery which was situated on Mont Ste Geneviève, or whether he lectured in some other building on the hill, is a matter upon which we have no evidence. But no sooner did William hear of this counter-march than he brought his own school back again, only to find however

1 *Ibid.* col. 119; for a discussion of these and other theories of universals, see *infra*, pp. 90 ff.

that his pupils deserted him for the greater attraction provided by Abailard's lectures, and he retired in consequence
to St Victor. For some time disputes between the students
of the two logicians continued, and in this struggle Abailard
tells us his side was not unsuccessful:

> si quaeritis hujus
> Fortunam pugnae, non sum superatus ab illo,

he quotes.[1] And this state of affairs went on until Lucia sent
word from Brittany to ask her son to return, as Berengar had
already taken vows and she intended to follow his example.

Contemporary writers give us but little information about
Abailard's character either at this or at any other time; the
audacity and the novelty of his opinions clearly monopolized
their attention. The anonymous author of the *Vita Gosvini*,
however, provides us with an interesting and invaluable
picture. When Gosvin came to Paris as a student, he found
Abailard lecturing on Mont Ste Geneviève where, although
none dared to attack him openly, his teaching aroused much
criticism. Gosvin was anxious to argue with him, but he was
dissuaded from so doing by Joscelin, later bishop of Soissons,
who declared that Abailard was not really a disputant but a
quibbling scoffer and that he more often played the part of a
jester than that of a teacher, throwing away like Hercules the
cudgel he had taken up in no spirit of levity.[2] Despite these
warnings, Gosvin attacked Abailard, a David against a
Goliath, and, the scriptural allusion notwithstanding, did no
apparent damage to the reputation of the master. The same
writer also gives us a description of Abailard's personal appearance. We are told that he was fair and of handsome
countenance, but slight in build and of short stature.[3] The
Historia Calamitatum gives us to understand that he was a

---

1 Ovid, *Metam.* XII. 89, quoted *Hist. Calam.* 2, col. 122 A.

2 Magistrum Petrum dicens disputatorem non esse, sed cavillatorem; et
plus vices agere joculatoris quam doctoris, et quod instar Herculis clavam non
leviter abjiceret apprehensam. Bouquet, *Recueil des Hist. des Gaules*, XIV.
pp. 442–3.

3 Erat enim albus quidem et decorus aspectu, sed exilis corpulentiae et
staturae non sublimis. *Ibid.* p. 443.

man who, fully aware of his own intellectual powers, could not brook the criticism of others; the views of those with whom he could not agree he always treated with the greatest disdain. He cannot have been a very amiable opponent.

When he came back once more from Brittany, Abailard found to his astonishment that William of Champeaux had been appointed to the bishopric of Châlons. As that see fell vacant on May 20th, 1113, we must date his election and consecration as having taken place some time in that year, and so Abailard must have returned to France either in the latter half of 1113 or in 1114.[1] But, instead of resuming his lectures at Paris, Abailard now decided to study theology under Anselm of Laon. The *Historia Calamitatum* does not tell us the reason for this decision. In character, the book is totally different from the *Confessions* of St Augustine; anxious to rehabilitate his character as a teacher and a theologian, Abailard does not reveal the conflicts of his inner self as did the great African. But from the little he does say, there can be no doubt that his action was due to the influence of Lucia either as the direct result of some conversation with her, or because of her profession as a nun. If his mother definitely persuaded him to abandon logic for theology, the question arises whether she looked forward to his advancement to some high preferment, or whether she wished him to be influenced and steadied by theological reading. It is abundantly evident that Lucia was a good woman, and it is unlikely therefore that her motives were purely mundane. Abailard himself must have realized that the distinction he had already won in the schools of Paris would obtain for him an equally successful career as a professor of theology, while at the time it was only natural for a student of logic to apply himself to theology, since the latter was then regarded as the Queen of the Sciences to which all human knowledge was necessarily subservient. But his own motive was not merely the desire to equip himself as a theological lecturer. Abailard appears to have been anxious to study the Scriptures for their own sake, as the

1 For the date of William's election, see Michaud, *op. cit.* p. 441.

most salutary branch of learning, since it was the Bible that
taught men how to save their own souls. Yet, he was already
thirty-four, too old it might seem to become a student again.
That this well-known teacher should have submitted himself
to the rule of another master is certainly attractive. Although
his pride and self-assurance made him a very difficult pupil,
not every professor of his standing and age would have left
his desk for the bench of a student. But for his own future
this change from dialectic to theology was of vast importance: it determined the character of his writing and teaching
henceforward.

Abailard could have chosen no better masters than Anselm
of Laon and his brother, Ralph. Anselm in particular was
exceedingly well read in patristic theology, and was a conservative theologian whom, John of Salisbury declares,[1] none
would attack with impunity. The two brothers were famous
throughout all France as the leading theological professors
of the day. In this general appraisement of their worth
Abailard, however, did not share; he says that although
Anselm possessed a wonderful command over language, his
lectures were far from clear and meaninglessly verbose. When
he lit the torch of his learning, Anselm only filled the room
with smoke; though at a distance his tree was conspicuous
for the wealth of its foliage, on close inspection it was barren.
And he applied to Anselm the lines in which Lucan compares
Pompey to an old oak tree:

> stat magni nominis umbra,
> Qualis frugifero quercus sublimis in agro.[2]

Gradually his attendance at lectures became less frequent,
much to the annoyance of his fellow-students, who rightly
concluded that his continual absences meant that he despised
the master in whom they took so much pride. One day, as
they were joking together after a lecture, one of them asked
Abailard how he thought he could teach theology without

1 *Metalogicon*, I. 5, col. 823 B; cf. his *Hist. Pontif.* ed. Poole, p. 20, and Otto
of Freising, *Gesta Fred.* I. 48, *ed. cit.* p. 68.
2 *Pharsalia*, IV. 135; *Hist. Calam.* 3, coll. 123–4.

a master, especially since he had not studied some of the sciences which were then considered indispensable to a theologian. To this enquiry Abailard answered that he was surprised that men who were so learned should rest content with the texts and usual glosses without the aid of something else. It was the dialectician and the teacher from Paris that spoke. The students, however, received his answer with laughter; they could not be expected to accept such a statement from one who, though perhaps their senior in years, was but a novice in their own subject. And so they challenged him to prove what he had said. Abailard, accordingly, invited them to a lecture on the very next day and chose for exposition the prophet Ezekiel, the most difficult of all the books in the Bible. So hard a task, they replied, should not be undertaken without due meditation at leisure, but, scorning their suggestion that his lecture should be postponed, Abailard indignantly said that it was not his practice to rely on long study but upon his own wits. His first lecture was not well attended; the apparent impossibility of his task kept men away. But those who came were profuse in their commendation, forcing him to continue with his exposition. Consequently, his audience at the second and third lectures increased, while those who had been absent from the first sought to transcribe his gloss from the beginning.[1] His success was bound to annoy Anselm; a new-comer, ill-equipped with the necessary knowledge, was stealing his own students. It was indeed a repetition of Abailard's earlier misfortunes at Paris; just as William of Champeaux used to torment him on account of his philosophical opinions, so Anselm of Laon was now persecuting him for his theological methods. In this, Anselm was urged on by two of his pupils, Alberic of Rheims and Lotulf of Lombardy. Alberic must have been a senior student, for in 1113–14 he became archdeacon of Rheims and head of the cathedral school there,[2] and at Rheims he was regarded with great respect as a man of suf-

1 *Hist. Calam.* 3, coll. 123–5.
2 Otto of Freising, *Gesta Fred.* 1. 49, *ed. cit.* p. 68.

ficiently wide reading, kind and eloquent, though not fluent in answering questions.[1] Nothing is known of Lotulf.[2]

The hostility which he had aroused made his departure from Laon imperative, and once more Abailard returned to Paris, where his reception was enthusiastic enough to satisfy his pride. He was offered a chair at the cathedral, and since William was now settled at Châlons, he was destined to enjoy peace for some long time. Dr Poole conjectures that he was also given a canonry at Notre-Dame; it seems highly probable that he must have held some official position on that cathedral body since he taught at the cathedral school. But, though he is mentioned as having been a canon at Tours, Chartres and Sens, he is never called by any contemporary writer a canon of Paris.[3] This does not necessarily disprove Dr Poole's theory; Abailard would have been better known as a teacher at Paris than as a canon. In his lectures he attempted to finish the commentary on Ezekiel which he had begun at Laon and which was so well received by the students of Paris. With the increase of his reputation Abailard obtained much honour and wealth from the courses which he gave on theology and dialectic.[4] But, as he realized afterwards, prosperity always puffs up the foolish, while peace in this world both weakens the vigour of the mind and unleashes the enticements of the flesh. Proudly regarding himself as the only philosopher that was living at the time, Abailard gave rein to his desires, and the more he progressed in theology and philosophy, the less he imitated in his life the examples of the philosophers and the saints. Through fastidiousness and his preoccupation with his studies he had

1 *Vita Hugonis abb. Marchian.* in Bouquet, *Recueil,* xiv. p. 398. Alberic afterwards became archbishop of Bourges, 1155-74.

2 Otto of Freising, *op. cit.* p. 69, calls him Letald of Novara.

3 See Poole, *Illustrations,* p. 124 note 11; p. 171 note 30. Also for mention of the other canonries, Rémusat, *Abélard,* 1. Paris, 1845, p. 39 note, and *Hist. Litt.* xii. p. 12.

4 It was not until 1138 (see the rescript of Innocent II given in Richard of Hexham, *de Gestis Stephani,* ed. R. Howlett, RS. p. 175, and du Boulay, *op. cit.* ii. p. 175) that payments exacted from their students by masters were forbidden.

always lived chastely; now he fell at once into love and into debauchery.[1]

Héloise was the niece of one Fulbert, a canon of Notre-Dame. In his affection the uncle had had her carefully educated in letters, and the extent of her knowledge, a rarity in the women of the day, added to her reputed physical charms. Greatly attracted, Abailard contrived to make her acquaintance, and on account of his fame as a scholar he succeeded in his aim. Through the good offices of a friend he obtained an introduction to Fulbert, who was proud of and curiously attentive to the studies of his niece. Flattering his weaknesses, Abailard persuaded him to give him a lodging in his house in the Rue des Chantres together with the entire supervision over the education of Héloise. His courtship had an ill effect upon his public lectures, for he no longer spoke from inspiration but, content with the repetition of old lectures, he taught from memory; and if he wrote poetry, it was now of love and not of philosophy. Something of the character of his love-poems may be gathered from the following verses of his *Planctus* of David over Jonathan with its felicity of rhythm and rime:

Vel confossus pariter
Morerer feliciter,
Quum, quod amor faciat,
Majus hoc non habeat.

Triumphi participem
Vel ruinae comitem,
Ut te vel eriperem
Vel tecum occumberem.

Et me post te vivere
Mori sit assidue,
Nec ad vitam anima
Satis est dimidia.

Vitam pro te finiens,
Quam salvasti totiens,
Ut et mors nos jungeret
Magis quam disjungeret.

. . .

Vicem amicitiae
Vel unam me reddere,
Oportebat tempore
Summae tunc angustiae;

Do quietem fidibus:
Vellem ut et planctibus
Sic possem et fletibus.
Caesis pulsu manibus,
Raucis planctu vocibus
Deficit et spiritus.[2]

1 *Hist. Calam.* 5, col. 126.
2 Coll. 1822–4. A translation is to be found in H. Waddell, *Wandering Scholars*, London, 1927, pp. 196–7. Cf. Dreves, *Analectica Hymnica*, XLVIII. p. 232.

David's lament, indeed, contains a sure mark of the affection
which Abailard himself bore for Héloise. With perfect justice
Miss Helen Waddell calls the love-lyrics of Abailard those of
a scholar.

Eventually Héloise was with child, and Abailard found it
necessary to take advantage of an absence of Fulbert and take
her away one night to Brittany. There, at the house of his
sister, a son, whom they called Astralabe, was born. Naturally,
Fulbert was beside himself with grief, and to pacify him
Abailard returned alone to Paris, where at length he was able
to reconcile him by promising to marry Héloise. Thereupon,
he went back home to fetch her and their child. But Héloise
refused to give her consent to their marriage on the ground
that she could take no pride in a marriage which would involve the curtailment of his future career. All she apparently
asked for was to be left in Brittany with her son so that
Abailard could pursue his studies unhampered by the possession of a family. She recognized that any chance of his
attaining to high preferment would be ruined once he married,
and she did not wish to stand in his way; instead, she desired
to remain his friend and lover. And so she quoted from St
Jerome to illustrate the anxieties of a married life, recalling
the quarrelsome nature of Xantippe and the words of Cicero
that it was impossible for a man to devote himself to philosophy and to a wife at the same time. What indeed had a
philosopher to do with the trappings of a nursery; what had
pens and quills in common with spindles, books with
colanders?[1] With eighteenth-century crudity Alexander Pope
made much of her refusal; it smacked of the illicit relations
which he himself wished to establish with Lady Montagu.
But there is no suggestion that Héloise wished to continue as
Abailard's mistress; she desired rather that the incident should
be regarded as closed and that she should always remain his
devoted friend. Finally, however, Abailard persuaded her to
leave the child with his sister and to return to Paris where

[1] *Hist. Calam.* 7, coll. 130–31; cf. Jerome, *c. Jovin.* 1. 48, PL. 23, col. 278,
from the now lost book of Theophrastus, *de Nuptiis*.

they were to be married. An agreement was made to keep the wedding secret, but Fulbert and his servants betrayed them. Angered by their betrayal and infuriated by Fulbert's harsh treatment of his niece, Abailard then took her away to a nunnery at Argenteuil where he knew the abbess and where Héloise herself had been brought up. There she made her profession as a nun.[1]

This action, evidently taken without consulting him, enraged Fulbert. Entering Abailard's room one night, accompanied by some companions, he attacked and robbed him of his manhood.[2] Such a dastardly act does not seem to have affected his physique, save naturally during a necessary period of convalescence, for most, if not all, of his books were written at a later date. Afterwards, when reviewing the events of his early life, he came to see in their deed the working of the finger of God. The reprisal was indeed justified and, since he was now freed from the lusts of the flesh and as he could henceforth devote both himself and his philosophy wholly to the service of God, Fulbert's action could not be entirely regarded as a misfortune.[3]

Ill and despondent, Abailard saw no other alternative than that of following the example of Héloise and of seeking refuge in a cloister. Accordingly, he entered the abbey of St Denys close to Paris, a house which exercised a great influence in French politics from the ninth to the fourteenth century. Then in 1118 or thereabouts he made his profession. At the time the abbot was named Adam, a man of even worse character than those under his rule.[4] The criticism which Abailard levelled against the evil condition of the monastery is supported by the attacks of St Bernard, who wrote some ten years later to stigmatize the abbey for the laxity of its discipline and to congratulate Suger, Adam's successor, upon his reforming work.[5] Bernard tells us that St Denys was a

1 *Hist. Calam.* 7, coll. 133–4. 2 *Ibid.* coll. 134–5. 3 *Ibid.* 8, coll. 134–5.
4 Cujus abbas ipse, quo caeteris praelatione major, tanto vita deterior atque infamia notior erat. *Ibid.* col. 136 c.
5 *Ep.* LXXVIII. PL. 182, coll. 191–2. Adam became abbot in 1094. Suger, born in 1081, succeeded him in 1122 and lived till 1151. Influenced by

place mainly devoted to the business of the palace and to the armies of the king, a true synagogue of Satan.¹ Its abbot, exulting in worldly pomp, never left its precincts without a train of at least sixty horsemen,² and within its walls were to be seen lords of castles and not monks, chiefs of provinces and not the rulers of men's souls.³ Otto of Freising says that in the abbey Abailard spent day and night in meditation and reading.⁴ His fellow-monks, however, soon grew anxious to rid themselves of the new-comer, whose reputation as a scholar did not altogether counterbalance their feeling of annoyance provoked by his criticism of their behaviour. As his former pupils wished him to resume his lecturing, he obtained the necessary permission from the abbot to retire from the monastery, and once more he opened his school. There his main concern was with theology, but he did not entirely forsake the secular subjects in which his own studies had been more thorough; as it was through dialectic that he had won his fame, he used dialectic as a bait with which to attract students to his theological lectures, thus imitating the example of Origen.⁵ In a letter written to commiserate with him upon his mutilation and upon his trial at Soissons, Fulk de Deuil speaks of his fame as a lecturer during this period. No distance, neither tall mountains, deep valleys, nor roads beset with perils and endangered by thieves prevented students from attending his lectures. Not only did students come from various parts of France; his fame brought him pupils from Flanders, from across the Rhine, and from England.⁶

St Bernard's reforming zeal, he set himself to eradicate the abuses at the abbey in 1127. See Vacandard, *Vie de St Bernard*, 1. Paris, 1920, pp. 178 ff.

1 *Ep.* LXXVIII. PL. 182, 4, coll. 193–4.   2 *Apologia*, 11, 27, col. 914 A.
3 *Ibid.*   4 *Gesta Fred.* I. 49, *ed. cit.* p. 60.
5 *Hist. Calam.* 8, coll. 138–9; for Origen, see Eusebius, *Hist. Eccles.* VI. 13, which Abailard quotes. Hugonin, *Suger et la Monarchie au XIIᵉ siècle*, Paris, 1855, p. 120, states that Abailard retired to Deuil. Here he must have met Fulk, perhaps for the first time.

6 Nulla terrarum spatia, nulla montium cacumina, nulla concava vallium, nullá via difficilis licet obsita periculo, et latrone, quominus ad te properarent retinebat. Anglorum turbam juvenem mare interjacens et undarum procella terribilis non terrebat: sed omni periculo contempto, audito tuo nomine, ad te confluebat. Remota Britannia sua animalia erudienda destinebat. Ande-

It was at this time that Abailard wrote his first theological book, an essay on the Unity and the Trinity of God, directed against the theology of Roscelin. We shall see later that this book was in all probability the tractate known as the *de Unitate et Trinitate Divina*.[1] Abailard tells us that it was written at the request of his students who desired an exposition of the doctrine of the Trinity based on philosophy and illustrated by human reason, a book of which the contents were to be intelligibly presented, not mere verbiage which could not be understood.[2] His aim was to correct the faults which he had himself discovered in the method of Anselm of Laon; he sought to render intelligible the doctrine of the Trinity by citing from classical authors statements which he considered as proofs of their belief in the Trinity of Christian theology, and by explaining through the use of dialectic the reasonableness of a faith in a triune Godhead. The book was widely read, but some of its statements aroused fierce criticism. Since Anselm of Laon and William of Champeaux were already dead,[3] Lotulf and Alberic now led the attack upon Abailard and, enlisting the aid of their archbishop who in his turn obtained the support of the papal legate, Conon of Praeneste, they procured the summoning of a council at Soissons in 1121 at which the book was to be examined.[4] Save for a reference in Otto of Freising, Abailard himself is the sole authority we possess for the events at this council. He tells us that before he had arrived at the city Alberic and Lotulf stirred up the clergy and people of Soissons against him, and that their hostility was responsible for the condemnation of his book, for the assembly could find nothing heretical in its pages. By Alberic the citizens were told that Abailard taught the existence of three gods; the actual charge, however, preferred against him at the council was that of Sabellianism.[5]

gavenses eorum edomita feritate tibi famulabantur in suis. Pictavi, Wascones, et Hiberi: Normannia, Flandria, Teutonicus et Suevius tuum calere ingenium. ...*Ep.* xvi. PL. 178, coll. 371-2.   1 See Appendix I.

2 *Hist. Calam.* 8, col. 141.   3 In 1117 and in January 1121 respectively.

4 *Hist. Calam.* 9, coll. 144-6.

5 Cf. *Gesta Fred.* I. 49, *ed. cit.* p. 69, and *Hist. Calam.* 9, col. 147. See also *infra*, p. 26 note 4.

The attempts made by Alberic to prove him heretical
resulted only in his own confusion at the hands of Abailard.
The council apparently did not know what steps should be
taken; but on the last day of their meeting Geoffrey of Lèves,
the bishop of Chartres, spoke in Abailard's favour, evidently
with the intention of obtaining his acquittal and of pointing to
the many supporters who wished to defend him. If indeed
they were anxious to proceed canonically against him, they
should give him the opportunity of answering the charges
brought against him, and not condemn him unheard.[1] But
this course did not appeal to the assembly, which was probably afraid of Abailard's skill in dialectical argument; the
worthy bishop accordingly proposed an adjournment on the
plea that there were few present who were competent to
judge the case. Meanwhile, Abailard was to be handed over
to the abbot of St Denys who was present at the council for
safe-keeping at his abbey, where a greater number of more
learned men were to examine his theology. The legate and
the council agreed to this proposal, but after Conon had risen
to say Mass, there were some who felt that nothing had been
accomplished, hastened to the legate to object to this decision, on the ground that his transference to another diocese
would deprive them of their jurisdiction over the matter.
They asked that the book in question should be burnt and
that Abailard himself should be sent to an abbey within the
diocese. The very fact, they argued, that he had presumed to
read the book publicly without the licence of either the pope
or the church ought to be sufficient to procure the condemnation of the treatise. His opponents were here referring
to the necessity of some ecclesiastical permission enabling a
man to teach theology,[2] a permission which would hardly

1 *Hist. Calam.* 9, col. 148. du Boulay (*op. cit.* II. p. 45) suggests that Geoffrey
had been a pupil of either Abailard or of William of Champeaux. He succeeded Ivo at Chartres in 1115 and lived till 1148, for which see Clerval,
Écoles, p. 153.

2 Dicebant enim ad damnationem satis hoc esse debere, quod nec Romani
pontificis nec Ecclesiae auctoritate eum commendatum legere publice prae-
sumpseram. *Hist. Calam.* 9, col. 149 c. Cf. H. S. Denifle, *Die Universitäten des
Mittelalters*, Berlin, 1885, pp. 764–5 and p. 765 note 31, whence I have
emended the text of this quotation.

have been granted to Abailard seeing that he had studied theology for so short a time. His post at Paris was evidently either overlooked or not considered a sufficient testimonial. It was therefore decided that the book should be burnt and that Abailard, after publicly reciting the Athanasian Creed, should be entrusted to the abbot of St Médard, another attendant at the council.[1]

This abbot was Geoffrey, surnamed Col de Cerf, who had been appointed in 1121 and was anxious to reform the discipline of the house. To this end he had chosen as his prior the same Gosvin whom we have already met as one of Abailard's pupils.[2] Abailard says that both Gosvin and the monks, confident that he would remain with them, treated him with great kindness.[3] The author of the *Vita Gosvini* also states that Gosvin hoped that a kindly reception would make it easier for him to learn resignation; the prior therefore talked to him both of the extent of his knowledge and of the victories which he had won in the schools, pointing out nevertheless the superior worth of the monastic life and of the monk's contempt for the world and of his service to God. Far from regarding as a misfortune his enforced residence at St Médard where he would not be looked upon as a prisoner, Abailard was to consider himself shut off only from the turmoil of secular affairs, a free man, not one in fetters. Only let him shew himself upright, and he would be a master to them all and an example of integrity.[4] But to a man who delighted in the freedom and adulation of the schools, whose fighting spirit had been aroused by the events at Soissons, St Médard could only appear as a grim prison.[5] To Gosvin he replied that though many talked of uprightness, none knew what it was, a reply which drew from Gosvin the curt answer

1 *Hist. Calam.* 9–10, coll. 149–50.
2 For Geoffrey see *Hist. Litt.* XII. p. 185.
3 *Hist. Calam.* 10, col. 151 A.
4 ...non deputaret infortunio nec adscriberet dispendio quod eo transmissus esset, ubi non reclusum ergastulo se experiretur, sed tantum exclusum a turbine saeculari, non compeditum sed expeditum; honestum tantum se haberet, et omnibus esset magister et exemplar honestatis. *Vita, loc. cit.* p. 445.
5 *Hist. Calam.* 10, col. 151.

that if he did or said anything dishonourable, their guest for one would soon know its character.[1] Frightened by this, "that rhinoceros" became quieter and more patient of discipline. Still, Abailard was immensely unhappy, and his bodily disablement appeared of little moment compared with the insult thus done to his fame. His predicament seemed only to be due to the hateful persecution of his enemies, for it was his love for the faith that had driven him with the best of intentions to set pen to paper. He says that his sentence awakened everywhere violent feelings of reprobation. Each of his enemies tried to put the blame on another, while the papal legate, deploring the animosity shewn by the French clergy, sent Abailard back again to St Denys.[2]

There he found old enemies amongst almost all the brethren, and a few months after his return chance gave them an opportunity to attempt his ruin. In obedience to the command of Louis the Pious, Hilduin, a former abbot (814–? 840), had written a life of their patron-saint and in this the Areopagite had been for the first time identified with Dionysius, bishop of Athens.[3] Reading a commentary of Bede upon Acts, Abailard came across a statement to the effect that Dionysius the Areopagite was bishop of Corinth,[4] and from this he concluded that this Denys was not the same as the Dionysius who was bishop of Corinth towards the end of the second century, but a third Dionysius, a contemporary of the bishop of Athens mentioned in the Acts.[5] When he spoke of his discovery to some brothers who happened to be near, they became infuriated at the insult offered to their patron-saint. Bede, they declared, was an impostor; since he had travelled to Greece for the express purpose of gathering information concerning the saint, Hilduin must certainly be regarded as an infallible authority. Dionysius the Areopagite

---

1 *Vita, pag. cit.*   2 *Hist. Calam.* 10, col. 153.
3 Hilduin's *Life* of St Denys is printed in PL. 104, coll. 23–50.
4 Cf. Abailard, *Ep.* XI. col. 344 CD, and *Hist. Calam.* 10, col. 154; Bede, *super Acta Apostol.* 17, PL. 92, col. 981 A.
5 Abailard's authorities for this later bishop of Corinth are Jerome, *de Viris Illustr.* 27, PL. 23, col. 645 B, and Eusebius, *Hist. Eccles.* IV. 21.

was bishop of Athens, not of Corinth, and was the first man to evangelize Gaul. The outcry against Abailard became general. Summoning all the monks, abbot Adam said that he would denounce him to the king as an enemy of the country, and in the meantime he was placed under surveillance. But, profiting by the sympathy of some of the brethren and with the aid of a few disciples, Abailard managed to escape one night, and he made his way to the lands of Theobald, count of Champagne, who knew him and his history, for he had previously stayed at a cell on his estate.[1] One of his former friends happened to be the prior of a cell at Provins which belonged to the monks of Troyes, and there he was joyfully received.[2]

Not long after his escape it happened that Adam visited count Theobald on business. Hearing of his arrival, Abailard besought the count to ask Adam for his pardon and for permission to allow him to live as a monk wherever he might find it convenient. He thought, however, that Abailard wished to enter another monastery and that this would be an affront to St Denys, for it was a triumph that so distinguished a scholar should have come to their house in preference to all others. Adam and his companions would not accede to the request. Instead, they threatened him with excommunication if he stayed at Provins, adding that they would extend the ban to include the prior of that cell if Abailard was allowed to remain. Shortly after his return to Paris, however, Adam died. We are thus able to date Abailard's escape from St Denys and his reception at Provins. Since Adam's death took place in 1122, these events must have happened in either 1121 or 1122.

Abailard now enlisted the aid of the bishop of Melun, who addressed to Suger, the new abbot of St Denys, the same request, namely that he should be allowed to live the monastic life in whatever place he might choose. But as Suger did not

---

1 *Hist. Calam.* 10, col. 156.
2 *Ibid.* This was the priory of St Ayoul belonging to the monks of St Pierre at Troyes, see Rémusat, *op. cit.* I. p. 103.

immediately give his consent, the support of Stephen de
Garlande, the royal seneschal, was also obtained. This
Stephen was a man of great influence, but largely because he
had succeeded his two brothers, Anseau and William, in their
office, he was very unpopular in many quarters. A man of
great industry and gifted with much worldly wisdom, he held
many ecclesiastical preferments and even enjoyed a military
command next after the king, despite the fact that he was in
deacon's orders.[1] To St Bernard it appeared an outrage that
a deacon should serve both God and Mammon, should be a
soldier as well as a clerk, and that the same hand should give
the king his cup at table and should administer the cup at
Mass.[2] None the less, Stephen proved a very useful ally, and
by his help Abailard obtained his request. In the presence of
Louis le Gros, Suger gave him permission to enter that
solitude which he desired, provided only that he did not make
himself dependent upon another religious house. Accordingly,
he returned to the diocese of Troyes where certain friends—
among them perhaps Theobald of Champagne, a faithful
patron of the church—gave him some land in the parish of
Quincey.[3] There, with the consent of bishop Hatto, he built
himself a mud-and-wattle oratory which he dedicated to the
Trinity.[4]

News of his retreat was soon noised abroad and students
flocked from all parts, leaving, he says, the towns for the
desert, their soft beds for couches of reeds and moss, their
tables for sods of turf.[5] And in so doing, Abailard asks,[6] were
they not imitating the first philosophers, spurning, like
Pythagoras, the attractions of the world to live in desert

1 See *Chronica Mauriniacensis*, II. 12, ed. L. Mirot, Paris, 1909, pp. 42–3.
Anseau died in 1117 (*ibid.* p. 22 note 2); William then succeeded him, dying
in 1120 (p. 14). Stephen succeeded William, and, marrying his niece to
Amaury of Montfort, he sought to obtain the appointment of Amaury as his
successor (p. 43). He was finally driven from court in 1127; for which see
Suger, *Vita Ludovici*, xxx, ed. A. Molinier, Paris, 1887, p. 116.
2 *Ep.* LXXVIII. 11, col. 197 B.
3 For Quincey, see Innocent II, *Ep.* LXX. PL. 179, col. 114 C, and Jaffé-
Löwenfeld, *Regesta*, No. 7513. Quincey lies to the south-east of Nogent-sur-
Seine.   4 *Hist. Calam.* II, coll. 159–60.
5 *Ibid.* coll. 160–61.   6 *Loc. cit.*

places, and, like Plato whose sumptuous bed had once been soiled by the muddy feet of Diogenes, choosing for their Academy an abode in the country far from the town, a place which was not simply a wilderness but a pestilential site in addition? Further, these scholars who sought him in his solitude, building round his little oratory huts which were those of hermits rather than those of students, were like the sons of the prophets who followed Elisha. Yet there was this great difference which somewhat marred the analogy: the river by which their master dwelt was the Arduzon, not the Jordan.[1] Force of circumstances as well as the arrival of these students compelled Abailard to resume his lecturing, for he was exceedingly poor and unable to till the ground, while he was ashamed to beg. Since they could supply his wants, the arrival of pupils seemed most opportune. Still, an economic difficulty presented itself; the tiny oratory was too small to accommodate so large a concourse of pupils. If he wished to lecture, something better had to be found. And so his students set to work and rebuilt the house more substantially of wood and stone, making it big enough to contain them all, and, because God had sent his Comforter to Abailard in his distress, their new convent was dedicated to the Paraclete.[2]

Like Echo his renown spread through the entire world, while his former enemies, unable to overthrow him themselves, roused up against him two new "apostles", a canon regular and a monk.[3] That Abailard was here referring to St Norbert, the founder of the Premonstratensian Canons, and to St Bernard cannot be doubted, but it is equally clear that at this period neither of these two men was actively engaged in attacking him. It has been thought that one of St Bernard's books, the de Baptismo written circa 1125, was directed against

1 Ibid. col. 161 c.
2 Ibid. col. 162 AB. Cf. Construxerat enim monasterium in episcopatu Trecensi juxta Nogentum super Secanum in quodam prato ubi degere solitus fuerat. William of Nangey, Chron. in Bouquet, Recueil, xx. p. 731. See also William Godell, Bouquet, Recueil, xiii. p. 575, and Robert of Auxerre, Chron. MGH.SS. xxvi. p. 235. All these references shew how well known was his residence at Quincey.
3 Hist. Calam. 12, col. 164 A.

Abailard, but there is no real evidence to support this theory.[1]
Very probably the sense of some impending danger was
merely the hallucination of a nervous man who had already
suffered so much at the hands of his enemies. The sentence
of the council of Soissons had never been fully carried out,
for after his removal to St Médard and then to St Denys no
steps had been taken to enquire further into his theological
views. At Quincey he was teaching without papal authority,
and his unrecognized lecturing had been one of the charges
brought against him. His nervous foreboding of some future
disaster, however, made him feel that it would be safer for
him to leave the Paraclete, and so, when *circa* 1125 the abbacy
of St Gildas de Ruys in the Breton diocese of Vannes fell
vacant and when the monks there with the consent of the
duke elected him unanimously, he accepted their offer. We
have no evidence to shew what orders Abailard possessed at
this time. Since when he left the Paraclete, he made no
arrangements for the celebration of the Offices there,[2] it seems
natural to suppose that he must then have been a priest. But
he could hardly have been a priest at the time of his affair
with Héloise, for none save those in minor orders were permitted to marry and, although this rule was frequently
broken, we find in the various reasons put forward by
Héloise against their marriage no mention of the breach of
canon law which their wedding would entail. Their subsequent separation each to a monastery would in the eyes of
the law dissolve the marriage disqualification debarring his
further ordination. From this it appears likely that he received ordination as a priest after his escape from St Denys,
probably from bishop Hatto, who not only took so great an
interest in him but was also his diocesan.

What was the precise reason which led the monks of St
Gildas to elect Abailard as their abbot we cannot tell. Being
themselves an unruly crowd, they perhaps thought that with
his record as an undisciplined monk his rule over them would

1 For a discussion of this see *infra*, pp. 214–15.
2 *Hist. Calam.* 13, col. 168 A.

be light. More probably they considered that his fame as a teacher would bring both repute to their house and, more especially, a steady flow of pupils who would aid their depleted finances. Exiled from France through the jealousy of his enemies, Abailard found his change of residence did not afford him that protection and freedom from worry which he earnestly required. Brittany was a barbarous land, and its language was unknown to him; the monks over whom he was to rule took no pains to conceal the disgraceful character of their lives.[1] Constantly in fear of the dangers that threatened his body and soul, he soon repented that he had ever left the quiet of the Paraclete. Profiting by the disordered state of the monastery, a neighbouring "tyrant", the most powerful man in the district, had converted to his own use all the land near St Gildas and had laid upon the monks heavier burdens than those which he imposed upon Jews. Since they had no common property and as each was consequently forced to support his concubines and his children on his own patrimony, the brethren pressed Abailard for their daily common necessities. Joyful at the sight of his difficulties, they stole whatever they could so that, when he eventually failed in his administration, he would be compelled either to desist from enforcing any discipline or to depart from Brittany altogether.[2] Thus, while the "tyrant" and his officials continually oppressed from outside, the monks within besieged him incessantly. His cares and the thought that no one had been left at the Paraclete to say the Offices made him long to return to France.

Matters at the Paraclete, however, righted themselves in a happy though unforeseen manner. By virtue of an old grant dating from the ninth century the abbey of St Denys claimed in 1123 the possession of the nunnery at Argenteuil where Héloise had taken her vows. If we may judge from the account given by Suger[3] and by the description of the behaviour of some of the nuns which is to be found in the *Historia Calami-*

---

1 *Ibid.* col. 165.   2 *Ibid.* col. 166.
3 See his *de Rebus in sua Administratione Gestis*, 3, PL. 186, col. 1215 B.

tatum, the condition of the nunnery was very unsatisfactory. But when the property was restored to St Denys and when in 1128 the nuns were rudely expelled and scattered throughout France, Abailard seized the opportunity and transferred the Paraclete to Héloise and the sisters who remained faithful to her. The deed of transference was first confirmed by the bishop of Troyes as diocesan, and later, in 1131, by Innocent II at the council of Rheims.[1] During the first year of their occupation, Héloise and her companions lived in great poverty, but the people of the district afterwards shewed themselves well disposed to the sisters and, Abailard allows,[2] in one year their property increased far more than if he had himself stayed there a century.

Abailard paid repeated visits to the nuns, and these visits only served to accentuate his despair. His zeal for monastic discipline had driven his monks to active revolt, and they made continual attempts to murder him, even by mixing poison in his chalice at Mass. Once, when he was staying at the house of one of his own brothers where the count at Nantes happened to be ill, they contrived that his servant should put poison in his cup. Though he did not himself drink from it, one of the monks attending him drained the cup and died. One day again, when he was riding, he was thrown and broke his collar-bone. Harassed by these and other difficulties, he tried to quell the revolt by issuing a ban of excommunication against the monks, and in this way he succeeded in forcing some of the most redoubtable to promise to leave St Gildas for good, but they did not keep their word. Finally, he obtained from Innocent II a papal legation to enquire into the state of affairs at the monastery, and in the presence of the legate the monks, who had broken their oath and had returned, were compelled to withdraw again. This legation must have taken place between October 1120 and March 1132, during the period when the pope was

1 *Hist. Calam.* 13, coll. 168–70. Innocent's brief is given in PL. 179, col. 114, and in Jaffé-Löwenfeld, *Regesta*, No. 7513, where it is dated, November 28th, 1131.
2 *Ibid.* 15, coll. 179–80.

in France; most probably it took place after January 1131 when we know Abailard visited Innocent at Morigny.[1] Nothing, however, could restrain the fury of the monks,[2] and Abailard finally left the abbey. The exact date of his departure remains somewhat of a mystery; Rémusat considered that it took place in 1134, but this seems too late, for he does not appear to have endured the hostility of the monks for so long a period after the appointment of the legation.[3] Hofmeister suggests that he may not have returned to St Gildas at all after his stay with Innocent in January 1131.[4] The *Historia Calamitatum* seems rather to infer that Abailard did indeed return for a time after the legation had been granted,[5] and this inclines us to date his departure from St Gildas in either late 1131 or in 1132.

His autobiography ends at this point, and, as we possess no other source of information, we cannot trace Abailard's activities during the next few years. The *Historia* itself appears to have been written as a pamphlet to prepare for his eventual return to Paris, and it is therefore natural to conclude that he was waiting for its circulation to provide him with a suitable opportunity to go back there. Most probably, he stayed either with his relations in Brittany or—and this appears more likely—somewhere within easy reach of the sisters at the Paraclete with whom he kept up a lively correspondence. There is the additional possibility that it was at this period that Abailard held one or other of the canonries associated with him, at Tours, Chartres, or at Sens.[6]

We do not hear of Abailard again until 1136 when John of Salisbury, who went to study at Paris in the year after the

1 See *Chronica Mauriniacensis*, II. 14, *ed. cit.* p. 154, for this visit. The pope dedicated an altar there to St Laurence and all the Martyrs on January 20th.
2 *Ep.* III. col. 192 A reflects the hostility of the monks.
3 Rémusat, *op. cit.* I. p. 139, quoting Brucker, *Hist. crit. phil.* III. p. 755.
4 See his "Studien über Otto von Freising", *Neues Archiv*, XXXVII. 1912, p. 636.
5 Cf. *Hist. Calam.* 15, col. 180 AB.
6 See *supra*, p. 10. A friendly bishop, knowing of his predicament at St Gildas, may well have given him preferment either at Morigny or at a session of the legation.

death of Henry I, became his pupil at Mont Ste Geneviève.[1]
Abailard then left Paris again, though he returned some time
before 1140 and resided at St Hilary, a church a quarter of a
mile to the north-west of Ste Geneviève. He seems to have
remained there until the council of Sens was summoned. It
was at this time that he joined with Arnold of Brescia who
had been banished from Italy as the result of his denunciation
at the Lateran Council of April 1139 and had fled to France.[2]
Thus, Abailard must have been in Paris between 1139 and
1140. Whether he actually taught after his final return to the
city, we are not told. Otto of Freising states that Arnold was
one of Abailard's pupils,[3] and this would naturally lead us to
suppose that Abailard was lecturing when Arnold arrived.
There is no evidence, however, to support Otto's statement;
the chronicler probably thought that the friendship of the
two men implied that the one was the pupil of the other.
Though Abailard, like many of his contemporaries, was not
blind to the deficiencies of the clergy of his day, there is nothing in his extant writings to shew that he would have
sympathized with the attacks made by Arnold upon the
wealth of the mediaeval church. The fact that both had been
harassed by ecclesiastical authority was sufficient to throw
them together. Evidence, however, will be put forward in
the sequel[4] to shew that St Bernard attacked Abailard's
pupils during a visit he paid to Paris in about 1140. It seems
therefore certain that Abailard was indeed engaged in teaching right up to his appearance at Sens. He could hardly have
stayed at Paris without occupying himself with lecturing.

II

Most of Abailard's various books were composed before the
council of Sens. The task of dating them, however, is one of

1 Henry I died on December 1st, 1135, and at Canterbury, with which John
was connected, Christmas Day was reckoned as beginning a new year (see
Gervaise, ed. Stubbs, RS. 1. p. 90). For John's visit to Paris, see *Metal.* II.
10, col. 867 B, and Poole, EHR. XXXV. 1920, p. 320.
2 John of Salisbury, *Hist. Pontif.* introd. pp. lx ff., and pp. 63–4.
3 *Gesta Fred.* II. 28, *ed. cit.* p. 133.   4 See *infra*, p. 227.

great complexity, and it therefore seems more prudent to relegate that to an appendix and to state here for the sake of future reference the conclusions which will be found below. His writings upon logic were certainly composed before the year 1120, although there is the slight, but improbable, possibility that a portion of one book—the *Dialectica*—may have been written after 1128. Of his theological writings the *de Unitate et Trinitate Divina* was certainly the first, and may be dated *circa* 1120. This was followed by the *Sic et Non* (1122–23). The *Theologia Christiana*[1] came next, and was not written, as many have thought, after the *Introductio*. The latter book, or to give it its proper name, the *Theologia*, was written and published in at least two parts, the first two books being composed in 1124–25, the third and subsequent books after 1136. The text we possess is incomplete. The *Expositio ad Romanos* and the *Scito teipsum* came after the first two books of the *Introductio*, and the *Dialogus inter Philosophum, Judaeum et Christianum* dates from the period after the council of Sens. The letters were written after the establishment of Héloise and her nuns at the Paraclete.

What may be called his theological "trilogy", the *de Unitate*, the *Theologia Christiana*, and the *Introductio*, is chiefly concerned with an explanation of the doctrine of the Trinity. They all begin with an account of Trinitarian beliefs which, Abailard maintains, were held by the writers of the Old Testament and by some of the classical authors of pre-Christian Greece and Rome. An attempt is then made in each to discuss the doctrine of the Trinity by the aid of logic. The *Theologia Christiana* and the *Introductio* also have an account of the reasons for the belief in one God, and a discussion of divine omnipotence, and of divine will. The *Introductio* probably contained a section upon Christology and upon the sacraments of the church. The *Sic et Non* is a collection of

1 It must be noted that Abailard was the first to use the word "theology" in its modern sense. Hitherto *theologia* meant Christology only; for Abailard it included all our knowledge about God and his acts. See C. C. J. Webb, *Studies in Natural Theology*, Oxford, 1915, pp. 205–6, and J. de Ghellinck, *Mouvement théologique au XIIme Siècle*, Paris, 1914, pp. 64 ff.

opposing statements gathered from the Bible and from the Fathers together with an interesting preface giving Abailard's object in compiling the book and theories concerning inspiration. The *Expositio ad Romanos* is, as its title shews, a commentary, but it has this great novelty which distinguishes it from the glosses of its predecessors. Instead of merely confining his attention to the elucidation of single words, Abailard includes in his book discussions of one or two doctrines which are connected intimately with the Epistle. An instance of this is his discussion of the doctrine of the Atonement which has since become so famous. The *Scito teipsum*, a book on ethics, discusses the meaning of sin, its forgiveness, the meaning of confession, and the power of absolution possessed by the clergy. The *Dialogus*, an unfinished treatise, is a discussion between a Philosopher, a Jew, and a Christian at which Abailard acts as a judge, though, unfortunately, his judgement was never pronounced. The book belongs to a series of such discussions,[1] but unlike them, Abailard proceeds upon a much more philosophical line, attempting almost a piece of natural theology.

We have already seen that Abailard knew nothing of mathematics; it now remains to enquire what intellectual equipment he possessed. Whether he knew any Greek or Hebrew is a somewhat difficult question to answer. The few Greek words that he gives, such as λόγος, νοῦς, ὕλη, ἀγαθός, might well have come from Macrobius or any other writer whom he had studied, and in the MSS. they are always written in Roman characters. He certainly did not know Aristotle in the original, but from the translations of Boethius and others.[2] For his acquaintance with Plato he was dependent upon Macrobius and the early Christian Fathers, while the only dialogue he could read was the *Timaeus*, in the translation of Chalcidius. He does indeed quote in the original the sentence, τὸν ἄρτον ἡμῶν τὸν

1 Cf. *Disputatio Judaei cum Christiano*, in PL. 159, coll. 342 ff., and J. A. Robinson, *Gilbert Crispin, Abbot of Westminster*, London, 1911.

2 For his knowledge of Aristotle, see Appendix II.

ἐπιούσιον, in the Lord's Prayer,[1] and he knew that it had been rendered in the Vulgate in two different ways. But neither his use of the original Greek nor his knowledge concerning the two translations proves that he knew any Greek; he could well have been relying upon a book of some previous writer. Yet, he transcribes Aristotle's περὶ ἑρμηνείας correctly as *Perihermenias*, and not, as was then usual, by the ablative *Perihermeniis*,[2] for he knew that in Greek a genitive would take the place of the ablative.[3] The evidence at our command indeed, although deemed sufficient by Deutsch to prove that Abailard knew the elements of Greek,[4] is extremely scanty. It is possible that he could perhaps transcribe the alphabet correctly and translate the words he uses, though these words were so frequent in Latin writers that the ability to use and translate them correctly would no more prove that a man knew Greek than a knowledge of the French expressions used by an English writer to-day would mean that he was a French scholar. It is safer to assume that at the best Abailard knew very little Greek.

The proofs that he knew any Hebrew are almost as scanty. He acknowledges his indebtedness to St Jerome for his various etymological derivations, but he is aware of the fact that in Hebrew there is no copulative verb,[5] and that in Genesis i. 7, *Dixit quoque Deus*, the conjunction does not stand in the original text.[6] Further, he knows that in Genesis i. 2, *Spiritus Domini ferebatur super aquas*, the verb could as well be translated by *volitabat*, as indeed it is in Deuteronomy xxxii. 11.[7] But though he transcribes the Hebrew for "spirit", doubtless from Jerome, he does not give the Hebrew for

1 *Ep.* x. col. 337 D.

2 Cf. *Theol. Christ.* III. col. 1213 B. *Introd.* III. 7, col. 1112 C, has on the other hand, according to the Codex Victor, *Peryarmenias*; see Deutsch, p. 59.

3 *Exposit. ad Romanos*, I. 2, col. 815 C.

4 Pp. 58–60. A passage in the *Logica*, p. 218, indicates his ignorance of the genitive constructions in Greek.

5 *Hexaem.* col. 745 B, where he compares the construction with Ps. i. 1, "Beatus est vir...".

6 *Ibid.* col. 741 C.

7 *Ibid.* col. 736 B, and *Exposit. ad Romanos*, IV. 9, col. 935 C. I cannot find this in Jerome, Origen, Augustine, or Ambrose.

ferebatur, which he could have found in that author.[1] Now, in answering one of her queries, Abailard tells Héloise that he had once listened to a Jew commenting upon the meaning of I Kings ii. 35–36,[2] and this statement is highly significant. It is very likely that he may have consulted this Jew, or one of the many that could then have been discovered in Paris, and thus have learnt the smattering of Hebrew which he uses in his writings.[3] Had he known more than the elements of the language, we should certainly have expected him to have displayed his knowledge in those portions of the *Dialogus* in which the Philosopher and the Jew discuss Hebrew religious ideas. But, as he refers so seldom to Hebrew except when he actually quotes St Jerome, it may be affirmed that the few rules of grammar and syntax which he gives represent the sum total of his knowledge, and that they perhaps came in the main directly from a conversation with a Jewish friend.

Abailard's Latin is that of his day. Especially in his letters to Héloise, his style is flowery and abounds in classical and patristic allusions. He made no attempt to follow closely the rules of Quintilian, and in this he is widely different from his pupil, John of Salisbury, who was deeply influenced by the literary tradition of the schools at Chartres and wrote exceedingly well. In his theological books and his treatises upon logic Abailard wrote with the single object of committing his ideas to paper. His poetry contains a great ease of diction and rime. It may have been that his love-poems were the reason for St Bernard giving him the name of "Goliath"[4]; the subject-matter of his verse was indeed the very antithesis of David's poetry.

1 Cf. *Quaest. Hebr. in Genesim*, PL. 23, col. 939 A.
2 *Problemata*, 36, col. 718 B.
3 Cf. Deutsch, p. 26.
4 See F. A. Wright and T. A. Sinclair, *A History of Later Latin Literature*, London, 1931, p. 296, and he may have also been the original of the famous bishop Golias.

Chapter ii

FAITH & REASON

I

IN THE PAST scholars used to regard Abailard as a prototype of the eighteenth-century philosopher and as a martyr to Rationalism in an age which was notorious for its obscurantist thought. By his supposed declaration that understanding must always precede belief, he was considered to have reversed the motto of the conservative St Anselm. No longer was faith to be the key which unlocked the mysteries of revelation; *intelligo ut credam* was thenceforward to be the watchword of every theologian.

Of late, however, this interpretation of his attitude has rightly been discarded. Abailard never aimed at employing human reason as a solvent of Christian orthodox belief, and nowhere in his writings can the phrase, "I understand so that I may believe", be found. Indeed, the whole trend of his thought shews quite clearly that he never contemplated its use. To be sure, he allowed reason an important part in theological discussion, but he employed logic with far less assurance than did some of his more orthodox contemporaries, and with greater limitations than some of his modern critics would be prepared to allow. That his dialectic brought him to adopt heretical conclusions was in no way due to any wish on his part to overthrow the accepted scheme of Christian dogmatics; again and again he protested that he was orthodox, teaching only the doctrines of tradition, while he begged that any errors of phrase or of understanding that might be found in his books should be forgiven on the score that they were not intended.[1] "I would not be a philo-

---

1 Cf. *Introd.* Prolog. col. 980 C, and *Theol. Christ.* III. col. 1228 D.

sopher", he declares,[1] "if that meant a denial of Paul, nor
an Aristotle if that involved separation from Christ".

We can best appreciate Abailard's method if we enquire
into the circumstances which prompted the writing of his
chief theological books. The *de Unitate* was written as an
attack upon the tri-theism of Roscelin, and in both the
Theologia Christiana and the *Introductio* the views of that
heretic are discussed and condemned. Reference is also made
to many heretics of the time, to Tanquelm, undoubtedly a
madman, who dared to call himself the Son of God, causing
a temple to be erected in his honour; to Peter de Bruys, who
was forcing men to be re-baptized, teaching them that the
Mass ought no longer to be celebrated and that all crucifixes
should be removed from the churches.[2] The refusal of the
Eastern Church to include in its creed the *Filioque* clause provoked constant controversial treatises from Western scholars
throughout the Middle Ages, and Abailard himself was at
pains to shew how the doctrine of the Double Procession
must needs command our acceptance. The *Introductio*, it is
true, was written at the express wish of his students, who
desired a *summa* of sacred knowledge to serve as an introduction to their study of the Scriptures,[3] but though its object is thus mainly didactic, the concern of its author with the
heretical thought of his day is everywhere apparent. His
students were certainly to be instructed, yet at the same time
they were to be warned against the heretical teaching of
certain perverse theologians. Like so many other professors
of theology, Abailard looked beyond the four walls of his
lecture-room, disproving for the benefit of his students that
part of contemporary thought which appeared to him in-
imical to Catholic truth. All the scholastic writers were to a
great extent apologists, and Abailard was no exception.

1 Nolo sic esse philosophus, ut recalcitrem Paulo. Non sic esse Aristoteles,
ut secludar a Christo, *Ep.* XVII. col. 375 C. Though these words were written
after the council of Sens, they yet represent his position all through his life.
2 For further information on these heretics, see Appendix I, p. 262.
3 Aliquam eruditionis summam, quasi divinae Scripturae introductionem.
...Prolog. col. 979 A.

Now among the Fathers as well as among the theologians of the Middle Ages there was a general belief that heresy would always exist, and this belief was shared by Abailard. Because they test the faithful, inciting them to a firmer faith, heretics, he says,[1] have their appointed place in the divine scheme of things; until the end of time tares will always be present in the church, and then the angels as the harvesters of God will gather them together and throw them into everlasting fire. But till that day dawns, apologetic work is necessary so that the church may be defended against her enemies. And it was to this task that Abailard largely applied himself, for he was no rationalist who sought to use his powers to effect the downfall of the church, but a zealous defender of her orthodoxy, a rationalist indeed, but one who employed his reason both for the instruction of students and for the protection of the church against her foes.

His training and interest in dialectic moulded Abailard's idea of faith as much as did his concern with the need for apologetic. For a logician of his calibre it was natural to approach credal matters more from an intellectualist than from an affective viewpoint, and so to regard Christian dogma as a set of propositions similar to those which he had met in his study of dialectic. Thus, Abailard came to hold an intellectualist conception of the meaning of credal assent. For him faith was "that which we hold firmly in our minds".[2] It was to be more than the pronouncement of an idle "Amen" at the conclusion of a credal statement the import of which was not understood.[3] He had little patience with those who confessed unblushingly that their faith consisted in the utterance of words rather than in a knowledge of their meaning, men who, indeed, prided themselves on believing matters which could be neither discussed nor conceived.[4] Against

1 *Introd.* II. 3, col. 1047 B. His theory is based on an exegesis of II Tim. iii. 3.
2 Id quod mente firmiter tenemus. *Epist. ad Romanos,* II. 6, col. 876 A. Cf. also the present writer in JTS. XXVIII. 1927, pp. 198 ff.
3 *Introd.* II. 3, col. 1051 C; cf. *Exp. Symb. Apost.* col. 620 D.
4 Credere se profiteri non erubescant, quasi in prolatione verborum potius

such men he declared that something at least of the meaning of the creeds must be understood; otherwise the faith of a man who believes quickly, and in a facile manner, will soon diminish.[1] God indeed is the inspector of our hearts more than the judge of our lips; our prayers will accordingly have little or no fruit, unless they are accompanied by the devotion of our minds.[2]

The great apologetic value of such an attitude towards faith will readily be seen. If Christians would but attempt to understand their beliefs, not only would their devotion to God be increased, but they would also be in a position to convince the heretic of his errors. A faith which is not thus founded on the intellectual acceptance of tradition cannot win for itself converts, save through example and through the power of rhetoric, methods which did not appeal to Abailard as a logician. In the *Dialogus*, accordingly, he makes the Philosopher reject the beliefs of both the Christian and the Jew on the sole ground that each refused to give intellectual proof for his doctrines. Jews seek only for signs, while Christians appeal to the authority of their traditional books alone; yet neither method of substantiating the truth of their creeds will satisfy the requirements of the Philosopher. For Jews the biblical account of the first Passover may be enough, but to the Gentile it is not a sufficient proof that the Children of Israel are a favoured people in the sight of God.[3] Further, the philosopher tells the Christian that men were originally converted to his faith by argument, and not by force, and that this fact was especially true in the case of the Greeks who were interested in philosophy, and were not, like the Jews, sensual and unable to discuss the problems

---

quam in comprehensione animi fides consistat, et oris ipsa sit magis quam cordis. Qui hinc quo maxime gloriantur, cum tanta credere videantur, quae nec ore disseri nec mente concipi valeant. *Dialogus*, col. 1615 B.

1 *Introd.* II. 3, col. 1051 C, quoting Ecclus. xix. 4.

2 Orationis fructus aut nullus est, aut parvus, quam devotio intelligentiae non comitatur, cum cordis potius quam oris sit inspector Deus. *Sermo* XIV. col. 489 C.

3 *Dialogus*, col. 1615.

of metaphysics.[1] In a letter to his son, Astralabe, Abailard
himself wrote:

Fides non vi, sed ratione venit.[2]

It is through reason, and not through compulsion, that men
can be brought to accept the Christian faith.[3]

Such an intellectualist conception of faith may well be
compared with the voluntarism of St Bernard. To the latter
faith is "a voluntary and certain foretaste of truth which has
not yet been made manifest";[4] voluntary not merely because
there is no force which compels us to believe,[5] but because
credal assent is a meritorious action of the will.[6] Faith, we
are told, comes from hearing, that is from the statement of
authority unsupported by any attempt to win our allegiance
by the performance of miracles, or to convince us that the
content of faith is tenable. Miracles only confirm the truth
of what we have already heard,[7] while the truth of the faith is
amply shewn by the testimony of the martyrs. The example
of previous Christians, "young men and maidens, old men
and children, who have chosen to die by a thousand deaths
rather than for a moment depart from their faith",[8] is for
Bernard a satisfactory proof of the tenability of Catholic
doctrine. His own method of converting the heretic was not
intellectual, but rhetorical. Throughout the south of France

---

1 Ibid. coll. 1637-8.

2 Monita, ed. Hauréau, Notices et Extraits, xxiv. part 2, p. 179. An interesting comparison is Alcuin's warning to Charlemagne: Cogi poteris ad
Baptismum, sed non proficit fidei. Ep. xxxv. PL. 100, col. 187.

3 Ratione potius quam potestate. Introd. ii. 3, col. 1048 D, and Theol.
Christ. iv. col. 1284.

4 Fides est voluntaria quaedam et certa praelibatio necdum propalatae
veritatis. De Consid. v. 3. 6, PL. 182, col. 791. Cf. Augustine's statement:
Quid est enim credere, nisi consentire verum esse quod dicitur? Consensio
autem utique volentis est. De Spiritu et Litt. 31. 54, PL. 44, col. 235.

5 The existence of such a force is stated in Summa Sentent. i. i, PL. 176,
col. 43. For the authorship of this book, which is not by Hugh of St Victor,
see infra, p. 244.

6 Cf. J. Ries, Das geistliche Leben nach der Lehre des hl. Bernard, Freiburg,
1906, p. 136.

7 Sermo in cant. cant. lix. 9, PL. 183, col. 1065 c.

8 In Vigil. Nativ. Domini, iii. 9, PL. 183, col. 99 c.

and northern Italy he preached to the unorthodox, winning men back by the sheer power of his words.

At first, Abailard's conception of faith may seem to have been claiming too much for the human intellect. Did he intend to assert that man has the power of understanding the secrets of God? Such a claim Abailard, however, was far from making. His statement that our beliefs must be understood does not mean that in his view a complete comprehension of divine matters was possible for men. No mediaeval scholar ever thought that the hidden things of heaven could be fully known by the human mind; indeed, many philosophers under the influence of the neo-Platonism of the pseudo-Dionysius went so far as to consider that nothing could be known of God. Abailard certainly maintained that the judgements and ways of the Creator are inscrutable; his actions, which we experience every day, cannot be investigated, for our reason is unable to discuss their secret nature. Nor can we know in itself (*per se*) the mind of God, the reason, that is, which he has in his prescience concerning the things which he intends to do.[1] But although we cannot comprehend, we are yet able to understand. And between understanding (*intelligere*) and comprehension (*comprehendere*) Abailard makes a sharp distinction which is fundamental to a proper appreciation of his point of view. Understanding is the partial knowledge to which men may attain, and is therefore compatible with faith; comprehension is a fuller knowledge, "the experience of things in themselves through their presence".[2] The attainment of this kind of knowledge is impossible for man, and therefore comprehension has nothing to do with faith; it is rather faith's negation. Here Abailard

---

1 *Epist. ad Romanos*, IV. 11, col. 937; cf. Rom. xi. 33–5.

2 Sed profecto aliud est intelligere seu credere, aliud cognoscere seu manifestare. Fides quippe dicitur existimatio non apparentium, cognitio vero ipsarum rerum experientia per ipsam earum praesentiam. *Introd.* II. 3, col. 1051 D. Cf. Grabmann, II. p. 190; Heitz, *Essai sur les Rapports entre la Philosophie et la Foi*, Paris, 1909, p. 17. The distinction is based on an opposition between *agnitio* and *intellectus* to be found in Gregory, *Homil. in Evang.* II. 2, PL. 76, col. 1083 A. Cf. also Augustine, *in Ps. cxviii.* 73, PL. 37, col. 1552, where *credere* and *intelligere* are connected. See Webb, *Studies*, p. 211.

was making a distinction between the knowledge of the
things which are seen, and those which are not. Standing
outside the veil, we can have no sight of the things of God,
and thus no comprehension of them. God, on the other
hand, knows things not only as they are but, as he is their
Creator, before they even came into existence. Dependent
upon the data of the senses, man cannot acquire such per-
ception. And so it happens that in regard to those matters
which are not subject to the senses we have opinion rather
than understanding, with the result that when we have
formed some idea of a city's character, we often find it different from what we had previously thought, once we come
to see it as it really is.[1] Yet, in a restricted way we can understand the things of God. Though any full comprehension of
his being is entirely beyond our power, our study of his
creation enables us to understand that he must be one.
Although a triune Godhead is a *quiddity* unknown to us, the
theologian has the power to understand through the use of
analogy how three persons can yet be one God.

This distinction between understanding and comprehension led Abailard to formulate a definition of faith which
was to arouse bitter criticism. In the *Theologia Christiana* he
adopted the traditional definition of faith: "faith is the substance of things hoped for, the evidence of things unseen".[2]
In a passage in the *Introductio*, however, he calls faith an
existimatio.[3] When they read the book, both St Bernard and
William of St Thierry objected to the changed definition on
the score that *existimatio* was equivalent to opinion, and for
them opinion was the same as the verisimilitude of the
academic philosopher.[4] Walter of Mortagne also charges
Abailard with teaching, not the true Catholic faith, but his
own opinions.[5] But in so interpreting his thought, it is clear

1 *Logica*, p. 23.   2 Heb. xi. 1; *Theol. Christ.* III. col. 1224 A.
3 See *supra*, p. 36, note 2.
4 Bernard, *Tract. in error. Abael.* IV. PL. 183, col. 1061; William, *Disput.
adv. Abael.* I. PL. 180, col. 249. Bernard defines *opinio* as follows: opinio sola
veri similitudine se tuetur, *de Consid.* v. 2. 5, col. 790 c.
5 *Epistola ad Abaelardum*, ed. H. Ostlender, *Sentent. Florianenses*, Bonn,
1929, p. 34.

that his opponents did Abailard a gross injustice; he was
never guilty of the Pyrrhonism for which he was attacked.
The word, *existimatio*, is a difficult term to translate, but it
certainly does not mean opinion. It can best be rendered by
its derivative, "existimation" or "mental apprehension".
And faith is called *existimatio*, not because it is in any way
lacking in certainty, but because it is the existimation by the
human mind of truths which cannot be fully comprehended.
Faith can never be complete knowledge; it must always be
the act of understanding by the mind of truths which are not
perceptible to man's senses. And, so far from being heretical
in his new definition, Abailard seems to me to have been
seeking to express an idea which was later accepted by
orthodox theologians when they defined faith as "below
knowledge, but above opinion".[1]

Now faith which is merely intellectual consent to dogmatic propositions would be lifeless unless it were animated
by some ethical principle. The truth of this was realized by
Abailard when he followed St Augustine in distinguishing
between three different kinds of belief in God. There is firstly
the simple belief that God exists (*credere Deum*); secondly, our
trust in God (*credere Deo*), that is, our trust in his words and
promises because they are true; lastly, there is our belief in
God (*credere in Deum*) which is "to love him, to cherish him
by our faith, and by our faith to strive to become members
of him".[2] The first two forms of belief are held by devils and
reprobates, for they know that God exists, but they do not
hold the third kind of faith, for they neither love him, nor in

1 Infra scientiam...sed supra opinionem. Cf. *Summa Sentent.* I. I, PL. 176,
col. 43; Hugh of St Victor, *de Sacrament. Legis Nat. ibid.* col. 330; Roland,
Sentenzen, pp. 11 and 13; John of Salisbury, *Metal.* IV. 13, col. 924. Aquinas
declares: Fides habet aliquid commune cum opinione, et aliquid cum scientia
et intellectu. *In Boetium de Trinitate*, quaest. III. art. I, ed. Mandonnet,
Opuscula Omnia, III. p. 61.

2 Aliud est credere Deum, ut videlicet ipse sit, aliud est Deo, id est,
promissis vel verbis ejus, quod vera sunt, aliud in Deum. Tale quippe est
credere in Deum, ut ait Augustinus, "amare, credendo diligere, credendo tendere ut membrum ejus efficiatur". *Epist. ad Romanos*, II. 4, col. 840 A, and
Exp. Symb. Apost. col. 621 BC. Cf. Augustine, *In Johan.* XXIX. 7. 6, PL. 35,
col. 1631.

their devotion do they seek to become members of his church.[1] A faith which can be held by devils, cannot be a faith by which men are saved. Justification, accordingly, comes from the third kind of faith alone, and this is more than intellectual assent. In consequence, Abailard can speak of the "beginnings of faith", by which he means a simple recognition of the truth of Christian doctrines. Of themselves these beginnings possess no justifying merit; that must be supplied by the addition of charity.[2] There is here no idea of two faiths which differ from each other in regard to their content; the distinction is purely one of time,[3] for the objects of faith remain the same throughout, although through the advent of charity the character of our faith is lifted to a higher plane. We may be orthodox theologians, but without charity we have no true religion, and certainly no merit. Here Abailard was both working from Augustinian conceptions and anticipating the technicalities of later scholasticism. St Augustine had spoken of a faith which was firmly fixed in his heart before his baptism, though as yet it was unformed and in many points fluctuating from the rule of doctrine.[4] As charity is the gift of the Holy Spirit and is given to members of the church alone,[5] the character of his faith underwent a change as a result of his baptism. This "unformed faith" is the same as Abailard's *primordia fidei*. In like manner, Anselm of Canterbury distinguished between the faith which is valueless since it is without love, and living faith which, as it possesses charity, is therefore meritorious.[6] Later theologians —among them Thomas Aquinas—spoke of *fides informis* and *fides formata*, of which the first lacks charity and with it

1 *Loc. cit.*
2 At nunquam si fidei nostrae primordia statim meritum non habent, ideo ipsa prorsus inutilis est judicanda, quam postmodum charitas subsecuta, obtinet quod defuerat. *Introd.* II. 3, col. 1051 A.
3 Deutsch, pp. 184–5.
4 *Confess.* VII. 5. 7, PL. 32, col. 737.
5 *De Bapt.* III. 16. 21, PL. 43, col. 149; cf. Loofs, *Dogmengeschichte*, 4th ed. 1904, pp. 372–3.
6 Inutile est fides, et quasi mortuum aliquid, nisi dilectione valeat et vivat. *Monolog.* 77, PL. 158, col. 219 C.

merit, while the second has charity and is in consequence a virtue.[1]

Such then is Abailard's theory of the nature of credal assent. The true Christian should understand something of the articles of his faith, for the statements of authority are not to be accepted by the action of the will, but are rather to be regarded as intellectual propositions. But in his claim that the believer must understand something of the meaning of the creeds, Abailard was far from asserting that the dogmas of Christianity can be fully comprehended by the limited intelligence of finite man. Complete knowledge of the secrets of the faith belongs to God alone, and a partial understanding of their nature is alone possible for men. This partial knowledge is, as we shall see, obtainable through the use of analogy and through an observation of the character of God as revealed in his creation. Still, mere intellectual acceptance of divine truth is of itself insufficient; the faith which justifies must be infused with charity so that it may be made to live.

Master Roland objected to Abailard's definition of faith as an "existimation of things unseen" on the ground that it was too inclusive. The addition of some clause, specifying the character of the things believed in, was in his opinion necessary; otherwise the heretic with his existimation of hidden things must be judged orthodox, no matter how inconsistent with Catholic truth his beliefs might be.[2] Such criticism was unjust in that it did not fully appreciate the object of the definition. Abailard was defining faith as a form of conviction, irrespective of any doctrinal associations which would delimit its content, and in his acceptance of the dogmas of Christian tradition he was as loyal as Roland. He tells us that there are many things which, though they belong to the power of God, we may believe or not as we choose; our eternal salvation is, for instance, totally unaffected by our belief in the nature of to-morrow's weather. But, if we look

1 Cf. Idem habitus fidei, qui sine charitate erat informis, adveniente charitate fit virtus. *In Romanos*, 1. lect. 6, VI. 18. Also *Summa Theol.* II. 2, quaest. IV. art. 4, and quaest. XIX. art. 5.
2 *Sentenzen*, p. 12.

for the reward of the saints, there are specified doctrines which we must hold, and these are contained in the Catholic faith which consists "partly of the character of the Godhead, partly of the benefits and other necessary dispensations and ordinances of God which are carefully described in the Apostles' Creed and the creeds of the holy Fathers".¹ And this faith is called "Catholic", because it is universal, and does not exist in any one part of the world alone.² The faith of a heretic is different, for it belongs only to a single man or at the most to a group of his adherents. We must enquire then into Abailard's attitude toward the character and authority of tradition.

To all mediaeval thinkers the Bible was the chief standard of truth, and was regarded as having been verbally inspired. Although he had his own peculiar view of what inspiration was, Abailard accepted the traditional notion of scriptural authority, and he says that to dissent from anything taught by the Bible is heretical.³ He did not, however, look upon the writers of either Testament as the amanuenses of the Holy Spirit, who recorded like stenographers the words dictated to them, a conception which was then generally accepted. He maintained instead that when the Spirit speaks in his chosen vessels, he first illuminates them in an inward fashion, and then leaves them free to convey to others their message in words of their own choice.⁴ Accordingly, inspiration is the indwelling of the Holy Spirit, and not the dictation of the actual words which the writer of Scripture was to employ. When he says that the Bible was composed

1 Fides autem Catholica partim circa ipsam divinitatis naturam, partim circa beneficia et quascunque Dei necessarias dispensationes vel ordinationes consistit, quae nobis diligenter apostolorum vel sanctorum Patrum symbolis expressa sunt. *Introd.* 1. 4, col. 986 D.

2 *Ibid.* col. 986 C. This definition of "Catholic" was, however, accepted by Roland, *Sentenzen*, p. 14.

3 *Sic et Non*, Prologus, col. 1347 A.

4 Spiritus autem sanctus cum in electis loquitur, primum intus illuminat ipsos, quam exterioribus eorum verbis alios. Unde bene hoc loco voci divinae, ut dictum est, vox humana dicitur addita, ut quod per inspirationem aliis nuntietur. *Sermo* XIX. col. 514 A.

at the dictation of the Spirit,[1] we must recognize that he is using the term in a special sense. He does not mean that the verbal form of revelation was given, but that through the action of the Spirit the conception of a truth was implanted in the mind of a scriptural writer.[2]

But despite its inspired character, the Bible contains many misstatements as well as passages which are difficult to explain. In St Matthew, for instance, we find Jeremiah erroneously given for Zechariah,[3] while St Luke says that the Virgin called Joseph the father of Jesus, a title which, Abailard adds, "is more according to the opinion of men than consistent with the truth".[4] The two versions of the Lord's Prayer in St Matthew and St Luke embroiled Abailard in a controversy with St Bernard, for under the influence of Abailard the sisters at the Paraclete used the Matthaean version in their daily Offices in spite of the general preference of the church for the Lucan text. To justify their practice, Abailard declares that, as St Matthew was present at the Sermon on the Mount, he had a complete text; St Luke, on the other hand, was not there, and had to depend upon the account of another absentee, St Paul.[5] Some of these misstatements, like the Virgin's application of the title "father" to Joseph, are but exaggerations, similar to those which we ourselves use in daily conversation, as when we speak of the moon growing greater or less.[6] Others are traceable to the calligraphical errors of scribes. For example, the difference in the times given for the Crucifixion by St Matthew and St John who declare that it took place at the sixth hour, and by St Mark who says that it was at the third, is due entirely to lack of sufficient care on the part of the copyists. Originally the sixth hour was written in St Mark, but "many have thought

---

1 *Epist. ad Romanos*, I. 1, col. 794 A; and v. 16, col. 976 D.
2 See Deutsch, p. 130 note.
3 *Sic et Non*, Prologus, col. 1341 C; Matt. xxvii. 9. Cf. also Isaiah for Malachi in the Vulgate text of Mark i. 2. Referred to in *Problemata*, 37, col. 718.
4 *Sic et Non*, Prologus, col. 1343 B; Luke ii. 48.
5 *Ep.* x. col. 335 D.
6 *Sic et Non*, Prologus, col. 1343 C.

that a Greek episemon was a gamma",[1] and have consequently been led to such errors in enumeration. And a
similar clerical error is responsible for the mention of Isaiah
instead of Asaph in the text of St Matthew.[2] Abailard further
realized that it is impossible to translate the idioms of one
language into those of another, and yet preserve the full
meaning of the original. And so in the past, both the Hebrews
and the Greeks, boasting in their own perfection, have sometimes been accustomed to insult our translations as imperfect,
instancing the fact that a liquid when poured into a succession
of vases must inevitably become lessened in bulk.[3] Hence
Abailard himself insisted upon the nuns of the Paraclete
studying Greek and Hebrew, so that they might be able to
read the Scriptures in their original tongues.[4]

Naturally in all this Abailard was not anticipating modern
textual criticism. His Greek was certainly insufficient to
allow him to emend the text of the Vulgate, and he had no
wish to disparage the authority of the Bible by pointing out
errors in its pages. From their study of patristic literature
mediaeval writers knew of the many mistranslations and inconsistencies in their Testaments, but that fact did not in any
way detract from the supreme authority of the Scriptures.
Abailard himself tells us that if a passage in either the Old or
the New Testament strikes us as absurd, we may not therefore conclude that its author was in the wrong; either we
shall find that the text is deficient, or our translation is faulty,
or else we have ourselves failed to grasp its true meaning.[5]
Often unusual words are employed by biblical writers so that
their statements may be prevented from becoming worthless,
and in order that the more their precepts are studied, the

---

1 *Ibid.* col. 1341 B. This is the ἐπίσημον βαῦ which was written for the
number six. Its sign ϛ would easily be read for a gamma, the letter which
denoted the number three. The ἐπίσημον was frequently used in Merovingian
times, but later became a source of much difficulty to scribes. See Cabrol and
Leclercq, *Dict. d'archéol. chrétienne*, v. ii. pp. 238–41.

2 *Sic et Non*, Prologus, col. 1341 B. For Asaph see Matt. xiii. 35, and cf.
Jerome, *in Brev., Ps. lxxvii.* PL. 26, col. 1045.

3 *Ep.* IX. col. 331 B.   4 *Ep.* IX. coll. 325 ff.; cf. *Sermo* XVIII. coll. 511–12.
5 *Sic et Non*, Prologus, col. 1347 CD.

more their acceptability is increased.[1] Both from his own attempt to explain the *Hexaemeron* and from the difficult passages which Héloise asked him to solve, Abailard knew very well how perplexing a task exegesis could be. Thus, by making our own possible lack of understanding and the errors of the text responsible for any absurd inconsistencies which the Scriptures may seem to contain, he insured the supreme authority of the Bible.

In one passage, however, Abailard allows that a prophet may have erred, not indeed through his desire to deceive his readers, but because he thought that he was inspired, whereas in reality the gift of prophecy had been withheld.[2] At first it is somewhat difficult to reconcile such a statement with his other opinions; the words follow so closely after his assertion of biblical infallibility that it seems impossible to think that they represent a change of view. A key to his meaning can perhaps be obtained from his statement that the grace of prophecy was often denied because God wished to teach a prophet a lesson in humility, and from his allusion to St Paul's intention to visit Spain, a journey which the Apostle was never able to accomplish.[3] Probably, Abailard was thinking of some historical personage in the Bible whose prophecy was either unfulfilled or, like that of the false prophets in Ezekiel, was actually condemned. A promised journey, like that of St Paul's visit to Spain, is also a case in point, for the Apostle referred to a future journey which he was not allowed to make.

Abailard was too much of a Catholic to regard the Bible as the only source of Christian teaching, or to regard it as the sole criterion by which the validity of a doctrine was to be judged. "After the Gospels were written", he says,[4] "much that is necessary to the faith, but has very little sanction from

---

1 *Sic et Non*, Prologus, col. 1339 C.   2 *Ibid*. col. 1345 A.
3 *Ibid*. col. 1346 C; Rom. xv. 28.
4 Multa profecto fidei necessaria post Evangelium ab apostolis vel apostolicis viris addita sunt, quae ex verbis evangelicis minime comprobantur, sicut est illud de virginitate Matris Dei etiam post partum jugiter conservata, et de aliis fortasse multis. *Introd*. II. 14, coll. 1076-7.

the Gospel words, has been added by the Apostles and apostolic men". As instances of this he cites the doctrine that Mary remained a virgin after the birth of the Lord, and "perhaps many other things". Yet, "it does not invalidate a true confession of faith", he holds,[1] "if some of its beliefs are not to be found in the canonical Scriptures, for it was on that account that the creeds were added, so that they could teach and discuss the things which are not apparent in the Bible".[2] In this way Abailard maintains the typically Catholic theory of post-scriptural development. The Fathers, too, demand our allegiance, though their authority is not to be considered equal with that of the Bible. That they often fell into error is amply evidenced by the need which impelled St Augustine to compose his book of *Retractations*, and by Jerome's avowal that his study of Origen unwittingly influenced his own opinions in an unfortunate manner.[3] But the Fathers must not be impugned because they sometimes taught doctrines which are not true; their mistakes, far from being intentional, were due to their regard for their own opinions rather than for the truth of the matter which they were discussing.[4] But, since the value of patristic literature is uneven, the student is not bound to acquiesce in the opinions of the Fathers, unless some sure reason or the direct command of authority compels him to do so.[5]

II

Abailard aimed to use dialectic both as an instrument by which he could disprove the errors of contemporary heretics, and as a method of explaining to his students the meaning of the Catholic faith. Men, like Roscelin, had erred through

---

1 Ob hoc enim maxime symbola conciliorum Scripturis illis sunt superaddita, ut illa doceant vel disserant quae ibi aperte non habentur. *Ibid.* col. 1076 D.

2 *Ibid.* col. 1076 D.

3 *Sic et Non*, Prologus, col. 1334 A; for Jerome, see *Ep.* CXXIV. 4, PL. 22, col. 1063.

4 *Sic et Non*, Prologus, col. 1346 C.   5 *Ibid.* col. 1347 D.

their excessive reliance upon dialectic, and it was necessary
to turn against them the very weapons they had so dis-
astrously used. "What, indeed", he asks, "is more needful
for the defence of the faith than that we should have something from unbelievers which we can use against their im-
portunities? If philosophers attack us, they must be convinced through their own philosophy".[1] Yet here Abailard
had to meet an attack from two quarters. The very applicability of logic to the problems of theology was denied by
many men, and thus he had to prove that he was justified by
authority in his use of dialectic to unravel the difficulties of
theology. On the other hand, he was forced to shew why, if
the dialectic of other philosophers had failed from the standpoint of orthodoxy, his own use of dialectic was yet permissible and valid.

In his earlier writings, the *de Unitate* and the *Sic et Non*, no
attempt is made to defend the applicability of dialectic to
theology. The criticism levelled against him by the pupils of
Anselm of Laon, the hostility of the monks of St Denys towards his method, the suspicion he entertained that St
Bernard and St Norbert were working for his destruction,
put Abailard on his guard. Consequently, in writing his later
theological books he felt constrained to defend himself
against the criticism of those who denounced the legitimacy
of his method. Since the full storm of his opponents' enmity
did not break until after the composition of the *Theologia
Christiana*, his concern with the task of defending himself is
far less apparent there than in the later *Introductio*. The *Theologia Christiana*, indeed, represents an intermediate stage during
which he was chiefly engaged in explaining the doctrine of
the Trinity by the aid of logic; hence, although the book
naturally contains a short account of his own method of
approach to theological problems, it is in tone more explana-

1 Quid etiam magis necessarium ad defensionem fidei nostrae, quam ut
adversus omnium infidelium importunitatem, ex ipsis habeamus per quod
ipsos refellamus? ut si nos impetunt philosophi, per ipsos convincantur
doctores suos et philosophos. *Introd.* II. col. 1038 CD; cf. *Theol. Christ.* II.
col. 1170 A.

tory than defensive. The *Introductio*, however, contains a very
forcible attack on those who denied the applicability of dialectic to theology. This change of front is very remarkable,
and can only be accounted for if we remember the hostility
with which his teaching was received and the feeling which
haunted him that Bernard and Norbert had been enrolled
among his enemies. St Bernard was well known as an ex-
ponent of mystical theology, and as a man who therefore
denied that dialectic could be rightfully used by theologians.
Abailard naturally realized the need of justifying himself before the criticism of such mystical theologians. But another
fact was probably also responsible for the absence of any defence of his method in his earlier writings. The *de Unitate* had
been directed against Roscelin, a man who had employed
logic in theology with disastrous results, and in attempting
to disprove his heretical conclusions it was natural for Abailard to stress as little as possible his own use of dialectic. He
was indeed meeting Roscelin with his own weapons, and, a
logician himself, would not of course be faced with the necessity of defending the use of dialectic. But once his attention
was directed away from Roscelin to the conservative theologians who, as he thought, were attacking him, he had to
place an account and a defence of his dialectical method in a
prominent position in the *Introductio*, his later book.[1] But it
must not be supposed, as some critics in the past have done,
that the *Introductio* marks a change in Abailard's methodology;
the difference between that book and the *Theologia Christiana*
in this respect is solely one of emphasis. There is nothing to
shew that his reliance upon the use of dialectic was any
greater during the latter period of his life. Again, the presence
in the *Theologia Christiana* of an abusive attack upon a certain
set of philosophers who were in reality sophists, for their
reasoning produced nothing save empty verbiage, shews
clearly his preoccupation during the period before their supposed hostility turned his attention towards the school of
mystical theologians. Then he was more anxious to expose

1 Cf. his defence of logic in *Epp.* XIII and XIV.

the foolishness of these sophists and to distinguish between
their method and his own than to defend the use of dialectic
itself against men who held that logic had no place in theology. Accordingly, in estimating Abailard's own position we
must first see how he proves that dialectic was permitted by
Catholic authority, and then enquire into the reasons for his
onslaught upon these pseudo-dialecticians.

To Abailard reason was the mark by which "man is particularly compared to the image of God, and man ought to
direct his reason to nothing more readily than to the God in
whose express image he was made, since it is through his
reason that he is like unto God. And he must further believe
that his reason is fitted to investigate perhaps nothing more
suitably than him of whom it has received a likeness".[1] It is
indeed the special property of reason to "transcend the senses
and to enquire into those matters to which the senses cannot
attain",[2] for while our knowledge of the world around us
necessarily depends upon the data of our senses, our reason
can enquire into the invisible thoughts of God. But Abailard
had a peculiar method of proving the validity of human
reasoning. Christ, he reminds us, is called the Σοφία as well
as the Λόγος of the Father, and therefore just as the word
"Christian" is derived from Christ, so logic comes from
λόγος. Accordingly, the more the disciples of Christ are
lovers of wisdom, the more can they be called philosophers.
When the Lord became incarnate, he made us at once Christians and philosophers, promising his disciples the power of
wisdom by which they can refute the arguments of those who
contradict the truth: "I will give you a mouth and wisdom,
which all your adversaries will not be able to gainsay nor

[1] Unde etiam cum per insigne rationis imaginis Dei specialiter homo com-
paretur, in nihil aliud homo pronius eam figere debuerat, quam in ipsum
cujus imaginem, hoc est expressiorem similitudinem, per hanc obtinebat, et
in nullam fortasse rem percipiendam pronior esse credenda est, quam in eam
cujus ipsa amplius adepta sit similitudinem. *Introd.* iii. col. 1086 c; cf. *Epist.
ad Romanos*, iii. 7, col. 896 c.

[2] Si tamen vim ipsam rationis diligentius attendamus, cujus proprium est
omnem transcendere sensum, et ea vestigare quae sensus non valet attingere.
Introd. loc. cit.

resist".[1] A similar promise is also contained in the words: "Ask and it shall be given you, seek and ye shall find, knock and it shall be opened unto you", a promise which Abailard interprets to mean that our search must be through prayer, our asking through disputation, and our knocking through our enquiries into the meaning of the faith.[2]

The need of reason for the purposes of apologetic was, Abailard maintained, recognized by St Peter when he advised us "to be always ready to give an answer to every man that asketh your reason for *the faith and* the hope that are in you".[3] The words italicized do not occur in either the Greek or the modern Latin text; they seem to have been an interpolation, dating from post-Carolingian times, which was pretty well known in the twelfth century.[4] And Abailard did not forget that St Augustine had called dialectic "the science of sciences which teaches men both how to teach and how to learn",[5] a quotation which was then very commonly cited by theologians in defence of the use of dialectic.

By these references to the statements of authority Abailard justified the applicability of logic to theology. What was then his guarantee that Christian truth was accessible to human

1 Cum ergo Verbum Patris Dominus Jesus Christus Λόγος Graece dicatur, sicut et Σοφία Patris appellatur: plurimum ad eum pertinere videtur ea scientia quae nomine quoque illi sit conjuncta, et per derivationem quamdam a λόγος logica sit appellata: et sicut a Christo Christiani, ita a λόγος logica proprie dici videatur. Cujus etiam amatores tanto verius appellantur philosophi, quanto veriores sint illius sophiae superioris amatores. Quae profecto summi Patris summa sophia, cum nostram indueret naturam, ut nos verae sapientiae illustraret lumine, et nos ab amore mundi in amorem sui; profecto nos pariter Christianos et veros effecit philosophos. *Ep.* XIII. col. 355 BC.

2 Petite, inquit (Matt. vii. 7), orando, quaerite disputando, pulsate rogando, id est interrogando. *Ibid.* col. 354 D.

3 I Pet. iii. 15; *Theol. Christ.* III. col. 1217 B.

4 M. de Ghellinck (*Mouvement théologique*, p. 170) has shewn that this text was correctly cited in Carolingian times, e.g. by Agobard in his *Liber adversum dogma Felicis Urgellensis*, PL. 103, col. 32 A. It is cited in the form given in our text by several of Abailard's contemporaries, e.g. by Hugh of St Victor, *Erud. didasc.* v. 10, PL. 176, col. 798 C, and by Peter the Venerable, *c. Petrobusianos*, PL. 189, col. 726 CD. That Hugh borrowed from Abailard is not impossible, but it is more likely that in an age of struggle for and against the use of dialectic it was a widely known interpolation.

5 Disciplina disciplinarum...haec docet docere, haec docet discere. *De Ordine*, II. 13. 38, PL. 32, col. 1013.

reason? If we wish to employ logic, we must first be assured
that theology is a science in which the rules of logic hold
good, for otherwise our discursive reasoning would prove
to be of no avail. Abailard, however, was fully convinced
that Christian doctrine was essentially rational and logical,
and that it lay within the province of human thought.¹ As the
Λόγος and the Σοφία Christ is the intellectual and eternal
speech of God, and in his providence the operation of all
things has been fixed since the beginning of time.² The world,
in short, is a rational whole governed by the reason of God,
and with the world theology itself must also be rational. To
lend authority to his conception of the inherent rationality
of the universe, Abailard quotes from Boethius a passage
which was popular through the Middle Ages because it provided Christian thinkers with a valuable doctrine so analogous
to their own in the Stoic theory of a universal all-controlling
Reason:

O qui perpetua mundum ratione gubernas
...stabilisque manens das cuncta moveri.³

It has been suggested that in his defence of dialectic
Abailard was influenced by John Scotus Erigena.⁴ That he
was acquainted with the writings of the Irish scholar is difficult to prove for certain, for as a rule Abailard made a point
of naming those writers to whom he was in any way indebted, and nowhere in his books does a reference to Erigena
occur. The teaching of the Irishman is certainly based on the
same equivalence of human and divine reason which we have
already noticed as existing in the *Introductio*. He declares
"that true authority never opposes correct reasoning, nor
correct reasoning true authority, since there is no doubt that
they both flow from one source, namely the divine Wisdom".⁵

1 Cf. Seeberg's statement: als nicht vernunftwidrig, als logisch, als denk-
bar. *Dogmengeschichte*, III. p. 164.
2 Cf. *Introd.* I. 11, col. 996 C; *Epist. ad Romanos*, IV. 2, col. 937 B.
3 *De Consolatione Phil.* III. metre 9. See *Introd.* III. 6, col. 1104 D.
4 M. de Wulf, *Hist. de la phil., médiévale*, p. 198, and H. Bett, *Johannes Scotus Erigena*, Cambridge, 1925, p. 173.
5 Vera enim auctoritas rectae rationi non obsistit, neque recta ratio verae
auctoritati. Ambo siquidem ex uno fonte, divina videlicet sapientia, manare
dubium non est. *De Div. Naturae*, I. 66, PL. 122, col. 511 B.

We know, however, that the *de Divisione Naturae* was read at the end of the eleventh century, for it is quoted with approbation by Abailard's former master, Anselm of Laon,[1] and it was not until 1225 that the book was condemned.[2] But although it might certainly seem more than a mere coincidence that the two men should have both stressed the validity of human reason to discuss matters of belief, on the score that reason and authority each have their origin in the divine Word and are therefore never at variance, and even if it cannot be definitely denied that Abailard was ignorant of Erigena's book, it seems safer to conclude from the lack of any reference in Abailard to the *de Divisione Naturae* that each was using the same philosophical idea independently. The connexion between human reason and the Word was a natural one for the early mediaeval thinker with his Augustinian conceptions of psychology to utilize; the idea that all creation was rational owing to its foundation in the Second Person of the Trinity was one which went unquestioned at the time.

In his championship of the use of dialectic Abailard had one especial difficulty with which to contend. Gregory the Great had maintained that "the faith for which human reason gives proof, has no merit",[3] a statement which became the war-cry of those who denied the rightfulness of logic to deal with the meaning of faith. The passage itself comes from one of Gregory's *Homilies*, where he discusses the appearance of Jesus to his disciples "when the doors were shut",[4] and he declares that it is no more possible to explain the Lord's

---

1 *Sentent.* ed. F. P. Bliemetzrieder, BGPM. xviii. (1919), 2–3, p. 22. See also the same editor's text of excerpts from Anselm in *Recherches de théologie ancienne et médiévale*, ii. 1930, p. 55 note.

2 Cf. letter of Honorius III to Bartholomew, bishop of Paris, dated Lateran, January 23rd, 1225, and printed in Denifle and Chatelain, *Chartularium Univ. Paris*, Paris, 1889, p. 106; his doctrine of the Eucharist was associated with that of Berengar and condemned at Vercelli in 1050, and at Rome in 1059. See Bett, *op. cit.* p. 172.

3 Nec fides habet meritum, cui humana ratio praebet experimentum. *Homil. in Evang.* xxvi. PL. 76, col. 1197 C.

4 John xx. 19.

entrance than it is to account for the miraculous nature of his birth. The anti-dialecticians, Abailard tells us, took Gregory's words to imply that no mystery belonging to the faith ought to be investigated by human reason, and that consequently all the doctrines of authority must be accepted no matter how remote from human reason they may seem to be. But he refused himself to admit that this was the meaning which Gregory intended. If the interpretation given by these anti-dialecticians was indeed correct, we should have to recognize that he went back upon his words, for again and again he made use of reason in his attempts to examine and recount the reasonableness of the Catholic faith.[1] The actual words in which Abailard continues his examination of Gregory's statement are of such great importance that we give them with a translation in our text. The passage which we quote has been the subject of much discussion which has often resulted in a totally false evaluation of Abailard's position. The text as printed in Cousin and Migne has, however, been shewn to be corrupt, for six words, which completely alter the sense, have been omitted through a homoeoteleuton from the MS. consulted. These have been supplied from a Balliol MS. by Dr Lane Poole, and are here indicated by italics:

Novimus quippe ipsum beatum Gregorium saepius in scriptis suis eos qui de resurrectione dubitant, congruis rerum exemplis vel similitudinibus ratiocinando ipsam astruere, pro qua tamen superius dixit: fidem non habere meritum, cui humana ratio praebet experimentum. Nunquid hi quos rationibus suis in fide resurrectionis aedificare volebat, has ejus rationes secundum quam ipsius sententiam refellere poterant, secundum quam scilicet astruere dicitur, nequaquam de fide humanis rationibus disserendum esse, qui nec hoc astruere dicitur, ipse proprie exhibuit factis. Qui nec etiam dixit, non esse ratiocinandum de fide, nec humana ratione ipsam *discuti vel investigari* debere, *sed non ipsam* apud Deum

---

1 Ex qua profecto sententia, ne videlicet inutilis sit fides et expers meriti, patenter asserunt nil ad Catholicae fidei mysteria pertinens ratione investigandum esse, sed de omnibus auctoritati statim credendum esse, quantumcunque haec ab humana ratione remota esse videatur (*leg.* videantur). Quod quidem si recipiatur, ipsum quoque Gregorium in his quae antea de dictis ejus collegeramus sibimet ipsi contrarium reperiemus. *Introd.* II. 3, col. 1050 B; *Theol. Christ.* II. col. 1226.

habere meritum, ad quam non tam divinae auctoritatis inducit testimonium, quam humanae rationis cogit argumentum.[1]

We know that very often in his writings St Gregory used to teach the resurrection to those who had doubts about it, by reasoning with suitable examples and analogies; yet he said in the foregoing that the faith for which man's reason gives proof has no merit. Those whom he wished to build up in the faith of the resurrection were not able to refute his reasoning according to his own opinion, by which indeed he is said to have taught that matters of faith must never be discussed by human reason, although the very man who is said to have taught thus, did actually use reason. But he did not say that the faith ought not to be reasoned about, nor that it should be discussed and investigated, but that only that faith has no merit with God, when it is not the testimony of divine authority that leads us to it, but the evidence of human reason that compels our assent.

In this manner Gregory's words, so often employed as a proof that dialectic ought not to be used in theological discussion, are made to serve the needs of a dialectical theologian in the very defence of his method. The validity of human reason to investigate credal matters is recognized, but it is clearly laid down that, if it is to be meritorious, faith must proceed from the witness of divine authority. Of itself the evidence of human reasoning is useless, unless the teaching of the church is first accepted. Dialectic has no right to explain how Christ in his risen body could enter the room where the disciples were assembled; any such explanation, if indeed it could be made, would entail the suppression of a mystery. Dialectic can only dissipate any doubts which the marvellous nature of the occurrence must engender, and serve as a means whereby the faith of a doubter may be strengthened and confirmed. Here, it will be noted, Abailard, far from attacking the motto of Anselm of Canterbury, *Credo ut intelligam*, was really adopting it as his own. Our understanding of credal matters by the aid of logic can only come after our acceptance of their truth; the results of our discursive reasoning have nothing in common with faith. When Abailard goes on to

[1] *Introd.* col. 1050 CD. Cf. CQR. XLI. 1895, p. 139 note 2, and *Illustrations*, p. 140 note 28. The emendations are from Balliol MS. ccxcvi, folio 29.

assert that "faith is not believed in because God has spoken, but because its truth convinces", and when he distinguishes between the faith which is built upon such understanding and that of Abraham who believed in hope against hope,[1] he is not making the tenability of a creed subject to a prior conviction that its doctrines can be shewn to be true. He certainly does not suggest that we should only accept those beliefs which satisfy our reason. Rather he distinguishes between the faith of Abraham which came from direct revelation and the faith of other men who owe their beliefs to some human teaching. Thus, to teach others we must ourselves be convinced and be prepared to offer more than a *Deus id dixerat* to those whom we are anxious to convert. "What, indeed, could be more ridiculous than that a man who wishes to teach others, should allow that he neither understands the matters of which he is speaking, nor knows what they are about, when someone asks if he does understand what he is saying".[2] These words are very characteristic of Abailard with his contention that the dogmas accepted from authority must be understood if we are to be able to convince others of our beliefs. His own pupils had clearly recognized that it was as easy for the blind to lead the blind as for the uninstructed to teach doctrines which neither they nor their audience could understand.[3]

We have already said that Abailard attacked a certain set of philosophers who were in reality nothing else but sophists, so valueless was their dialectic. He claims that these thinkers were disturbing the peace of the church by their empty logic. Such was their arrogance that they held that nothing existed

1 Nec quia Deus id dixerat, creditur, sed quia hoc sic esse convincitur, recipitur. Distinguitur itaque fides talis a fide Abrahae, qui contra spem in spem credidit. *Introd.* coll. 1050 D–1051. Cf. Anselm's assertion that whatever cannot be understood must yet be believed, *de Fide Trin.* 2, PL. 158, col. 263 C.

2 Quid denique magis ridiculosum quam si aliquis alium docere volens, cum requisitus fuerit de his quae dicit utrum intelligat, neget seipsum intelligere quae dicit vel se nescire de quibus loquitur? *Introd.* II. 7, col. 1054 C.

3 Cf. *Hist. Calam.* 9, col. 142 A.

which could not be either comprehended or expressed by
their little reasonings (*ratiuncula*), and, disdaining the universal authority of the church, took pride in trusting in their
own powers alone.[1] Both the character of their lives and the
never-ending flow of their words made their logic nothing
more than intolerable verbosity,[2] and where their aim should
have been to edify, they succeeded only in destruction.[3] "It
is", Abailard retorts,[4] "one thing to enquire into the truth by
deliberation, but quite another to make ostentation the end
of all disputation, for while the first is devoted study which
strives to edify, the second is but the mere impulse of pride
which seeks only for self-glory. By the one we set out to learn
the wisdom which we do not possess; by the other we parade
the learning which we trust is ours". And the sole offspring
of the knowledge flaunted by these pseudo-philosophers was
ignorance;[5] for what they did not understand, they called
foolishness, while whatever they could not comprehend, was
termed nonsense.[6] In no way could their reasoning be called
dialectic, for they busied themselves with the semblance of
reason, its caricature, and not with its truth, and thus instead
of refuting their falsity they propounded false arguments.[7]
Who these pseudo-philosophers were we are not told; but
it seems highly probable, nay almost certain, that they were
the same sophists who were later attacked by John of Salisbury and were called by him the followers of a certain
Cornificius. John indeed tells us that Abailard was among
the many logicians who inveighed against their doctrines.[8]
The account given by John of the life and tenets of Cornificius
and his followers strongly suggests that they were identical

1 *Theol. Christ.* III. col. 1218 BC.   2 *Ibid.* col. 1215 D.
3 *Ibid.* col. 1216 C.
4 Aliud quippe est conferendo veritatem inquirere, aliud disputando con-
tendere ad ostentationem. Illud quippe devotionis est studium ad aedifica-
tionem; hoc elationis impetus ad gloriationem. Ibi scientiam quam habemus
percipere nitimur, hic eam ostentare quam nos habere confidimus. *Ibid.* col.
1217 C.
5 *Ibid.* col. 1218 C.
6 Quidquid non intelligunt, stultitiam dicunt: quidquid capere non possunt,
aestimant deliramentum. *Ep.* XIII. col. 353 A.
7 *Ibid.* coll. 353-4.   8 *Metal.* I. 5, col. 832 B.

with the pseudo-philosophers mentioned in the *Theologia Christiana*. Cornificius is described as a man of bad character and evil fame, so foul indeed that John forbears to enter into the details of his moral turpitude.[1] He plainly attempted the impossible task of trying to teach philosophy without tears.[2] In his school everything was made new: the grammar was altered, dialectic changed, rhetoric condemned, and while discarding the old rules, he discovered new approaches to philosophy.[3] There they discussed every inane syllogism, and, spurning what they had previously learnt, these scholars suddenly became great philosophers. The pupil who came to Cornificius as an illiterate did not stay longer in his school than it takes for a chick to become a fledgling.[4] His pupils had no regard for the theological opinions of others, and strove to darken those splendid lights of Gaul—Anselm of Laon and his brother Ralph.[5] Judged by the account given by John, the moral characters of these sophists were not a whit better than the reputation Abailard accords them; we are told they made bad monks, unscrupulous physicians, and dishonest courtiers.[6] It is indeed very unfortunate that John of Salisbury does not give the real name of this Cornificius, preferring to call him by that of one of Virgil's detractors mentioned by Donatus in his life of the poet. Attempts to identify Cornificius, however, have not proved entirely unsuccessful. There is very good reason to suppose that he was really a certain Gualo, described by Wibert in 1149 as a logician who was responsible for inane syllogisms, such as the following: "mouse" is a syllable; a syllable does not gnaw cheese; therefore a mouse does not gnaw cheese.[7]

1 *Metal*. I. 2. col. 827 D.

2 Faciet (auditores) eloquentes et tramite compendioso sine labore philosophos. *Ibid.* col. 828 D.

3 ...et novas totius quadruvii vias, evacuatis priorum, regulis de ipsis philosophiae aditis proferebant. *Ibid.* col. 829 D.

4 *Ibid.* col. 829 C.   5 *Ibid.* I. 5, col. 832 CD.

6 *Ibid.* I. 4, coll. 829 B–831 C.

7 See his letter in Martène and Durand, *Vet. Script. Ampl. Collectio*, II. p. 337, and cf. P. Mandonnet, *Siger de Brabant*, Louvain, 1911, I. pp. 122 and 143–4. John's statement, "rodere nomen auctoris", seems to strengthen this identification; cf. *Metal*. I. 2, col. 828 A.

This attack upon the Cornificians is very instructive, for it clearly shews the limitations which Abailard imposed upon the use of dialectic. He would have nothing to do with their claim that they could explain in full the mysteries of the faith, and that anything which they could not understand must therefore be regarded as having no meaning. Human reason has but a limited scope in matters of theology; "that which cannot be explained, must be accepted to our profit".[1] Reason can never teach the actual facts (res) of theology, but only "as it were a certain resemblance", for it is God alone who knows the full truth of reality.[2] Critics thought that such a statement meant that he only aimed at teaching his own opinion, and not the truth,[3] but such an attempt was far from his thought. In contradistinction to these sophists, he denied that human reason had the power to grasp the complete truth, but that does not imply that he substituted his own opinion for the tradition of the church. Dialectic only has the power to demolish false arguments and to sift the false from the true;[4] unable to comprehend reality, it must be content with a likeness of the real. And although Abailard insisted that such doctrines, as that of the Trinity, could not be known in themselves, he maintained none the less that analogy would illustrate their reasonableness and enable men both to understand and explain their truth. Hence his emphasis upon Gregory's use of "suitable examples and analogies". That Father was not cited as a theologian who taught that human reason could lead men to a full comprehension of the content of faith, but as one who used similitudes in an attempt to make plain the soundness of the creeds. From his

1 Credi igitur salubriter debet quod explicari non valet. *Theol. Christ.* III. col. 1226 A.
2 Quidquid ita de hac altissima philosophia (the dogma of the Trinity in particular) disseramus, umbram non veritatem esse profitemur, et quasi similitudinem quamdam, non rem. Quid verum sit, noverit Dominus. *Ibid* col. 1228 D.
3 Cf. Walter of Mortagne: Quis autem orthodoxus de fide Catholica trac taturus, non veritatem, sed sensum opinionis suae promittat exponere? Ed. Ostlender, *Sent. Florianenses*, p. 35.
4 See *Ep.* XIII. col. 353 A.

perusal of Macrobius, Abailard obtained further authorization for his analogical method. There he learnt how Plato
had employed analogies when he wished to the Agathon, a
being about which only one thing is known, and that is that
no human mind can know its nature.[1]

A further instructive fact about his criticism of these
sophists is that Abailard makes much of the unsavoury character of their lives. The thought of the early Middle Ages
was essentially Augustinian and so Platonic; in consequence
it was generally taught that morality was an indispensable
pre-requisite to all true knowledge. Although God might
employ an evil man to effect some good thing, a man can
never attain to knowledge unless he practises some kind of
catharsis or self-purification. From the words of the Psalm,
"a good understanding have they all that do his commandment", we learn that understanding which proceeds from a
strictness of life avails far more with God than any subtlety
of intellect.[2] Only by the road of humility and by righteous
living can knowledge of God be acquired.[3] The truth of this
had been taught by no other authority than St Paul himself
when he said that the "natural man receiveth not the things
of the Spirit of God".[4] Further, to enable a man to study
philosophy—and one must assume theology as well—some
gift of grace is necessary. Thus in his *Dialectica*, Abailard
declares:

> However long you exert yourself in dialectic, you will consume
> your labour in vain, unless grace from heaven makes your mind
> capable of so great a mystery. Daily practice can, indeed, furnish
> any mind with knowledge of the other science, but philosophy is
> to be attributed to divine grace alone, and, if this grace does not

1 Sic Plato, cum de Τἀγαθῷ loqui esset animatus, dicere quid sit non ausus
est, hoc solum de eo sciens, quod sciri quale sit ab homine non posset, solum
vero ei simillimum de visibilibus solem repperit. *Comment. in Somn. Scrip.* I.
2. 15, ed. F. Eyssenhardt, Leipzig, 1893, p. 482, quoted *Introd.* I. 10, col.
1022 D.

2 ...ex hoc aperte doceamur, PLUS PER intelligentiam apud Deum ex religione vitae, quam ex ingenii subtilitate proficere. *Theol. Christ.* III. col.
1220 D.

3 *Ibid.* col. 1221 D.   4 I Cor. ii. 14.

prepare your mind inwardly, your philosophy merely flogs the air outside to no avail.[1]

Since it requires genius, dialectic is not a science which can be learnt by routine; it must depend upon the gift of divine grace. And, in addition, we are told that there are few of us who are able to persevere farther than its beginnings, so confused do we become by its subtleties.[2] Just because they failed to understand these things, the sophists were unable to produce anything except idle verbosity. They attributed all that they did to their own prowess alone, and they did not recognize in their lives the essential connexion of knowledge with ethics. And they lacked so evidently the needful gift of divine grace. Surely, Abailard declares,[3] it was against men such as these that St Paul, no hostile critic of learning, warned his correspondents to be on their guard.

Faced with the problem of combating the results of such empty dialectic, Abailard compares himself to the slight David attacking the immense, elated Goliath.[4] The dialectic of which these idle sophists made so disastrous a use was to be turned against them, but it was to be utilized in a proper fashion; logic was not to be regarded as capable of probing into every theological mystery, for the full meaning of Christian doctrine could not be comprehended by the limited human mind. The sophists had made dialectic into a philosophers' stone, a solvent for every difficulty. Ignoring the complexities of theological problems and failing to grasp the fundamental fact that the secrets of God lie beyond the knowledge of men, they had allowed their logic to investigate all the articles of the Catholic faith, a task for which they were not fitted since they lacked the necessary gift of grace and

1 Quantocunque enim tempore in ejus doctrine desudaveris, laborem inaniter consumis, nisi mente tua arcani tanti capacitatem coelestis gratiae munus effecerit. Caeteras vero scientias quibuslibet ingeniis potest exercitii diuturnitas ministrare; haec autem divinae gratiae tantum adscribenda est, quae nisi mentem praestruat interius, frustra verberat exterius. P. 436.

2 *Ibid.*   3 Coloss. ii. 8.

4 Nam et divino fretus auxilio parvulus David immensum ac tumidum Goliam proprio ejus gladio jugulavit; et nos eodem dialecticae gladio.... *Theol. Christ.* III. col. 1227 C.

were not equipped with the required knowledge. In Abailard's eyes dialectic had no such powers. It had no right to
probe into the mysteries of the faith in such a way that men
judged those things which they could not understand as
meaningless. Dialectic was not to be employed as a criterion
of the truth of a credal act; its rôle was to indicate the reasonableness, not the truth, of a given doctrine, for the validity
of dogma depended upon the statements of authority, not
on the results of human reasoning. Dialectic indeed was a
defensive weapon in the hands of the Christian apologist.
All that it was entitled to do, was to shew that orthodox
belief was reasonable, and so at once to enable students
to fit themselves with that partial understanding of the
creeds which Abailard considered so necessary for a true
believer, and to provide them with the means of defending
Catholic orthodoxy against the attacks of the heretic.[1] But in
so doing the logician must always remember that there are
many matters which he can never understand. The content
of faith was revealed to men, and whatever cannot be understood must therefore be believed.

It will be seen that Abailard cannot be called a rationalist
if we give to that term its modern connotation; he was, as we
have said, an intellectualist in his attitude toward the assent
to faith. Yet in a restricted sense he was a rationalist. Like
Anselm of Canterbury and Thomas Aquinas, indeed like all
the great scholastics till the rise of Ockhamist Nominalism,
he believed firmly in the power of human reason to grasp
at least something of reality. Reason was the valid instrument of all human thought.

---

[1] Cf. the advice given by Aquinas: Ad hoc igitur debet tendere Christiani
disputatoris intentio in articulis fidei, non ut fidem probet, sed ut fidem de-
fendat. *De Rationibus Fidei ad Cantorem Antiochenum*, 2, ed. Mandonnet,
Opuscula Omnia, III. p. 253.

Chapter iii

HIS USE OF
PRE-CHRISTIAN WRITERS

THE first two books of the *Theologia Christiana* as well as the earlier portions of the *de Unitate* contain a long account of what Abailard held to be a sure indication that many writers before the Incarnation believed in the trinitarian Godhead of Christian orthodoxy. In his own efforts to explain the reasonableness of Catholic truth, this assurance that some at least of the pre-Christian thinkers had taught typically Christian beliefs was a valuable asset. He intended therefore to use the faith of men who lived before the Incarnation to support the claims of orthodox theology and to shame the unbelief of the heretical. If men before the Incarnation of Christ had held truly Catholic doctrines, there could be no excuse for the heretic of the twelfth century who refused to accept the teaching of the church.[1] His reference to these pre-Christian thinkers was also due to the recognition that, if the doctrine of the Trinity is accessible to human reason, it must have also been accessible to the enquiry of men of every age. But in citing the beliefs of these philosophers, Abailard stood far removed from the standpoint of his contemporaries. Even Anselm of Canterbury, despite his firm belief that the dogma of the Trinity could be proved by man's reason, unaided by revelation, never allowed that classical authors could in any way be regarded as orthodox trinitarians. Only a few patristic writers had noted parallels between the tenets of Christian theology and those of classical philosophy; their method had been useful for apologetic, but their example was never copied. Authors, like Plato and Virgil, had been invested with a considerable amount of

---

1 Cf. *Introd.* 1. 25, col. 1034 C.

authority by the Middle Ages, and their statements would have accordingly carried much weight, but that was not the reason for their citation by Abailard. By reproducing their beliefs he sought only to appeal to the power of human reason. The classical philosopher worked solely through the aid of his reason, knowing nothing of a written revelation. If the result of such reasoning was correct, as Abailard claimed that it was, the men of his day could prove the reasonableness of a belief in a Trinity by use of dialectic alone. Yet in one way his reference to these philosophers indicates a certain distrust in the power of logic. By instancing the soundness of much pre-Christian thought, he seems to be appealing to men to accept a belief which has the support of the philosophy of thinkers who were guided by their reasoning alone.

The Old Testament had early been stolen from the Jews and had been converted into a Christian book. The fashion of seeking in its pages for indications of Christian doctrine was set by the writer of the *Epistle of Barnabas* at the end of the first or the beginning of the second century, and was continued throughout patristic and mediaeval times. Following in this tradition, Abailard interpreted the plural use of *Eloim* with a singular verb in the first chapter of Genesis as a clear proof that Moses had believed in the Christian doctrine of the Trinity.[1] He further maintained that God's words describing how Adam had "become one of us" indicated the same belief,[2] while the three-fold repetition of "God" in Psalm lxvii. 6–7 was an indubitable sign of David's trinitarian orthodoxy.[3] Both the Psalms and the prophecies of Isaiah were taken as providing ample proof that the doctrine of the Son's generation was known to the Jews; the identification of the Word with wisdom, the special attribute of Christ, was considered by Abailard as a sign of the Christian character of the Wisdom literature. A belief in the personal existence of the Holy Spirit was evident from the phrase, "the Spirit

---

1 Cf. *Introd.* I. 13, col. 998 C.
2 Gen. iii. 22; *Introd.* I. 13, col. 999 D.
3 *Ibid.* col. 1000 A.

of God moved upon the face of the waters",[1] and from the many references to the Spirit throughout the Psalms and the book of Isaiah. To detail further the various quotations which are given by Abailard as proofs of the Christian beliefs discoverable in the Old Testament would be tedious.

The propriety of reading classical literature was, however, quite a different matter. Apart from any idea of utilizing the books of pagan Greece and Rome to support the claims of Christian orthodoxy, many men, both in patristic and medi-aeval times, denied that these writings should be read at all.[2] The criticism levelled against the reading of the classics was to a large degree actuated by pietistic considerations. With his fierce idea that man's earthly life should be regarded as a period of abstinence from all the pleasures and enticements that the world could offer, the ascetic naturally looked upon secular learning as unnecessary. Thus, in the eleventh century Peter Damiani warned monks against the "feigned schools of the grammarians" on the ground that worldly knowledge rendered men earthly and bastard, whereas heavenly wisdom made them spiritual and the legitimate sons of the church.[3] St Bernard again inveighed against his monkish friends who gave themselves to scholarship,[4] though he was often a patron of scholars. Two further reasons why secular learning should not be indulged were often put forward. One was that science puffed men up;[5] another, that the conclusions of secular learning were in many instances incompatible with the teaching of the church. This latter line of criticism was more often used during the thirteenth century when, under the influence of Averroïst commentaries, Aristotelian doc-

1 Gen. i. 2; *Introd.* 1. 13, col. 1003 B.

2 See, among others, E. K. Rand, *Founders of the Middle Ages*, Harvard, 1928; C. H. Haskins, *The Renaissance of the Twelfth Century*, Harvard, 1927, and relevant chapters in J. E. Sandys, *A History of Classical Scholarship*, Cambridge, 1903, vol. I.

3 Theatralia grammaticorum gymnasia, *de Perfect. Monach.* 11, PL. 145, col. 307 C; *de Vera Felicitate*, 3, PL. 145, col. 833 B.

4 *Ep.* CIV. PL. 182, coll. 238 ff.

5 Cf. I Cor. viii. 1. Cf. also qui scholastica inflantur disciplina, Joachim da Fiore, P. Fournier, *Études sur Joachim de Flore*, Paris, 1909, p. 10.

trines, such as those of the eternity of matter and the unity
of the human intellect, were being spread abroad. But, even
in the eleventh century, we find Manegold of Lautenbach
stigmatizing those who held the common Greek theories
that the Antipodes were inhabited,[1] and that the human soul
was composed out of the elements.[2] Still, the renaissance of
learning under Charlemagne had given a great impetus to
classical learning. Chroniclers, such as Adam of Bremen,
abound in classical references, while Bernard of Chartres
could teach in the early twelfth century that his contemporaries were but dwarfs mounted upon the shoulders of the
Greek and Roman philosophers.[3]

In no way can Abailard be called a classical scholar. Like
all his contemporaries, he regarded Latin and Greek literature chiefly as a mine from which useful statements could be
drawn with which his own opinions could be either neatly
rounded off or better substantiated, and even with the Latin
classical authors he had little real acquaintance. He knew
something of both Cicero and Virgil, but most of his knowledge of other classical writers can be traced to the books of
the Fathers, and it was from them that he picked out passages
which would be of service to him. And in so doing, he felt
no qualms either in seeking for secular learning or in turning
it to the defence of Christian truth. To those who argued that
knowledge "puffeth up", he replied that that was not due to
any fault on the part of learning; science makes men proud
only when students take pride in their accomplishments.[4]
And, had not St Paul himself quoted from a Greek philosopher, Aratus?[5] If the apostle had done so, was it not permissible for a Christian to study and use classical literature?
Like Rhabanus Maurus,[6] who allowed that it was legitimate
to spoil the Egyptians, Abailard pointed to the use made of
pagan letters by the early Christian Fathers.

1 *Opusculum c. Wolf.* 4, PL. 155, col. 154.
2 *Ibid.* 22, PL. 155, col. 170.
3 See John of Salisbury, *Metal.* III. 4, col. 900 C.
4 *Introd.* II. 2, col. 1045.   5 Acts xvii. 28.
6 *De Cleric. Institut.* III. 26, PL. 107, col. 404 B.

Acting upon these principles, Abailard takes as his first example of a classical thinker who held Christian beliefs Hermes Trismegistus, whom he ignorantly equates with the god of that name.[1] From the pseudo-Augustinian treatise, the *adversus Quinque Haereses*,[2] he learnt that Hermes had written a book, the Λόγος τέλειος, in which he had taught that the universe had been created by a single God and that he had made, prior to his creation, a second God who was both unique and true.[3] That Hermes had distinctly said that this second God was made did not militate against his orthodoxy, for had he not corrected his error by declaring that this second God was indeed born?[4] And, we are reminded, similar mistakes by which *fecisse* has been written for *genuisse* occur in patristic, and even scriptural, writers.[5]

Abailard makes much of the Platonic Trinity, composed of God, the νοῦς and the World-Soul; this Trinity he considers identical with that of Christian revelation. Here again, as with Hermes, the fact that Plato had said that the νοῦς was made does not vitiate the essential correspondence of his teaching with that of the church; Plato's use of the word "made" was purely a verbal error.[6] Abailard himself was not the originator of this identification. The equivalence of the Christian and the Platonic Trinity had been first noted by Claudianus Mamertus, a pupil of St Augustine,[7] and it is clear that he knew of the writings of Claudianus. But his claim that the Platonic World-Soul was the same as the Holy Spirit of Christian theology roused the fury of his adversaries. For his knowledge of the World-Soul, Abailard was dependent upon the commentary on Cicero's *Somnium Scipionis* written

1 Et magni nominis occurrat Mercurius, quem pro excellentia sua deum quoque appellaverunt. *Introd.* 1. 16, col. 1009 D.

2 PL. 42, col. 1103.

3 Dominus, inquit (*scil.* Hermes), et factor omnium deorum secundum fecit Dominum, hunc fecit primum, et solum et primum. *Adv. Quinque Haereses*, 3, col. 1103, quoted *Introd. loc. cit.*

4 *Introd.* 1. 16, coll. 1010–11.

5 He instances Eccl. i. 3–5, 8–11.

6 *Introd.* 1. 17, col. 1013; *Theol. Christ.* 1. 5, col. 1144.

7 In his *de Statu Animae*, 11. 7, ed. A. Engelbrecht, CSEL. XI. p. 122.

by Macrobius, and it has been shewn that all his quotations relative to the World-Soul come from that source.[1] He also found in the *Aeneid* references to the Soul, and these, together with a description of it by Pythagoras, he proceeds to quote.[2]

In his treatment of the World-Soul, Abailard had no interest in Greek philosophy either as a subject enthralling in itself, or as an aid to the understanding of cosmological and metaphysical problems. Here he was utterly different from Bernard Sylvester of Tours, a contemporary Platonist, who incorporated in his philosophy many of the chief theories of the *Timaeus*.[3] Bernard adopted the Platonic idea that the universe owed its beginning to the two principles of the One and the Many, the world being made by God out of the pre-existent matter, which is eternal. The first parent, that is God, ordered the diversity, bounded the indeterminate, shaped the infinite, and evolved the tangled matter into the elements.[4] But it was the World-Soul—the knowledge and will of God—that was the means whereby the universe was made.[5] The entire world is indeed an animal, and the νοῦς literally its Soul. Abailard, however, had no wish to found a metaphysic upon the basis of the theory of the Platonic World-Soul; Plato's thought at this point only appealed to him because he regarded it as an instance of the

1 See E. Kaiser, *Abélard critique*, p. 15. It must not be thought that Abailard was ignorant of Chalcidius' translation of the *Timaeus*. *Timaeus*, I. 4–5 is quoted (*Introd.* I. 15, col. 1007 D) as part of the *Republic*, and the translation corresponds to that of Chalcidius. It may be noted that Manegold of Lautenbach (*c. Wolf*. col. 153) states that in his day Macrobius was the main authority for the World-Soul of Plato.

2 *Aeneid*, VI. 724 ff.; *Introd.* I. 20, col. 1025 B, and *Theol. Christ.* I. 5, col. 1150 A. For Pythagoras, see *Introd.* I. 18, col. 1019 D, from Salvian, *de Gubern. Dei*, I. I. 2, CSEL. VIII. p. 3; cf. Cicero, *de Natura Deorum*, I. II. 27.

3 Cf. his *de Mundi Universitate*, ed. C. S. Baruch and J. Wrobel, Innsbruck, 1876, who err in identifying Bernard with Bernard of Chartres, two widely different men; Clerval, p. 258.

4 Erant igitur duo rerum principia, unitas et diversitas. Diversum longe retro antiquissimum. Unitas non inceperat: simplex intacta, solitaria, ex se in se permanens, infinibilis, et aeterna. Unitas deus. Primiparens igitur divinitas diversitatem excoluit, limitavit interminatam, figuravit informem, explicuit obvolutam hylen ad elementa. *Ibid.* II. 23, p. 61.

5 *Ibid.* I. 2, pp. 9–10.

acceptance of Christian beliefs before the time of the Incarnation. And so he maintained that the doctrine of the *anima mundi* must not be strictly interpreted, for otherwise we should condemn Plato, the greatest of philosophers, as being the greatest of fools.[1] That the universe could be regarded as an animal appeared to Abailard an untenable doctrine. By definition, an animal must be equipped with senses, but which of them, he asks, save perhaps that of touch, can be said to belong to the world? In explaining why the world has no need of the other parts of the human body, such as eyes or nostrils, Plato had indeed affirmed that it lacks the instruments of the other senses. Are we then to believe that the universe feels the impact of the spade, and that it suffers more than do the trees when they are hewn down, since both the trees and the world are animated by the same soul?[2] Yet everyone knows that trees and plants are without feelings, and that they may not therefore be thought of as animals. And, as the *anima mundi* is infused in our own bodies, why does Plato say that our own souls were created? Either our souls or the World νοῦς are superfluous, for the one or the other would by itself be sufficient to quicken our bodies. If, in addition, both the νοῦς and our own souls are present in our bodies, it is difficult to understand why the *anima mundi* does not enliven our bodies when our souls have departed at death.[3] But if, on the other hand, we follow the example of Macrobius and do not interpret the theory of the World-Soul in a literal fashion,[4] we shall be able to accept Plato's doctrine as being consistent with the teaching of the church. Abailard accordingly strips the World-Soul of its original cosmological attributes and makes it equivalent with the spirit which animates our individual souls. "Unless I am mistaken", he says, "the philosophers understood the Holy Spirit as the spiritual life of our souls, acting through the distribution of its gifts. Just as our souls are the life of our bodies, so the

1 *Ibid.* I. 3, p. 31. 2 *Introd.* I. 20, col. 1023 C.
3 *Ibid.* col. 1023 D.
4 Ex hac itaque Macrobii traditione clarum est quae a philosophis de anima mundi dicuntur, per involucrum accipienda esse. *Ibid.* col. 1023 B.

Spirit is the life of our souls for, by quickening them, it moves us to the performance of good deeds ".[1] Thus, Abailard can speak of the Spirit as dwelling within us as if we were its temples.[2] But, it will be noted, he emphasizes the fact that the Spirit distributes gifts; by this he fully shews that he does not interpret the World-Soul in any pantheistic sense. That Soul does not dwell within us as the life-giving principle of our physical life; both the personality and the transcendence of the Holy Spirit are clearly maintained, for the Spirit is the charity of God poured into our souls. And in this way the orthodoxy of Plato is in Abailard's eyes sufficiently upheld.

Throughout the Middle Ages the fourth eclogue of Virgil was regarded as a prophecy of the Incarnation, and as such it is quoted by Abailard.[3] Further, by reading *trina* for *terna* in the first word of a passage in the eighth eclogue:[4]

> Trina tibi haec primum triplici diversa colore
> Licia circumdo, terque haec altaria circum
> Effigiem duco; numero deus impare gaudet,

our author proved to his own satisfaction that the Roman poet not only believed in the coming of Christ, but was also an orthodox trinitarian. The prophecy of the Sibyl is also given and, following in a well-worn tradition, Abailard notes that the first letters of the lines:

> Judicii signum, tellus sudore madescet,
> Et caelo rex adveniet per saecla futurus,
> Scilicet in carne praesens, ut vinceret orbem,

when written in Greek characters, form the divine Monogram and witness no less than does the matter of the poem

1 Nisi fallor, Spiritum sanctum intellexerunt philosophi ipsis animabus nostris vitam spiritalem, distributione scilicet suorum donorum, ut sicut singulae animae vita corporum, Spiritus sanctus vita animarum, quas vegetando ad profectum bonorum operum promovet. *Introd.* I. 18, col. 1024 B.

2 Quas ipse (*scil.* Spiritus sanctus) per aliquod gratiae suae donum quasi templum inhabitat, et virtutibus vivificat. *Loc. cit.*

3 Lines 1 ff.; *Introd.* I. 21, col. 1031 A; *Theol. Christ.* I. 5, col. 1163 B· Cf. *Ep.* VII. col. 247 B.

4 Lines 73–75; *Introd.* I. 21, col. 1032 B. As far as I know, this altered reading has not been noticed before.

that the Sibyl was indeed referring to the Incarnation of Christ.[1]

But how did it happen that these pre-Christian thinkers came to know of so essentially a Christian doctrine as that of the Trinity? One answer to this question was ready at hand, but Abailard refused to take it; Clement of Alexandria had held that both Plato and the Sibyl were familiar with Jewish thought.[2] St Augustine himself had once accepted Clement's theory, but he had later retracted it.[3] Following St Augustine in his final position, Abailard refuses to allow that Plato could either have listened to Jeremiah or have read the Hebrew Scriptures, for when the Greek philosopher visited Egypt, Jeremiah had long been dead and the translation of the Septuagint had not yet been made.[4] Instead, Abailard claims that Plato and other pre-Christian thinkers had grasped the truth, because they used dialectic in the correct manner, and this enabled them to attain through their reasoning to some knowledge of reality. Unlike the sophists against whom Abailard railed so vehemently in the *Theologia Christiana*, these pre-Christian thinkers did not boast of their own unaided capabilities in philosophy; they attributed all their knowledge to God. In whatever they were about to do, whether it was of importance or not, these philosophers, we are distinctly told, were accustomed to call upon God, and the omission of such an invocation they considered as the height of folly.[5] And, unlike the sophists of Abailard's time, the Greek and Roman philosophers realized that pride and knowledge were mutually incompatible. Cicero says that God himself can be understood in no other way than as a mind that is unrestricted, free, and separated from every

1 *Oracc. Sibyll.* VII. 217, ed. J. Geffcken, Leipzig, 1902, pp. 153–4, quoted *Introd.* I. 21, col. 1031 B, and *Theol. Christ.* I. 5, col. 1162 C. Though Abailard refers to Lactantius, his translation comes from Augustine, *de Civit. Dei,* XVIII. 23, PL. 41, col. 579. Lactantius has the original Greek.

2 *Protrepticus,* 6 and 8, ed. O. Stählin, Leipzig, 1905, pp. 51 ff. and 59.

3 *De Doctrina Christ.* II. 43, PL. 34, col. 56; *Retract.* II. 4. 2, PL. 32, coll. 631–2. Cf. *de Civit. Dei,* VIII. 11, col. 235.

4 *Introd.* I. 20, col. 1028 CD; *Theol. Christ.* I. 5, col. 1160 B.

5 *Timaeus,* I. 4–5, p. 27 BC, quoted in *Introd.* I. 15, coll. 1007–8.

union with mortality.[1] This Abailard takes to imply that God can only be honoured by a mind which is cleansed from imperfection and adorned with virtue. He adds,

> Si Deus est animus nobis, ut carmina dicunt,
> Hic tibi praecipue sit pura mente colendus.

So convinced, indeed, was Abailard of the ethical greatness of many classical writers which enabled them to apprehend something of reality, that he even proceeded to defend that part of Socratic teaching which could easily be considered as directly opposed to the principles of Christian morality. Because he had been thought to have advocated the communism of women, Socrates had often been regarded with horror. Such an interpretation of his meaning, Abailard held, was completely mistaken. The Greek moralist had never maintained that polyandry should be practised; all he proposed was that children should be brought up together by the state, and not by their parents. The result of this common education would be that children would not attribute to themselves but to the community all that they seemed to possess.[2] Abailard was apparently much struck by the advantages of the plan; had children thus been reared by the community in ancient Rome, he says, there would have been none like that son of Aulus Fulvius who took a part in the conspiracy of Catiline, for would they not all then have been the sons of the state?[3] And he proceeds to equate the teaching of Socrates, thus understood, with that contained in the words of the Psalm, "Behold, how good and pleasant it is for brethren to dwell together in unity".[4]

Abailard does not explain how he thought that these philosophers attained to such great moral perfection, but we think it highly probable that he would have done so, had he been asked, by referring his questioner to the theory of *jus naturale*. This theory had been borrowed by Christian theo-

---

1 *Tusc. Dispp.* I. 27. 66, quoted from Salvian, *de Gubern. Dei*, I. 5, *ed. cit.* p. 4, in *Introd.* I. 19, col. 1020 A. Cf. John of Salisbury, *Metal.* IV. 20, col. 927 D.
2 *Theol. Christ.* II. col. 1181 A.
3 Valerius Maximus, V. 8, quoted *loc. cit.*   4 Ps. cxxxiii. 1.

logians from the Roman lawyers, whose influence with some modifications is apparent in the definition of Natural Law given by Isidore of Seville and adopted by subsequent writers. Isidore says that "Natural Law is common to all peoples, and is that which is held everywhere through the inspiration of nature, and not through any human constitution".[1] The examples he gives are those which are to be found in the *Digest*. It seems clear that both lawyers and theologians in Abailard's day were unable to distinguish clearly between Natural and Divine Law. Thus, Gratian, who follows Isidore in his definition, could not distinguish between them; Natural Law, he says,[2] "is that which is contained in the Law (of Moses) and in the Gospels, and by it everyone is commanded to do what he would that men should do unto him and forbidden to do what he would not wish them to do unto him". Abailard certainly could not separate the teaching of Natural Law from much of the teaching which he found in the Gospel. Thus, he declares that both the Law of Nature and the Scriptures command us to love God and our neighbour,[3] while in the *Theologia Christiana* he goes so far as to state that the Gospel is nothing else than a reformation of the Natural Law which was followed by the philosophers.[4]

But what is of the greatest importance to our present discussion is Abailard's equation of Natural Law to human

1 Jus naturale (est) commune omnium nationum, et quod ubique instinctu naturae, non constitutione aliqua habetur. *Etymolog.* v. 4. 1, PL. 82, col. 199 B. The whole matter is well discussed in Grabmann's paper, "Das Naturrecht der Scholastik von Gratian bis Thomas von Aquin", reprinted in his *Mittelalterliches Geistesleben*, Munich, 1926.

2 Jus naturale est, quod in lege et Evangelio continetur, quo quisque jubetur alii facere quod sibi vult fieri, et prohibetur alii inferre, quod sibi nolit fieri. Decret. 1. dist. 1, PL. 187, col. 29 A. The first distinction between the two laws occurs in Rufinus, Gratian's first commentator, who wrote 1160–70; see Grabmann, *Geistesleben*, p. 69.

3 Verba autem legis naturalis illa sunt, quae Dei et proximi charitatem commendant. *Epist. ad Romanos*, I. 2, col. 814 C, with reference to Tobit iv. 16, and Matt. vii. 12.

4 Si enim diligenter moralia Evangelii praecepta consideremus, nihil ea aliud quam reformationem legis naturalis inveniemus, quam secutos esse philosophos constat. *Theol. Christ.* II. col. 1179 D.

reason.[1] "Concupiscence", he says,[2] "is contrary to the natural law of my mind, that is, to the reason which ought to rule me as if it were a law". In our bodies we have a law which is the same as reason—though it is opposed to grace— and by this we are governed.[3] It follows therefore that, since it is natural, this law was present in men who lived before the Incarnation of Christ, and that its character is identical with the Gospel teaching in regard to moral and ethical behaviour. Such a theory was by no means novel. Abailard was but developing a doctrine found in St Augustine that the image of God is not obliterated even in the mind of an unbeliever, a doctrine which led Augustine to conclude that Gentiles are justified, provided that they do naturally (*naturaliter*) the things which Natural Law commands.[4] To Abailard their obedience to its teaching gave to the pre-Christian philosophers the moral pre-requisite to knowledge, which they had themselves recognized as an absolute necessity. The same reasoning faculty which enabled men to seize upon at least some portion of Christian truth, enabled them also to know and practise the Christian mode of life.

Upon the whole question of the means whereby pre-Christian thinkers had attained to a knowledge of doctrines, such as that of the Trinity, Abailard's thought is not entirely clear. Either he did not think out his own position fully, or he regarded the question as one which needed no exhaustive examination, so convinced was he of the definitely Christian character of so much of their philosophy. In one place, however, he actually declares that God had announced through eminent philosophers or seers the tenor of the Catholic faith to the Gentiles, just as he had proclaimed it to the Jews

---

1 *Epist. ad Romanos*, I. 1, col. 805 AB.

2 Legem illam concupiscentiae dico repugnantem, id est, contrariam *legi naturali meae mentis*, id est, rationi quae me quasi lex regere debet. *Ibid.* III. 7, col. 896 D; cf. Ephes. iii. 2.

3 *Ibid.* col. 897 B.

4 *De Spiritu et Litt.* 28. 49, PL. 44, coll. 230–1. Cf. Jerome's allowance of merit gained through the observance of Natural Law in his *super Matthaeum*, 25. 24, PL. 26, col. 188, quoted *Epist. ad Romanos*, I. 1, col. 807 D.

through the medium of the Old Testament prophets.[1] We are told again elsewhere that God revealed the doctrine of the Trinity to men who lived before the Incarnation of his Son, because his divine Trinity became known from his visible works through the reason which God conferred on men, and in this way the Creator himself imprinted upon mankind the knowledge of his nature through the effects of his own handicraft.[2] Such a quotation might lead us to suppose that Abailard viewed those pre-Christian thinkers who believed in the doctrine of the Trinity as amanuenses of the revelation of God, but this supposition would do violence both to his thought in general and to his conception of inspiration in particular. Abailard certainly followed closely in the footsteps of St Augustine, who had constantly taught that all human knowledge was given by God; quite definitely he says that the understanding of human reason is truly one of the gifts of the seven-fold Spirit.[3] But there is nothing to shew that he considered the knowledge of these pre-Christian thinkers to have been derived from any direct suggestion of the revealing grace of God guiding their thoughts. It must, however, be noticed that he lays much stress upon the part played by human reason in leading these thinkers to the truth. This fact induces us to conclude that it was through the character of their reason, not through any suggestion of the truth, that pre-Christian men were brought to beliefs which were so typically Christian. Possibly, Abailard may have coupled the Stoic idea of the λόγος σπερματικός with the *jus naturale* of the Roman lawyer, and, like Justin Martyr, have accounted for the trinitarian beliefs of pre-Christian thinkers by the presence and operation in man of this innate principle of rationality. His method of citing instances of their beliefs is of course that of the early apologists, though

1 Cum itaque Dominus et per prophetas Judaeis, et per praestantes philosophos seu vates gentibus catholicae fidei tenorem annuntiaverit. *Introd.* 1. 25, col. 1034 CD.
2 Deus illis revelavit, quia per rationem quam Deus contulit, ex visibilibus ipsius operibus divina ejus Trinitas innotuit, et per effecta sua ipse artifex sui notitiam impressit. *Epist. ad Romanos*, 1. 1, col. 803 B.   3 *Ibid.*

while they wrote with a view to convert those outside the church, Abailard sought to educate his students and to disprove the errors of contemporary heretics. How far he was actually acquainted with the writings of the apologists is a difficult matter to decide; he does, indeed, quote Lactantius and other writers of a similar type, but again it is impossible to say whether he possessed any first-hand knowledge of their books. A theory analogous to that of the λόγος σπερματικός was, however, indigenous to the Augustinian thought of the early Middle Ages. Thus Anselm of Laon, Abailard's *quondam* master, held that in man there exists an innate reason by which we have knowledge of the Trinity.[1] We have, further, Abailard's own identification of logic with the divine Λόγος, an identification which he cannot have thought applicable only to the logic employed by definitely Christian philosophers. Apart from the etymological connexion between logic and λόγος, there is in his defence of the use of dialectic a plain indication of his firm belief that logic is a valid instrument because of its close connexion with the Word of God. And so, in using their reason subject to the necessary concomitants of a good life and to the recognition that they owed their success to God alone and not to their unaided powers, these pre-Christian thinkers actually worked out their belief in a trinitarian Godhead by means of their reason, a God-given, valid instrument of thought. In all his discussion of the thought of these philosophers, however, Abailard was certainly more interested in the perfection of Natural Law. The entire *Dialogus* is an ethical treatise, dealing with the ethics of men, a Philosopher, a Jew, and a Christian, all of whom stood outside the Christian church. Their ethical ideas were considered by him as something, not only of great interest, but of great effect. The law of Christ was indeed more perfect and more able to win merit for men because it is later.[2] The emphasis here is clearly placed upon the late-

1 *Sentenzen*, ed. cit. p. 7.
2 Cujus (*scil.* Christi) quidem lex tanto debet esse perfectior et remuneratione potior, ejusque doctrina rationabilior, quanto ipsa est posterior. *Dialogus*, col. 1634 D.

ness of Christ's legislation; the laws, which preceded it, are
not condemned as having been invalid. The question is one
of degree, and, despite its imperfection, Natural Law was
sufficient to enable men to act in such a way as would render
their reason capable of attaining to some knowledge of truth.

In thus claiming that the doctrine of the Trinity was a
doctrine of Natural Theology, Abailard's standpoint is
widely different from that of Aquinas in the succeeding century. Aquinas refused to accept the theory that innate ideas
are present in the human mind, for Aristotelian psychology
taught him that all knowledge was derived from the senses
alone, and that, prior to the advent of sense-knowledge, the
human mind is a *tabula rasa*. From an observation of the
world of phenomena it is, he held, possible to prove both
the existence and the necessary unity of a God; the triunity
of the Godhead, however, lay beyond the field of sensual
experience, and was therefore a matter for the truth of which
man must be dependent upon the authority of revelation.[1]
Now, this rejection of the Platonic theory of innate or seminal
reason made it possible for Aquinas to include under the
head of philosophy all those things which can be known by
the human mind through the medium of the senses. In
consequence, all those Christian beliefs, which could not be
known in this way, are matters which belong solely to the
province of revelation. A clear-cut distinction between
Natural Theology and the theology of Christian revelation
was thus effected. But for Abailard such a distinction was
impossible. It is of course true, on the one hand, that the
beliefs of these pre-Christian thinkers were not, strictly
speaking, revealed; but, on the other hand, they cannot properly be called natural. They proceeded from an indwelling,
spermatic reason in man.

1 *C. Gentiles*, IV. I.

Chapter iv

THE *SIC ET NON*

WITH the sole exception of the *de Unitate*, the *Sic et Non* was the earliest of Abailard's theological writings, and its method is traceable in all that he afterwards wrote. Consequently, there is no better place to study his aim in applying logic to theology than in the programme which is outlined in this book. We have already noticed that he drew the attention of his readers to the many misstatements and inconsistencies which are to be found in the Bible and the Fathers, and we have seen how he declared that the writers of Scripture have a far greater claim upon our allegiance than have the Fathers. The statements of patristic literature need not be accepted as binding unless we are compelled to do so by some sure reason. But while passages could easily be quoted to shew how frequently a single patristic writer contradicts himself, differences of opinion become all the more common when two or more authoritative writers are compared. The *Sic et Non* itself is a collection of such contradictory statements, gathered together as they occurred to him and, on account of the dissonant opinions which they seemed to contain, inviting the student to a close investigation of their true meaning. The statements are grouped under chapter-headings indicative of the subjects with which they deal, and the fact that the book has a hundred and sixty-eight such chapters shews how varied were the topics which Abailard discussed. The larger proportion of these headings shews also that he was mainly concerned with specifically doctrinal problems, but questions of ethics are included as well. Some idea of the comprehensiveness of the treatise may best be gained if we quote some half-dozen of these chapter-headings:

Ch. IV. Quod sit credendum in Deum, et contra.
  XVI. Quod Filius dicatur a Patre gigni, non tamen genitus, et contra.
  XLIV. Quod solus Deus incorporeus sit, et non.
  CXI. Quod ficto etiam baptismo peccata dimittantur, et non.
  CXXV. Quod sit conjugium inter infideles, et contra.
  CLIV. Quod liceat mentiri, et contra.

A glance through the book shews that Abailard drew upon the writings of practically all the Latin Fathers together with a number of the Greek patristic writers, such as Origen, whose books had been translated into Latin. It must not be thought, however, that he possessed a first-hand acquaintance with them all. Though at St Denys he had gained the reputation for being a constant student in the conventual library, it appears more than improbable that Abailard had read all the authors from whom he quotes. It had long been a common practice for scholars to compile collections of passages culled from the writings of the Fathers, issuing these in the form of anthologies, or, as they are technically called, *Florilegia*.[1] To judge from the number of these collections discoverable in the various libraries of Europe, they seem to have been very popular. Indeed, the *Florilegia* would naturally have been exceedingly useful to the mediaeval scholar who desired to learn the opinion of authority upon a certain subject. It seems therefore highly probable that Abailard must have derived much of his stupendous knowledge of patristic theology from such collections. He would also have obtained much acquaintance with the Fathers from the very frequent citations from their writings which are to be found in the pages of the great canonists of the eleventh and early twelfth centuries, and it has been shewn that many of his own quotations came straight from the books of Ivo of Chartres.[2]

It might seem, indeed, that the *Florilegia* served as a model

1 See further Denifle in ALKG. I. p. 587; Grabmann, I. pp. 179 ff.; and de Ghellinck, *Mouvement théologique*, chap. I.
2 Cf. P. Fournier, "Les Collections canoniques attribuées à Yves de Chartres", in the *Bibliothèque de l'École de Chartres*, LVIII. 1897, pp. 661-4. Abailard quotes Ivo thrice: *Theol. Christ.* IV. col. 1302 C; *Sic et Non*, CXXV. and CXXXI. coll. 1548 D, 1562 C.

for the composition of the *Sic et Non*, for like them the book is a collection of patristic statements. But how far Abailard definitely modelled his work upon these *Florilegia* is a matter which cannot be determined. The *Sic et Non* contains certain very fundamental differences, for unlike the *Florilegia* it is concerned not with the statements of authority, but only with those statements in which authoritative writers disagree. Further, it covers a far greater range of patristic literature than do the *Florilegia*. The student then cannot go to the *Sic et Non* and find in it a handy-reference book of patristic opinion; he is faced with a collection of contradictory statements which cannot be utilized, unless some method is found whereby harmony can be brought out of so many discords among the authoritative writers of the church.

But, though in the *Sic et Non* no attempt is made to reconcile these many opposing statements, Abailard outlines in his preface several ways in which the necessary reconciliation may be effected, and in his other writings there are passages in which these methods of harmonizing the contradictions in the Fathers are actually put into practice. Thus, he notes that the address of the Epistle to the Romans presupposes the existence of Christians at Rome before the arrival there of St Peter, and the question, By whom were they evangelized? has therefore to be met. A difficulty, however, presents itself; there seems at first to be no consensus of opinion upon the whole matter. The traditional theory, which is to be found in Eusebius, Jerome, and Gregory of Tours, held that the Romans were converted first by St Peter. But against this Haymo would appear to assert that the Gospel was first brought to Rome by some baptized Jews who were visiting the city.[1] Amid what seems to be an insoluble difference of opinion, Abailard was supremely confident that a solution could be found. Eusebius, he points out, does not say that Peter was the first man to preach Christ at Rome, but that he

---

1 Cf. Eusebius, *Hist. Eccles.* II. 14, from the translation of Rufinus; Jerome, *super Romanos*, I. PL. 30, col. 648; Gregory, *Hist. Franc.* I. 24, PL. 71, col. 173; Haymo, *in Romanos*, proem. PL. 117, col. 361.

was the first of the Apostles to go there. The words of
Jerome do not prevent us from concluding that the disciples
of St Peter may have arrived there before their master came.
We may accordingly conclude that the Gospel was first
brought to Rome by some of the disciples of St Peter. This
does not contradict the truth of Haymo's statement for,
although that writer does not deny that St Peter ever went
to Rome, he does not maintain that he was the first to
give Christian instruction there, and when he says that
Christ was first manifested at Rome by St Peter, he only
means that those Christians, who had before been hidden,
were at his arrival brought to the light for the first time.[1]
Thus, out of what appeared at first to be an irreconcilable
diversity of opinion, Abailard held that harmony could be
produced.

The general rules which Abailard gives in the preface to
the *Sic et Non* for the reconciliation of these contradictory
biblical and patristic statements are as follows. Care must be
exercised to prevent the reader from being led astray by the
false inscription of a title or by the corruption of the text
itself. Many opinions, we are told,[2] have been ascribed to
authoritative writers, which they have never held, while the
errors of scribes have corrupted much, even in the pages of
the Bible. And as many patristic writers composed books of
Retractations, the student must enquire whether a given
quotation represents the true opinion of its author, or one
which has been corrected at some later date. Abailard says
that he was himself always careful to see whether any passage
he quoted from St Augustine had not been corrected in the
Retractations and, if it had, he made a point of citing the correction as well.[3] As it was then a common practice for writers

1 *Epist. ad Romanos*, Prolog. coll. 786-7.
2 Illud quoque diligenter attendi convenit, ne, dum aliqua nobis ex dictis
sanctorum objiciuntur, tamquam sint opposita vel a veritate aliena, falsa tituli
inscriptione vel scripturae ipsius corruptione fallamur. Pleraque enim
apocrypha ex sanctorum nominibus, ut auctoritatem haberent, intitulata sunt;
et nonnulla, in ipsis etiam divinorum Testamentorum scriptis, scriptorum
vitio corrupta sunt. *Sic et Non*, Prolog. coll. 1340-41.
3 *Ibid.* col. 1349 C.

to give the opinions of others, care again must be taken to
attribute to an author only those views which he really held,
and not those which he quotes as questionable or as indicative
of the theories held by his opponents.[1] And when canons and
decretals are discussed, many things have to be gone into.
The incidents of a given decision must be discovered; whether
it was made to remit some indulgence or to excite men to
perfection, and, if it is an actual command and not a counsel
that is being discussed, whether it was intended to concern
all men or only certain specified people. The reasons for an
ordinance and the date of its enactment have to be investigated, because what is permitted at one time is often pro-
hibited at another, while a decree which is made for the sake
of enforcing strictness is sometimes tempered by a dispensation.[2] Again, the same words are not always used with the
same meaning; if that is remembered, an easy solution for
many difficulties will readily be found.[3] But even so, it will
be discovered that many contradictory statements cannot be
harmonized; the conflicting authorities must then be brought
together and the opinion which has the strongest support
and the greatest confirmation adopted.[4]

Since Abailard made no attempt in the *Sic et Non* to

1 Nec illud minus attendendum esse arbitror, utrum talia sint ea quae de
scriptis sanctorum proferuntur, quae vel ab ipsis alibi retractata sint et,
cognita postmodo veritate, correcta, sicut in plerisque beatus egerit Augustinus; aut magis secundum aliorum opinionem quam secundum propriam
dixerint sententiam. *Sic et Non*, Prolog. coll. 1341–2.

2 Diligenter et illud discutiendum est, cum de eodem diversa dicuntur, quid
ad praecepti coarctationem, quid ad indulgentiae remissionem vel ad pro-
fectionis exhortationem intendatur, ut secundum intentionum diversitatem
adversitatis quaeramus remedium; si vero praeceptio est, utrum generalis an
particularis...Distinguenda quoque tempora sunt et dispensationum causae,
quia saepe quod uno tempore est concessum, alio tempore reperitur pro-
hibitum; et quod ad rigorem saepius praecipitur, ex dispensatione nonnun-
quam temperatur. *Ibid.* col. 1344.

3 Facilis autem plerumque controversiarum solutio reperietur, si eadem
verba in diversis significationibus a diversis auctoribus posita defendere
poterimus. *Ibid.* col. 1344 D.

4 His omnibus praedictis modis solvere controversias in scriptis sanctorum
diligens lector attentabit. Quid si forte adeo manifesta sit controversia, ut
nulla possit absolvi ratione, conferendae sunt auctoritates, et quae potioris est
testimonii et majoris confirmationis potissimum retinenda. *Ibid.* coll. 1344–5.

harmonize the many contradictory opinions which he cites, what was his object in writing the book? He tells us himself that he wished to provoke his young readers to the greatest exertion in the search for truth, and through this exertion to sharpen their wits.[1] It has been suggested that he aimed at establishing a harmony of the truths of the faith, and at fixing a foundation for positive theology. In attempting to do this, he sought to arouse his younger readers to investigate the truth, while he himself attacked the traditionally accepted methods of teaching theology.[2] But this suggestion is not borne out by the facts. There is nothing to shew that the book was left in an unfinished state, and that he intended to complete it later by the addition of his own conclusions to each of the several chapters. It seems therefore impossible to conclude that either a harmonization of different contradictory statements or the foundation of a positive system of theology was the aim which Abailard had in mind. Nor can we regard the *Sic et Non* as a piece of apologetic written to vindicate his own use of dialectic in theology. In his preface Abailard does not attempt to defend the use of logic, nor does he claim for it the right to make independent decisions in cases where the authorities of the church are found to be in disagreement. Only one chapter—the first—is concerned with the problem whether faith may be furnished with reason, and as no special emphasis is laid upon it, no significance can be attached to its leading position.[3] Had the *Sic et Non* been intended as a statement of his theological method, we should have found in the preface some lengthy account of his purpose in applying dialectic to theology. Further, the book was composed at a time when he was little concerned with the need of self-defence. We must indeed accept his own account

1 ...quaestionem contrahentia, quae teneros lectores ad maximum inquirendae veritatis exercitium provocent et acutiores ex inquisitione reddant. *Ibid.* col. 1349 A.

2 E. Kaiser, *Pierre Abélard critique*, Freiburg, 1901, p. 52.

3 And on this point the authoritative writers of the church were in great disagreement. Hence, apart from his own difficulties, Abailard would have been bound to cite contradictory opinions on this problem.

of his objective in writing the treatise; he aimed only to incite others to the investigation of truth. His aim was thus didactic; he wished to provide students with material which would be of use to them in their dialectical exercises in the problems of theology.[1] The creation of a system of positive theology was to be their work, and, although in both the *Theologia Christiana* and the *Introductio* he attempted to form such a system, in the *Sic et Non* at least he was content to collect material for younger scholars and to shew them the way in which their task was to be accomplished. Hence his emphasis upon the youth of the readers whom he wished to incite. He quotes indeed the opposing statements of the Bible and the Fathers in the same spirit as that which led Aquinas later to give in his two *Summae* the opinions of theologians who held different theories upon the problem which he himself wished to discuss.[2] But, unlike Aquinas, he did not set out to compose a *summa* of Catholic dogma from a harmonization of the various inconsistencies which are quoted in the *Sic et Non*. He made his collection of these contradictory statements because he was convinced that, while the authority of tradition must in no way be impugned, the contradictions which it contains must first be reconciled before any system of positive theology could be built. Thus, the *Sic et Non* is really a syllabus from which he intended that his students should work, and its object is consequently to teach.

Both Reuter and Deutsch claimed that Abailard sought to make a free use of criticism whenever the statements of tradition were found to be at variance.[3] Their arguments, however, cannot be substantiated. Certainly, Abailard states in his preface that "by doubting we come to enquire, and by enquiry we perceive the truth",[4] but by this he did not mean to imply that the individual critic has the right to accept or

---

1 Cf. Grabmann, II. pp. 207 ff.   2 *Ibid.* p. 209.

3 Reuter, *Geschichte der religiösen Aufklärung in Mittelalter*, I. pp. 220, 335; Deutsch, pp. 159 ff.; cf. Grabmann, II. pp. 204 ff.

4 Dubitando enim ad inquisitionem venimus; inquirendo veritatem percipimus. *Sic et Non,* Prolog. col. 1349 B.

reject whatever opinion he may desire. He was but applying to theology a principle which he had already used in his logic. The statement which I have just quoted from the *Sic et Non* was reproduced verbally from his gloss on the *Categories*; there he was commenting upon an opinion of Boethius that it is perhaps dangerous to decide upon some problems in logic. Abailard agrees with Boethius, but he proceeds to add that it is none the less advantageous to doubt, for it is by doubting that we arrive at the truth.[1] All that he means is that there are many matters which lie beyond the scope of our understanding, and therefore our judgement of them must necessarily be suspended. Doubt, however, is permissible in such matters, because it is the first step to belief since it compels men to enquire into the meaning of their faith, and this enquiry, far from leading them either to adopt an agnostic attitude towards their beliefs or to accept only those beliefs which appeal to them in debated questions, is to lead them to a fuller and deeper understanding of the creeds. Thus, in both logic and theology Abailard clung fast to the idea that a sure knowledge of the truth can only be attained if we seek, that is, if we question the meaning of our beliefs and enquire into the sense which lies behind those statements of authority which seem to disagree. And it will be noted that throughout his discussion of these contradictory authoritative statements Abailard assumes that in very many cases disagreement is more apparent than real. In a great number of instances enquiry will shew that what seems to be contradiction will disappear when once the true meaning of the authorities concerned is investigated.

How little scope Abailard assigned to dialectic must also be noted. Dialectic, as we have seen,[2] he regarded as the science by which true arguments could be discerned from the false, and its proper business was the weighing of the meaning of words and the enquiry into the import of every statement

1 *Logica*, p. 223; Boethius, *in Categ.* II. PL. 64, col. 238 D; quoted also in *Hexaem.* praefatio, col. 732 B.
2 Cf. Hugh of St Victor, *Erudit. Didasc.* II. 31, PL. 176, col. 765 A.

and expression.[1] Thus, dialectic is not the judge of the truth
of a doctrine, but the instrument whereby the pronouncements of authoritative writers are to be investigated, so that
their meaning may be made plain. Faced with a difficult
statement, the mediaeval exegete had indeed no other alternative than that of employing dialectic, and, as historical and
comparative scholarship did not then exist, verbal scholarship had necessarily to take its place. In all this the mediaeval
theologians were embarking upon a task which was very
similar to that of the suppliants who came to Delphi only
to be given hexameters which, as they contained no apparent
meaning, could only be interpreted by a process of verbal
jugglery. The outlook of the Middle Ages in scholarship too
was largely moulded by the tradition which it inherited from
classical antiquity. In the Silver Age of Greek and Roman
literature, when the writings of the great authors became text-
books for elementary instruction, it was inevitable that peda-
gogues should concentrate upon the minutiae of grammar and
style, pointing out to their pupils the various turns of expression that were worthy of imitation. Aristotelian logic with its
stress upon the need of analytical verbal study formed the basis
of mediaeval higher education, and intensified an already present tendency to pay special attention to the study of words.
We can accordingly well understand Abailard's insistence upon a form of scholarship which may seem to us mere verbal
quibbling. The use and even the omission of words provided
him with the means of understanding and reconciling contradictory patristic statements which were otherwise unintelli-
gible to men ignorant of our modern critical apparatus. And
so he could claim with perfect justice that the peculiarity and
the correct use of words were far more important and worthy
of attention than the essence of the things they expressed.[2]

1 Hoc autem logicae disciplinae proprium relinquitur, ut scilicet vocum
impositiones pensando, quantum unaquaque oratione aut dictatione discutiat.
Dialectica, p. 349.
2 Est autem illud maxime notandum, quam maxime in enuntatione conse-
quentiarum vocum proprietas et recta impositio sit attendenda ac magis
quidem quam rerum essentia consideranda. *Ibid.* p. 351.

But how far may Abailard be called the inventor of the *Sic et Non* method? In the past scholars maintained that the famous method was indeed his own creation; recent developments in historical scholarship prove that it was less original than had once been supposed. We know that in both canon law and theology there had long been in existence movements which were tending to the production of some such method. In the tenth century Gerbert of Aurillac, later pope Sylvester II, made in his treatise, the *de Corpore et Sanguine Domini*, a brave attempt to bring some kind of order into the mass of contradictory patristic opinions, the presence of which he was only too consciously aware.[1] In canon law especially the existence of discrepancies between different pieces of ecclesiastical legislation was very apparent. Hincmar of Rheims realized this,[2] but he maintained that when he had the necessary leisure he could shew that this lack of harmony was but superficial and that at bottom no real difference of opinion existed in the pronouncements of the various councils.[3] Gerbert of Aurillac again pointed out the extreme difficulty of observing many canons, because they conflicted with the decrees of earlier legislation.[4]

That Abailard himself was familiar with some of the canon lawyers and their writings seems certain. We have seen that he derived part of his knowledge of patristic literature from Ivo of Chartres; in the preface to the *Sic et Non* he alludes to the difficulty of interpreting the legislation of ecclesiastical councils, for their canons were so often contradictory.[5] It

1 PL. 139, coll. 179–88.
2 See H. Schrörs, *Hinkmar, Erzbischof von Reims*, Freiburg, 1884, pp. 406–8.
3 De canonum formis, quas quidem non attendentes sollertius ecclesiasticas regulas inter se autumant discordare, quae et quot sint, et quas singulae canonum conplectantur sententias...si Dominus spatium et otium dederit... scribere temporis processu disponimus, quibus nihil discors, nihil sibi dissidens in sacris canonibus lector quilibet facillime valebit dignoscere. *De Praedest.* II. 37. 11, PL. 125, col. 413 C. Cf. Pro temporum varietate et causarum atque medicatione morborum, per diversa organa, ut ab uno multiplici prolata spiritu, cuncta consona, cuncta reperiet (lector) temporis, necessitatis atque infirmitatis causae convenientia. *Ibid.*
4 *Ep.* CCXVII, ed. J. Havet, Paris, 1889, p. 209.
5 Col. 1344 D; see *supra*, p. 80.

seems clear that Abailard sought to do for theology what Ivo, and Hincmar before him, had done for canon law. Just as their various Decretals had been designed as handbooks constructed for the use of lawyers, so the *Sic et Non* was to be a source-book for theological students to serve as a basis from which a definitely organized and articulated system of theology should eventually be built up. There was in the twelfth century nothing strange in this close connexion between theologians and canon lawyers. Although attempts were being made to distinguish clearly between the respective spheres of theology and canon law, there was in the early twelfth century no real differentiation between the interests of the theologian and those of the canonist. The latter knew his theology as well as did the theologian his canon law, and it was no uncommon thing for one man to be a master of both sciences. Thus, Roland Bandinelli and Omnibene were authors of theological books and of treatises upon canon law.

The comprehensiveness of the *Sic et Non* is one of its notable characteristics. Hitherto theological books had been for the most part confined to the discussion of single subjects, the annotation of a single book of the Bible, the elucidation of one particular doctrine, or the refutation of some specified heretical opinion; the *de Divisione Naturae* of Erigena and the *de Universo* of Rhabanus Maurus are alone magnificent exceptions. The *Sentences* of Anselm of Laon do indeed betray a new movement; they are concerned with the whole area of theology. The comprehensive character of the *Sic et Non* may have been the result of Abailard's very intermittent attendance at Anselm's lectures, but it seems more probable that comprehension of the book was due to the influence of the canon lawyers, whose decretals by the very nature of their subject included the varied questions dealt with by the legislation of the church councils. The fact that the method of the *Sic et Non* is to be found in the *Sentences* of Anselm of Laon does not necessarily force us to infer that that method was borrowed from Abailard's former professor. His references to the difficulties of interpreting canon law prove, as I have argued, that he took the method from the writings of the canonists. But the presence of the *Sic et Non* in Anselm's *Sentences* proves at once that the methods of the canon lawyers were finding their way into theology and that Abailard himself was not the first theologian to make use of them.

Nor does it seem to us possible to trace the *Sic et Non* to the influence of any single canon lawyer over Abailard. Dr Grabmann, indeed, would have us believe that Abailard borrowed the method directly from Bernold of Constance, who used it in his *de Sacramentis Excommunicatorum*.[1] Bernold was a distinguished canonist as well as a liturgiologist and a chronicler of repute who died in the year 1100; thus Abailard could well have known his work. That he employed the famous method cannot be denied, but this in itself does not prove that he influenced Abailard. As we know, Abailard usually quotes those authorities to whom he was in any way indebted, and in none of his extant writings is there any mention of Bernold. We should certainly have expected some such reference if Abailard had indeed taken the method from the pages of Bernold's treatise. There is, of course, the possibility that, as the *Sic et Non* was not concerned with the defence of the use of logic nor with any attack on the theological methods of other theologians, he may not have considered it necessary to mention Bernold as the authority for his use of the method. Still, Grabmann's thesis can hardly be said to be either proven or convincing. It appears therefore more critical to maintain that both Bernold and Abailard were utilizing independently a method which was then being developed among canonists. To make Bernold responsible for Abailard's use of the *Sic et Non* method seems to be entirely unnecessary and critically unwarrantable.

---

1 Grabmann, I. pp. 234–46, II. p. 216; Bernold's *de Sacramentis* is printed in PL. 148, coll. 1061–8.

Chapter v

ABAILARD'S LOGICAL THEORIES

RADITIONALLY, logic had always been divided into two portions; first dialectic or the judgement of the validity of arguments, and then topics dealing with the discovery of arguments themselves. Cicero had taught that the second was the more important section of the two, both by nature and because of its utility.[1] Otto of Freising tells us that Abailard was also more concerned in his logical studies with the discovery of arguments than with their judgement,[2] and the truth of this statement is amply confirmed by Abailard's own words in his gloss upon Porphyry.[3] Thus, in his view the primary use of logic was practical. The importance of this emphasis is great, for it amplifies our knowledge of his aim in applying logic to theology. Logic he regarded as the method whereby arguments could be discovered by which the truth and reasonableness of Catholic doctrines could be defended and the false opinions of the heretical disproved; by it arguments necessary for the explanation of the doctrines of the church were to be discovered. Dialectic, on the other hand, was the implement whereby the contradictions in authority were to be reconciled.

Abailard naturally founded his logic upon those Aristotelian treatises which were accessible in Latin at the time;[4] he also used the *Topics* of Cicero and the various commentaries of Boethius. From the *Isagoges* of Porphyry he borrowed much, and it was in them that he met with the main problem with which he had to deal. This was the question of

1 Cf. Cicero, *Topics*, II. 6; Boethius, *Comment. in Topica*, PL. 64, coll. 1044 ff.; Prantl, pp. 167–8.

2 *Gesta Fred.* I. 48, *ed. cit.* p. 69.

3 Ad utramque autem logicae partem, maxime vero ad inventionem haec scientia pertinet. *Logica*, p. 3.

4 For the Aristotelian texts known to Abailard see Appendix II.

the nature of universals, a problem which at some time or another has to be faced by every philosopher. The question at issue was whether genera and species subsist, that is, whether they signify some truly existent thing; or are they merely located in the intellect, as being simply the empty creations of the understanding, lacking all real existence? It is the old problem which divided the philosophy of Aristotle from that of his master, Plato, and it had been bequeathed to the mediaeval logicians by Porphyry, who had refused to decide between the rival interpretations of the Platonist and the Aristotelian.[1] In the eleventh and twelfth centuries especially, when a new renaissance of European learning dawned, the problem bulked large in the ever-increasing philosophical and theological literature. To theologians who were engaged upon expositions of the doctrine of the Trinity the nature of universals was fundamental, for their orthodoxy so largely depended upon a proper distinction between the individual Persons of the Godhead and their own substance.

Following his usual practice, Abailard prefaces his own account of the problem with a discussion of some of the different theories concerning the nature of universals propounded by the logicians of his day. If we would understand his position, we must therefore see what were his chief objections to the theories advanced by his contemporaries. Here, as we should expect, his objections are all based upon a criticism of the fact that these logicians did not sufficiently distinguish between the individual and the species or genus to which this individual belongs. Indeed, the whole problem of the nature of universals is identical with that of the one and the many. Further, in his attempt to disprove the theories of those philosophers with whom he disagreed, Abailard employed the logic of both Aristotle and Plato indiscriminately. Characteristically enough, he seems to have thought that the doctrines of these two thinkers differed more often in their terminology than in the nature of their tenets, and, apparently ignorant of the fundamental opposition be-

1 Boethius, *in Porphyr.* col. 82 B, and ed. S. Brandt, CSEL. XLVIII. p. 147.

tween them, and anxious to safeguard Plato's reputation as
the chief of the philosophers, he was inclined to attribute
Aristotle's criticism of the thought of his former master to
envy and to the desire for an equal reputation.[1]

In the *Logica Ingredientibus* Abailard has little to say of the
Nominalist theories put forward by Roscelin;[2] passages in
the *Dialectica* make it plain that he considered Nominalism
little worthy of attention.[3] Since the various forms of Realism
occupy him far more, I shall proceed straightway to describe
his attitude towards the different philosophers who taught
that universals were things with a subsistence of their own.

The first group of philosophers whom he criticizes are the
Platonic Realists who treated of universals as follows. In
those things which differ in form, they locate a substance
which is essentially the same in each and is the material essence
of the things in which it is. This universal is in itself one, and
it is only differentiated by the forms of the things "below"
it, that is, by the less general than itself.[4] This identical substance exists in both Plato and Socrates, despite the fact that
by virtue of the presence of different accidental forms belonging to each, these two men are distinct as individuals.
So, while the substance is in itself universal, it becomes
individual and singular through the addition of forms; while
it is in its own nature self-subsistent, it cannot exist apart
from these accidental forms in the world of reality. Thus, the
one substance is in itself universal, though in actuality individual. In itself the universal is not perceptible to the senses,
since only when accidents adhere to it does it become corporeal and sensible.[5] And in this way, we can say with

---

1 Cf. Novimus etiam ipsum Aristotelem et in aliis locis adversus eundem
magistrum suum et primum totius philosophiae ducem ex fomite fortasse
invidiae aut ex avaritia nominis, ex manifestationibus adversus ejus sententias
inhiantem dimicasse.... *Dialect.* pp. 205 ff. See Prantl, pp. 176–7.

2 P. 10.   3 P. 471.

4 Quidam enim ita rem universalem accipiunt, ut in rebus diversis ab
invicem per formas eandem essentialiter substantiam collocent, quae singu-
larium, in quibus est, materialis sit essentia et se ipsa una, tantum per formas
inferiorum diversa. *Logica*, p. 10.

5 *Ibid.* p. 11.

Aristotle that singulars exist, while universals are understood.[1]

Such a theory did not commend itself to Abailard, and among his reasons for its rejection he gives the two following. According to Aristotle there are ten "categories" or essences of all things, these being the ten *summa genera* or most inclusive classes into which things can be grouped. In each several category there is one single essence, and this essence is differentiated only through the forms of the subordinate classes. Consequently, apart from these forms the essence would possess no variety. As in Plato's theory all substances are at bottom one and the same, so in Aristotle's logic all that falls under each several category is the same. Since therefore the actual Socrates and the actual Plato have in themselves things belonging to each of the ten categories, and since the things in each category are essentially the same, all the forms of the one are also the forms of the other with no essential difference. Accordingly, we cannot rightly regard the nature of their forms as differentiating the single identical essence of Platonic logic, nor do the ten essences of Aristotle effect any differentiation, for the one single essence and the ten essences are at once both in the actual Plato and the actual Socrates.[2] Further, if their diversity was due only to forms, while the substance in which these forms inhere remained the same, how, Abailard asked, could numerical distinctions be explained? The one Socrates is not to be called many because he sustains many forms; he is himself one despite their plurality.[3]

The doctrine which holds that individual things owe their existence to the presence of accidental forms is untenable for another reason. If individual things derived their being from accidents, it would necessarily follow that these accidents must be prior to the species to which they give existence.[4] As man considered as a species is distinct from the genus

---

1 Cf. Boethius, *in Categ.* ii. col. 210 B.   2 *Logica*, p. 12.
3 Amplius quomodo multa numero consideremus in substantiis, si sola formarum diversitas eadem penitus subjecta substantia permanente? Neque enim Socratem multa numero dicimus propter multarum formarum susceptionem. *Ibid.* p. 13.   4 *Ibid.*

animal owing to the formation of difference, namely reason, so these Realists allege that Socrates is distinct from other individual men through the addition of accidents. Hence neither can the species exist without difference, nor the individual without accidental forms, and therefore Socrates cannot be prior to, nor the basis of, accidents, nor can man for that matter be prior to, nor the basis of, difference. But if accidents are not in individuals as in subjects, that is, if individuals are not both prior to, and the basis of, accidents, then accidents are most certainly not in universals. For it is part of this theory that whatever is in first substance, that is in individuals, as in subjects, is likewise in second substance, in species and genera, as in subjects.[1] Accordingly, the doctrine which claims that the same essence subsists in diverse things at the same time cannot reasonably be held.

Opposed to these Realists, as they are called, holding that universals were ultimate realities, come a group of philosophers who taught that individual things differ from each other not only through their accidental forms, but in that they are also discrete in their own essence, as indeed individual persons are. Thus, that which is in one thing, whether it be matter or form, cannot be present in any way in another. And so, if the forms were removed, the things would still subsist equally discrete in their essence, since their discreteness—according to which this individual is not that—does not arise from the presence of forms, but exists in consequence of the diversity of their essence.[2] Although they hold

1 Nam sicut homo ex formatione differentiae distat, ita Socratem ex accidentium susceptione appellant. Unde nec Socrates praeter accidentia sicut nec homo praeter differentias esse potest.... Si autem in individuis substantiis ut in subjectis accidentia non sunt, profecto nec in universalibus. Quaecumque enim in secundis substantiis ut in subjectis sunt, eadem in primis ut in subjectis esse universaliter monstrat. *Logica*, p. 13. For the use of the terms, first and second substances, i.e. individuals as opposed to species and genera, see Boethius, *in Categ.* I. col. 182 B; *Logica*, p. 140.

2 Res singulas non solum formis ab invicem esse diversas, verum personaliter in suis essentiis esse discretas nec ullo modo id quod in una est, esse in alia, sive illud materia sit sive forma, nec eas formis quoque remotis minus in essentiis suis discretas posse subsistere, quia earum discretio personalis, secundum quam scilicet haec non est illa, non per formas sit, sed est per ipsam essentiae diversitatem.... *Ibid.* p. 13.

that all things are in this way different from each other, so that none of them participates in another either in the same matter essentially or in the same form essentially, yet these same philosophers still cling to the universality of things. To reconcile what appears to be a contradiction in their thought, they call those things which are discrete the same thing not indeed *essentially* but *indifferently*. And so they say that individual men, though discrete in themselves, are yet the same in that they are men, that is, they do not differ in the nature of their humanity, and the same men whom they term individual on account of their discreteness the one from the other, they also term universals because of their indifference and the agreement of their likeness.[1] Abailard tells us elsewhere that William of Champeaux came to adopt a theory of indifference as the result of his own criticism. Before the arrival of Abailard at his school, William had held the ultra-Realist view criticized above, that diversity is due only to the presence within the same substance of different accidents.[2] Abailard further tells us that this school of philosophy was not unanimous; some held that the universal was but a collection of things, and others that the species, man, is not only a collection of men, but also that the individuals, in that they are men, form a species. And thus when the latter say that the thing which is Socrates is predicated of man, they mean that many men are the same as he, that is, that they agree with him, or that he agrees with the many, in that all are alike men. And so there are as many species as there are individual things; yet corresponding with the likeness of their natures these philosophers also posit a smaller number of universals.[3] Abailard does not tell us to which of these two

1 Cum autem omnes res ita diversas ab invicem esse velint, ut nulla earum cum alia vel eandem essentialiter materiam vel eandem essentialiter formam participet, universale tamen rerum adhuc retinentes idem non essentialiter quidem, sed indifferenter ea quae discreta sunt, appellant, veluti singulos homines in se ipsis discretos idem esse in homine dicunt, id est non differre in natura humanitatis, et eosdem quos singulares dicunt secundum discretionem, universales dicunt secundum indifferentiam et similitudinis convenientiam. *Ibid.* pp. 13–14.

2 *Hist. Calam.* 2, col. 119 A.   3 *Logica*, p. 14.

schools of indifferentists William of Champeaux belonged. We may, however, mention the two types of indifferentism taught by Adelard of Bath and Walter of Mortagne, both of whom rejected the idea that universals were self-subsistent entities. To these men genera and species appeared to be nothing else than individual things regarded under different aspects, but both gave to the character of these "aspects" a different name. Adelard, who wrote his treatise, the *de Eodem et Diverso*, some time between the years 1105 and 1116, taught that these aspects were merely *respectus* of the same thing. In his view the distinction between genus, species, and individual was solely a distinction made by the finite human mind according to whether an individual object was regarded as belonging to a genus or to a species or by itself in its own individuality.[1] Walter of Mortagne, on the other hand, held that these aspects were *status* of the same things, and, save for a changed terminology, his thought is practically the same as that of Adelard. Thus, he looked upon Plato as an individual in that which is Plato, as a species in that which is man, and as a genus in that which is animal in him.[2] The theories of these two philosophers then agree with the second group of indifferentists mentioned by Abailard.

Abailard takes first those who maintain that a whole collection of men taken together form a universal. He allows that their theory appears to be substantiated by a statement by Boethius to the effect that a species is the thought collected from the substantial likeness of individuals, and genus is the likeness similarly collected from species.[3] These philosophers do not indeed allege that the actual Plato and Socrates are in themselves species, but they hold that all men when collected together are that species which is man, and that all animals, when they are likewise collected, form the genus, animal. But even so the actual Socrates could be predicated in the same manner of many through the plurality of the forms which he sustains, and, because of his many parts,

---

1 The treatise is printed by H. Wilner in BGPM. IV. 1903.
2 Cf. John of Salisbury, *Metal.* II. 17, col. 875 A.
3 *In Porphyr.* I. col. 85 B; ed. Brandt, p. 166.

he would also become numerically a universal. Further, it
would be right to call any group of men a universal, for they
would be a collection of like things, and in the same way we
could properly apply to them the definition of a universal or
even of a species, so that then the whole collection of existing men would include many species.[1] But, according to
the logic of Plato, a universal is prior to its own individuals;
a collection, however, is necessarily posterior to its com-
ponent parts. From Boethius we know that while the part is
not identical with the whole, species is always the same as
genus.[2] Yet how could the entire collection of men regarded
as a species be identical with the multitude of animals, the
genus?[3]

Abailard now turns to criticize those who apply the term
universal to single individuals, because they agree with other
similar individuals, and allow that the same individuals may
be predicated of many, not indeed that these individuals are
identical with the many in essence, but because the many agree
with them. To such a view of the nature of universals Abailard
replies that, if "to be predicated of many" is the same as "to
agree with many", how do we say that the individual may
be produced of only one thing, since it is evident that there
are no things which agree with only one thing? To be sure,
a man as man, and Socrates in as much as he is man, both
agree with others of the same species. But neither does a
man in so far as he is Socrates, nor Socrates in as much as he
is Socrates, agree with other men. What man has, Socrates
has, and in the same way;[4] but Socrates as Socrates, an indi-

---

[1] *Logica*, p. 15.   [2] *De Divisione*, col. 879 c.   [3] *Logica*, p. 15.

[4] Restat autem nunc ut eos oppugnemus qui singula individua in eo quod
aliis conveniunt, universale appellant et eadem de pluribus praedicari con-
cedunt, non ut plura essentialiter sint illa, sed quia plura cum eis conveniunt.
Sed si praedicari de pluribus idem est quod convenire cum pluribus, quomodo
individuum de uno solo dicimus praedicari, cum scilicet nullum sit quod cum
una tantum re conveniat? Quomodo etiam per "praedicari de pluribus" inter
universale et singulare differentia datur, cum eodem penitus modo quo homo
convenit cum pluribus, conveniat et Socrates? Quippe homo, in quantum est
homo, et Socrates, in quantum est homo, cum caeteris convenit. Sed nec
homo, in quantum est Socrates, nec Socrates in quantum est Socrates, cum
aliis convenit. Quod igitur habet homo, habet Socrates et eodem modo.
Ibid.

vidual entity, cannot be predicated of others. Thus, no real distinction is made between the universal and the singular by thinkers who regard universals in this way.

The reason for the failure of all these theories concerning the nature of universals was, Abailard maintained, the fact that things, whether regarded singly or collectively, cannot be called universals and be predicated of many. He therefore ascribed universality to words alone. "Certain nouns", he declares, "are called by grammarians appellative, while others are termed proper. Dialecticians, on the other hand, call some simple words universals, and others particulars, that is, individuals. A universal word is one which on account of its invention can be predicated singly of many, while a singular word is one which is apt as the name of only one person." Thus, the noun, "man", can be conjoined to every individual to whose nature it is suitable; "Socrates", however, belongs only to a single individual. The universal word, therefore, is plural in signification, although in itself singular, for it signifies many equivocals. The singular noun, "man", accordingly, names many individuals, each of whom is substantially separate from the others.[1]

The problem, therefore, of Abailardian logic was to determine the manner in which the universal noun is discovered, and then to see whether that universal noun denotes a really existent thing or whether the universal is merely a creation of the understanding. But before we can follow Abailard's thought further, we must first enquire into his psychological theories. Prior to the publication of the *Logica Ingredientibus*, it was generally thought that he knew but little psychology;[2] but we are now in a position to appreciate the acuteness with which he understood the workings of the human mind, and his views upon the problem of cognition are naturally of prime importance to his theory of universals.

---

1 *Logica*, p. 16. Abailard is here utilizing Priscian, *Instit. gramm.* ed. Hertz, I. p. 145. His definition of a universal word as "that which can be predicated singly of many", comes from Boethius, in Περὶ Ἑρμ. ed. Meiser, II. p. 135; see *Logica*, p. 9.   2 Cf. M. de Wulf, *Hist. de la phil. méd.* I. 4th ed. p. 225.

Abailard's logic was essentially a logic of diction, based upon a philosophical understanding of grammar derived for the most part from Priscian. His philosophy indeed was not the natural philosophy of Chartrain scholars such as Bernard Sylvester, nor was it the *a priori* deduction and construction of Anselm of Canterbury; it was built upon a critical analysis of the meanings of words.[1] In this lies his great importance in the history of mediaeval philosophy and logic. More than any other man, he was the founder of a school of logicians, active throughout the Middle Ages, who based their logic upon a careful investigation in the meaning of grammar and language.[2] The result of this new emphasis in logic can be seen in the statement of John of Salisbury, Abailard's own pupil, to the effect that the cradle of all philosophy is grammar.[3] Further, his close linking of logic to grammar and diction enables us to understand why he regarded logic as so fundamentally important in resolving the discordant statements which he found in the pages of authority.

Abailard based his theory of cognition upon the Aristotelian distinction between the understanding (διάνοια) and the imagination (φαντασία). There are, he says,[4] three properties of the soul, the vegetal, the sensitive, and the rational. The first is that which gives life to the body, and is common to plants, animals, and men alike. The second, belonging to both men and animals, is that property of sense which can only be exercised through bodily instruments, for the senses can only perceive corporeal things and those accidents which are proper to bodies, such as colour, size, and sound.[5] Thus the senses cannot apprehend Rome save when it is visible to the eyes or accessible to the touch. The rational soul, on the other hand, which is composed of the imagination (*imaginatio*) and the understanding (*intellectus*) and belongs only to man, does not require the senses for its operation; and both imagination and understanding are not only able to perceive

---

1 Geyer-Ueberweg, *Die patristische und scholastische Philosophie*, Berlin, 1928, p. 216.   2 See further, Grabmann, *Geistesleben*, pp. 104–46.
3 [Grammatica] est totius philosophiae cunabulum. *Metal.* I. 13, col. 840 A.   4 *Logica*, pp. 312–13.   5 *Ibid.* p. 313.

incorporeal things, such as soul and paternity,[1] but can also retain an image of an object once seen, but no longer present. Between the imagination and the understanding, however, there is this great distinction. Without the operation of the reason there can be no understanding, for understanding is the product of reason; on the other hand, if objects have once been perceived by the senses, we can have an *imaginatio* of them without any operation of the reason. The senses, thus, are merely receptive; the understanding active.[2] Both the imagination and the understanding retain from the objects perceived certain representations (*effigies*) which, since they are solely mental products, are but forms, signs, and pictures of those things which we wish to remember.[3] As such, these representations do not possess any reality, as do the Ideas of Plato, for the proportions of a tower that we have once seen, but which has since been destroyed, are not the actual forms of that tower, since true squareness and true loftiness can exist in subject bodies alone.[4] Further, while the imagination is concerned with the conception of images, the understanding has to do with their distinction,[5] and it is the function of the understanding to consider and determine the nature or properties of things.[6]

Thus, human understanding cannot exist without the imagination; the action of the imagination in receiving representations from objects perceived by the senses precedes the act of cognition, and must exist before either the nature or the properties of things can be distinguished. "By means of the imagination we merely receive the object, without as yet considering any property or nature which it may possess; by the added action of the understanding we consider and determine its nature or property".[7] To imagine is thus to

---

1 *Logica*, pp. 20, 314.   2 *Ibid.* p. 313.
3 *Ibid.* p. 314, quoting [Cicero], *ad Herennium de Arte Rhet.* III. 16.
4 *Logica*, pp. 21, 314.   5 *Ibid.* p. 328.
6 *Ibid.* p. 329.
7 Per imaginationem rem simpliciter accipimus, nondum aliquam ejus naturam vel proprietatem attendendo, per intellectum vero supervenientem rei naturam aliquam vel proprietatem distinguimus vel attendimus. *Ibid.* p. 317.

fasten the mind on an object; to understand is to consider that object's nature.[1] It is as if we were to take a piece of wood in one hand, and with the other to carve and paint it.[2] In the same way the understanding gives shape to the representations of the imagination.

Now in grammar nouns and verbs have a double signification; they designate both objects and our understanding of them. They signify objects representing the understanding which belongs to them; they denote understanding either in the speaker or in the listener. The actual word used by a speaker Abailard calls a *vox*,[3] a term which he employs to signify the purely physical aspect of language. These *voces* are the representations of our understandings (*notae intellectuum*), by which we convey to another what we have ourselves already understood.[4] Accordingly the office of the *voces* is solely one of signification;[5] they direct the attention of the listener, not to themselves, but to the objects which they represent, just as, when we see a statue of Achilles, we consider the hero represented, and not the statue itself.[6] Moreover, the *voces* are of human origin, since their physical character varies from language to language, although the objects which they represent always remain the same. Thus, it does not matter whether the *vox* "*homo*" or the *vox* ἄνθρωπος is used, the substance "man" remains unaltered.[7]

Our conceptions of things are necessarily very different from those of the divine mind. God's ideas are creative; they are the preconceptions of the things which God intends to create, while our minds are perforce dependent upon the data of the senses, and we are thus incapable of conceiving the nature of created things in their fullness.[8] But, as matter and form always exist conjoined, the human mind has yet the power of considering matter by itself, form by itself, or both

1 *Ibid.* pp. 317–18.   2 *Ibid.* p. 318.
3 *Ibid.* p. 307.   4 *Ibid.* p. 310.
5 Officium itaque earum, ad quod institutae sunt, significare, hoc est intellectum constituere. *Ibid.* p. 309.
6 *Ibid.* pp. 315–16.   7 *Ibid.* p. 323.
8 *Ibid.* pp. 22–3.

matter and form together. The first two processes are
effected by means of abstraction; the third by conjunction.[1]
We are not like dogs or apes whose recognition of their
master is due to love, fear, or some other compelling motive,
and not to discernment; in any given object men can discern
its nature or property, if it is wood, distinguishing it as body
or as neither fig nor oak.[2] Despite the fact that matter and
form do not exist apart in subsisting objects, the human mind
can by abstraction perceive matter and form each in its own
simplicity; but, because this process of abstraction is effected
without in any way altering the subsistence of the object considered, the simplicity of both matter and form is therefore a
mode of intellection, and not of subsistence. The mind cannot consider them as separated in fact, for then the understanding would be false.[3]

In regard to composite things the senses often operate in
different ways, so that, if a statue is half gold and half silver,
I can discern the gold and the silver separately although they
are conjoined, considering now the gold, now the silver in
itself, looking upon them separately, but not as separate, for
otherwise the understanding would be empty.[4] Our understanding can refer to the true substance of an object, regarding it as when it is at one with the senses in the world of
phenomena, or, when that object is no longer present, our
understanding can refer to the conceived form of that object,
whether that form is common or proper, although the object

---

1 *Logica,* p. 25; cf. Abstrahens (*scil.* intellectus) vero dicitur, qui unum sic
attendit, quod alterum non capit. *Ibid.* p. 331.

2 *Ibid.* p. 329.

3 *Ibid.* pp. 25–6; cf. Per abstractionem autem illos dicimus intellectus, qui
vel naturam alicujus formae absque respectu subjectae materiae in se ipsa
speculantur, vel naturam quamlibet indifferenter absque suorum scilicet in-
dividuorum discretione meditantur. The pseudo-Abailardian *Tract. de Intel-
lectibus,* ed. Cousin, *Ouvrages inédits,* II. p. 745.

4 Sensus etiam saepe de compositis divisim agunt, veluti si statua dimidia
aurea et dimidia argentea, aurum et argentum conjuncta separatim cernere
possum, modo scilicet aurum adspiciens, modo argentum per se, conjuncta
cernens divisim, non divisa, quippe divisa non sunt. Sic et intellectus per
abstractionem divisim attendit, non divisa, alioquin cassus esset. *Logica,*
pp. 25–6.

is considered in itself as one thing.[1] Thus, without in any way altering the simplicity of the object, the understanding can conceive it either in regard to the forms which it has in common with other objects of the same species or genus, or in regard to its own proper forms as an individual. In the same way we can paint one picture to represent the common nature of all lions, and a second to shew certain individual characteristics, such as those of a particular lion, which may be portrayed either as limping, or as wounded by the spear of Hercules.[2] Since the human mind can direct its attention to one nature or property in an object to the exclusion of others, we can discern either the individual property of an object or those general properties which it shares with other objects of the same species or genus. And it is by a process of abstraction that we collect the universal from a set of like particulars furnished to the understanding by the senses.[3] The likeness abstracted by the understanding from a group of particulars Abailard calls a *status*, a term which is expressed in speech by the universal *nomen*. But since all nouns signify both the general and the particular, the universal noun also represents the individual things as they exist in the world of actuality.[4]

It should be evident that the universal noun represents a likeness which is wholly undetermined. Thus, when I hear the universal noun "man", I have a conception, neither differentiated nor discrete, of an animal which is both rational and mortal, yet lacking those other accidents which go to form an individual. But when I hear the word "Socrates", a certain form rises in my mind, but now it is one which represents only the likeness of a single individual, certifying and determining a certain definite thing, while the word "man", the understanding of which rests upon the common form of all men, expresses an undifferentiated commonness.

1 *Ibid.* p. 22.   2 *Ibid.* p. 22.
3 Cf. Est itaque universale ex particularibus colligere. *Ibid.* p. 142.
4 *Ibid.* p. 141, and cf. B. Geyer, *Die Stellung Abaelards in der Universalienfrage*, BGPM. Supplementband, 1. 1913, p. 110.

The word "man", accordingly, may not be taken to mean any individual man, either Socrates or anyone else, for although the general names the particular, "man" does not signify any one individual. The word "Socrates" not only denotes a stated individual, but it also differentiates the individual nature of that person.[1] We may, therefore, call our understanding of universals alone, naked and pure. They are alone in that they are considered apart from the object's appearance to the senses, naked because they are considered separately from all and every form, and pure because in the understanding of universals nothing, whether it be matter or form, is designated. And it is because our understanding of universals is pure that Abailard calls our conception of them undifferentiated.[2] Yet, the universal noun, just because it represents the universal and the particular, is both incorporeal and corporeal.[3]

Now if the process of abstraction of universals is to be valid, some guarantee must be given to shew that our understanding corresponds to the modes of subsistence in the object. Abailard finds this guarantee in the fact that objects are not understood in another state than that in which they subsist. "When I consider this man only in the nature of substance or of body, and not also of animal, man, or grammarian, I certainly understand nothing except what is in that nature, but not everything which that nature has." And this "only" refers to my consideration alone, and not to the mode of the object's subsistence, for otherwise the understanding would be empty. For the object not only has it, but is considered as having it. And yet in one way it is said to be understood otherwise than it is, not indeed in another state than it is, but only otherwise in the sense that the mode of understanding is other than the mode of subsisting. Thus, when we consider only one of the natures or properties which are in an object, our understanding does not understand that object otherwise than it is; our consideration is solely a mode of understanding, and in no way alters or misrepresents the subsistence of the object considered.[1]

We can now approach the famous problem to which Porphyry had refused to give an answer; Do universals signify some truly existent thing, or are they located in the understanding alone, being like such words as chimera or goat-stag (*hircocervus*) which do not represent any rational things?[2] According to Abailardian logic, universals indeed signify things which really exist, but they do so only by nomination, just as the singular nouns, "cat" or "dog", name really existent things.[3] But universals exist only in the human understanding as the direct result of a process of abstraction in the way we have already described, and have, therefore, no basis in objective reality. And universals can be imposed on no things whatsoever, for then they would not be common, but particular; and again as universals cannot name anything, for there is nothing in which they agree, universals seem to derive no meaning from things, especially because they constitute no understanding of anything.[4] Understanding, as we have already seen, comes from something which we seize upon through the senses and which we record in the intellection and in the imagination; a universal can give rise to no such understanding. Further, as Boethius pointed out, the word "man" gives rise to doubt concerning its meaning, for, unless some one defines the word by saying "all men walk", or at least "certain men walk", the understanding of the hearer has nothing which he can understand reasonably.[5] Hence, universal words are of purely human origin and application, similar in this to the *voces*, the physical expression given to our understanding. Yet, although the form of all *voces* varies from language to language, there is still a certain naturalness in their use dictated by the obvious

---

1 *Ibid.* p. 25. Geyer-Ueberweg, *op. cit.* p. 218, points to the similarity here between the thought of Abailard and of Aquinas in *Summa Theol.* 1. quaest. 85, art. 1, ad. 1.

2 *Logica*, pp. 27–8.   3 *Ibid.* p. 28.   4 *Ibid.* p. 18.

5 Boethius, *de Divisione*, PL. 64, col. 889; *Logica*, p. 18; cf. Lunel gloss, f. 16 v., cited Geyer-Ueberweg, *op. cit.* p. 218.

necessity for mutual understanding in two persons speaking the same tongue. In consequence, Abailard was afraid that his logical theories might be considered similar to the Nominalism of his opponent, Roscelin, who held that universals were merely *voces*. Accordingly, in his later gloss on Porphyry, contained in the still unpublished Lunel MS., he differentiates clearly between *voces* and *sermones*, applying the latter term to denote universals. *Vox* is, as we have seen, the spoken word regarded as physical sound and as something natural in origin; *sermo*, on the other hand, is the word in regard to the meaning imposed upon it by human choice.[1] Further, as the spoken word, in that it is sound, is a thing, it cannot therefore be predicated of anything.

But what of the *status*, the universality which is abstracted by the human mind from a set of particulars belonging to the same species or genus? Abailard refused to allow that this universality may be regarded as an independent reality, as did Plato and the ultra-Realists who followed him in his logic; Socrates did not owe his being to any Socrateity, nor Plato his to any Platoneity, and, for that matter, individual men do not owe their humanity to external reality in which they all agree.[2] For Abailard, however, this common *status* is neither a thing nor a nothing. He declares that we must, it seems, avoid considering the agreement in which all men unite, as nothing, since we saw in fact that this and that man agree in the *status* of man, that is, in that they are men. Yet by this *status* we understand nothing else than that they are men, although we refer to no essence.[3] And that is as far as Abailard will go towards positing the reality of any common *status* in

1 Geyer-Ueberweg, p. 217; see also Hoc enim quod est nomen sive sermo, ex hominum institutione contrahit. Vocis vero sive rei nativitas quid aliud est, quam naturae creatio, cum proprium esse rei sive vocis sola operatione naturae consistat? Lunel MS. f. 15 v.

2 Omnes res discretae sunt oppositae numero, ut Socrates et Plato, eaedem etiam sunt convenientes ex aliquo, ex eo scilicet quod homines. Neque tamen ex socratitate vel platonitate neque ex aliqua re, quam inter se participant, eos convenire dico et tamen ex aliquo convenire, id est aliquam convenientiam habere, ex eo scilicet quod sunt homines. Lunel MS. f. 20 r.; Geyer-Ueberweg, p. 218.

3 *Logica*, p. 20.

which particulars of a similar species or genus agree. It may perhaps seem that such an indefinite statement makes a disappointing conclusion to so long and so careful an enquiry into the nature of universals; yet it has to be remembered that this conclusion was one held by Aquinas, Duns Scotus, and the Nominalists of the fourteenth and fifteenth centuries. Despite their greater knowledge of logical literature, none of these was able to put forward a more complete statement than that advanced in the *Logica Ingredientibus*.

Although his theories of cognition and of the nature of universals were Aristotelian, Abailard was too greatly imbued with the Platonism of traditional theology to reject the Platonic theory of Ideas. Following Macrobius, he placed the Ideas in the divine mind, regarding them as the original forms of things.[1] They are, as Priscian had said,[2] the general and special forms of things which are constituted intelligibly in the divine mind before they are produced in bodies. In this, God works like an artist who forms in his mind a preconception of what he is about to create.[3] And it is only as concepts of the divine mind (*conceptus mentis*)[4] that the Ideas, so dear to the Platonic logician, can be said to exist.

The difference between this theory of universals put forward by Abailard and those advanced by his contemporaries must now be described. Against the Realists who taught that universals exist *ante rem*, that is prior in time and subsistence, Abailard maintained that universals cannot be either things or words, for neither can be predicated singly of many. Universal nouns denote a common *status* abstracted from particulars of a similar species or genus, and this status only exists *in re*, in the particulars themselves. Roscelin and the Nominalists taught that universals were merely *flatus vocis*,

---

1 Macrobius, *in Somn. Scip.* I. 2. 14, ed. Eyssenhardt, p. 482; *Introd.* I. 9, col. 991 A; *Theol. Christ.* IV. col. 1307 B.

2 *Inst. gramm.* XVII. 44, ed. Hertz, II. p. 135; Abailard, *loc. cit.* and *Logica*, p. 22.

3 *Logica*, p. 22; see further, *infra*, p. 133.

4 *Theol. Christ.* I. col. 1159 B; cf. Aquinas, *Summa Theol.* I. quaest. 15 art. 3.

signifying no reality. Against them Abailard argued that the very fact that these empty breathings are sound makes them also things, and therefore they cannot be predicated singly of many, while the common *status* which is expressed by universal nouns cannot be thought of as nothing. In the psychology of the Nominalists the only knowledge to which men can attain is that knowledge which is derived from the data of the senses; hence all generalizations derived from that knowledge have no validity. Abailard, too, followed Aristotle in holding that all human knowledge begins with particulars and progresses thence to the more general; but, unlike the Nominalists, he maintained that the results of cognition are valid and therefore that the *status* abstracted by the human mind from a set of similar particulars corresponds to some reality. And, it will be noted that Abailard uses the term *status* with a different meaning than that applied to it by either Adelard of Bath or Walter of Mortagne. For him a *status* is not the aspect under which an object is viewed according to whether it is regarded as an individual or as a member of a species or genus; it is a common likeness which the mind abstracts from a set of like particulars.

Historically, Abailard's theory of universals was of great importance, for until the rise of Ockhamist Terminism in the fourteenth century it was the accepted theory of the schools. Nominalism seems to have disappeared very soon after the death of Roscelin; the ultra-Realism which William of Champeaux originally taught succumbed not only to the attacks of Abailard, but also to those levelled against it by the various groups of indifferentist philosophers already mentioned. Nor did indifferentism fare any better than Platonic ultra-Realism. John of Salisbury states that although Walter of Mortagne had at first a few disciples, his theories were accepted by no logician in 1159, the year in which the *Metalogicus* was finished.[1] Certainly, the later translations of the *de Anima* facilitated the psychological discussions of subsequent thinkers, while the new translation of the entire

1 *Metal.* II. 17, col. 875 A.

Organon provided scholars with a fuller knowledge of Aristotelian logic; yet for a long time after Abailard's death no professor taught that universals were *voces*, nor that they existed *ante rem*. The theory advanced by Abailard is essentially the same as that taught by St Thomas Aquinas. Only his own pupil, John of Salisbury, criticized Abailard's theory. For the logical skill possessed by Abailard John, indeed, had the greatest respect, and he paid him a great compliment by calling him *Peripateticus Palatinus noster*. Further, when he says that Abailard called universals *sermones*,[1] he described his logical theories correctly. But Abailard was not the only professor of logic whose lectures John attended, and his progress from master to master resulted in his own logical theories being somewhat eclectic. Like Abailard, he held that universals are merely figments of the human mind,[2] possessing no reality save in the individual objects whence they are abstracted, for universals can only be understood in individuals.[3] His studies under Gilbert Porrée, however, led him to champion a theory that universals do indeed possess an objective reality, and so that they cannot be called *sermones*. Gilbert had taught the existence of native forms (*formae nativae*), which are the images of the Ideas in the mind of God, although they only exist in direct connexion with matter, being individual, sensible, and inseparable; yet, in that they are images of the divine Ideas, they are also insensible and more universal. This conformity of native forms in objects of the same species or genus constitutes their universality.[4] It will thus be seen that according to Gilbert universals have a certain reality; John of Salisbury, indeed, did not shrink from declaring that things can be predicated of things,[5] a doctrine which Abailard had denied so roundly. Gilbert further taught that subsistence can be understood in

1 *Metal.* II. 17, col. 874 C; Otto of Freising, on the other hand, says that Abailard called universals *voces seu nomina*, *Gesta Fred.* 1. 48, p. 69.

2 *Metal.* II. 20. col. 885 C.   3 *Ibid.* col. 885 AB.

4 *Ibid.* II. 17, col. 875 D; Gilbert, *in Boeth. de Trin. Comment.* PL. 64, col. 1267; Clerval, *Écoles*, p. 262, and *infra*, p. 147.

5 *Metal.* II. 20, col. 887 D.

two ways, both as *quod est sive subsistens*, and as *quo est sive subsistentia*, the first being for instance body, and the second bodiliness.[1] This latter *subsistentia* can again be taken in two ways; there is *subsistentia singularis*, which is only in the individual, the *Platonitas*, for instance, which is in Plato; and there is *subsistentia specialis* and *subsistentia generalis*, giving to the individual the attributes common to the species and genus to which it belongs. It follows, therefore, that species and genera are nothing else but the special and general subsistencies which are united to individual objects as *formae nativae*.[2] John of Salisbury could indeed follow Abailard in holding that universals are figments of the mind, for, according to Gilbert, universals are collected from particulars by our understanding. Yet, just because the native forms can only exist in matter, and are inseparable, universals are immanent in things as a metaphysical reality which cannot be abstracted and is in itself concrete.[3] And that John held Gilbert's realist conception of the nature of universals is shewn by his statement that species and genera do not merely denote quiddity, but quality and certain manner as well.[4] His phrase *quodammodo* especially indicates his belief in the concrete existence of native forms which give special and general subsistence to individuals. Hence, Abailard's term, *sermo*, does not rightly determine the nature of universals.

The reason for the general acceptance of Abailard's theory of universals lies in the Aristotelian character of both his logic and his psychology. Abailard, as we know, was not familiar with the entire *Organon* or with the psychological writings of Aristotle, yet he was able to discover in Boethius a pretty complete account of those Aristotelian and Stoic theories which were integral with the formation of his own logical theories. Any attempt to trace in Boethius the actual

---

1 Gilbert, *in Librum de duabus Naturis*, coll. 1374 ff.
2 Cf. Seeberg, iii. p. 147.
3 *In Trin. Comment.* col. 1267 A.
4 Ergo ex sententia Aristotelis (*Cat.* 5. 3 b 20) genera et species non omnino quid sunt, sed quale quodammodo concipiuntur. *Metal.* ii. 20, col. 885 c.

sources from which Abailard drew his inspiration must be
tentative; he does not always refer his readers to passages to
which he was indebted. There are, however, in Boethius
some very close parallels to his thought, and these provide us
with evidence concerning the origin of at least some of the
principal tenets held by Abailard.

Now Boethius, I think, provided Abailard with his theory
that in the act of cognition the mind comprehends the likeness of things, for Boethius states that when a man has seen
a sphere, he considers in his mind an image of it, and, having
once experienced the image of an object, he will always
recognize similar objects by that very image. Such indeed
was the regular Stoic idea of ἔννοια and πρόληψις. I do not
for a moment suggest that Abailard was fully acquainted
with the Stoic theory of general conceptions, but I think
that it was from such descriptions of phantasia and of the
likenesses drawn by the mind from sensible objects that
Abailard arrived at his theory of abstraction. Further, this
Stoic theory of ἔννοια and πρόληψις is to be found in the
Topics of Cicero, a book with which Abailard was familiar
through the commentary which Boethius made on it. There
the two Greek words are translated by the term *notio*, a word
which Cicero also used for genus.[1] To be sure Abailard does
not actually refer to the passage in question, although John
of Salisbury, who attended his lectures, quotes it. Though
strictly speaking this is not real evidence, there is at least a
strong possibility that John had had his attention drawn to
the term by Abailard himself. At all events, the passage is one
which no careful reader of the text would have lightly passed
over. But be that as it may, Cicero plainly states that a genus
is a *notio* appertaining to many different things, and also that
a *notio* is indigenous to the mind, a first-conceived cognition

1 Genus est notio ad plures differentias pertinens....Notionem appello
quod Graeci tum ἔννοιαν tum πρόληψιν dicunt. Ea est insita et ante per-
cepta cujusque formae cognitio enodationis indigens...Formae igitur hae in
quas genus sine ullius praetermissione dividitur. *Topics*, 7. 31. Cf. Boethius,
Comment. in Topica, ii. PL. 64, col. 1106 D; John of Salisbury, *Metal.* ii. 20,
col. 878 B.

of some form into which a genus is divided without the omission of anything naturally belonging to it, and, lastly, that a primary conception is one which requires further elucidation. Commenting upon this statement, Boethius gives us the Aristotelian theory that species and genera are conceived likenesses of many things which differ among themselves. Thus, although a man and a horse differ through the rationality of the one and the irrationality of the other, the conceived likeness of them both constitutes their common genus, animal. Again, the individual persons, Plato and Cicero, although they are different in regard to number and accidents, are none the less of the same species through a common likeness, their humanity.[1] We have already seen that in discussing the theories of the indifferentist logicians, Abailard quotes with approval the statement of Boethius that both species and genera are collected from individual subsistencies. It appears to me most probable that Abailard discovered in these descriptions of the Aristotelian phantasia and the Ciceronian *notiones* an explanation of the means whereby the general was abstracted or collected from the particular. His conception of the mental process of abstraction would enable him to escape from the predicament of the indifferentists with their theory that a mere collection of like things constituted a species or genus.

It would perhaps have been easy for a man of less logical acuteness than that possessed by Abailard to have recognized that the words expressing the common *status* thus abstracted denoted no other reality than that contained in the singular subsistencies themselves. The process of abstraction is one of human activity, and so its results must of necessity be real only in the human mind. Yet again, there are passages in Boethius which very probably suggested his theory to Abailard. We have already seen that he quotes from the *de Arte Rhetorica*—then attributed to Cicero—to the effect that the images which the mind makes of the things which it wishes to remember are but forms, signs, and representa-

1 Boethius, *loc. cit.*

tions. Now the word which we have translated "signs" is
nota, a term which Cicero himself uses elsewhere as a translation of the Aristotelian σύμβολον.¹ Aristotle's theory that
words are but symbols is worked out by Boethius in his commentary on the Περὶ ἑρμηνείαν, whence Abailard drew his
own account of the use in various languages of different
words to denote the same subsistencies. And we are also told
that the Peripatetic philosophers divided language into three
parts: that which is written in the form of letters, that which
is uttered by the voice, and, finally, that which is put together
by the mind.² The words and nouns uttered by the voice are
called *notae* or symbols of the impressions received by the
understanding, and those which are written down are in turn
called the *notae* of the words which we speak. Aristotle,
Boethius adds, was therefore correct in his statement that
whatever dwells in words and nouns signifies neither the
senses nor the imaginations, but the quality of understanding
alone.³ In addition to all this, words and nouns, we are told,⁴
are not merely physical things, *voces*, but just because they are
voces, they possess a proper signification and have in a certain
way a figure of positive meaning impressed upon them. The
example which Boethius takes is that of a *nummus*. Just as a
coin is not only bronze impressed with a certain figure, but
is also the price of something else, so verbs and nouns are
not only *voces*, but signify something understood.⁵

Here, it would seem, is the origin of the special terminology which was used by Abailard. Like the Peripatetics, he
employed the term *vox* to express the physical form of words,
and again like them he used *vox* with a double, to express
both the actual object and the thing understood from that

1 *Topics*, 8. 35; Boethius, *op. cit.* col. IIII.
2 Ed. Meiser, II. p. 21.
3 Quare recte Aristotelis sententia est: quaecunque in verbis et nominibus
versantur, ea neque sensus neque imaginationes, sed solum significare intellectuum qualitatem. *Ibid.* p. 29.
4 Ergo haec Aristotelis sententia qua ait ea quae sunt in voce nihil aliud
designat nisi eam vocem, quae non solum vox sit, sed quae cum vox sit,
habeat tamen aliquam significationem impressam. *Ibid.* pp. 32–3.
5 *Ibid.* p. 32.

object, the *nota*. *Sermo* is the word employed to express the common *status*, that term rather than *vox* being chosen so as to emphasize the purely human application and the unreal character of the universal noun. Small wonder then that, once the full Aristotelian corpus was accessible, the later Aristotelian schoolmen could accept the theory of universals as formulated by Abailard.

Chapter vi

ABAILARD'S DOCTRINE OF GOD AND OF CREATION

I

IT is a noteworthy fact that none of the early mediaeval scholastics took much interest in the problem of the existence of God.[1] For the most part they were content to rely on the statements of Christian authority, or else they tacitly assumed that a God existed and made no attempt to prove their assumption. Thus, Rhabanus Maurus thought it sufficient to cite the words of the Bible, while on the very first page of the *de Divisione Naturae* Erigena takes his reader's belief in the existence of a God for granted.[2] John of Salisbury scoffed at those who declared that there was no God,[3] and even Peter Lombard considered it enough to quote the statements of St Augustine and the Ambrosiaster. When indeed Peter did attempt a proof, it was highly unsuccessful.[4] Borrowing from Platonic and Ciceronian conceptions, Anselm of Canterbury alone formulated proofs worthy of the name.[5] No one, indeed, questioned for an instant the existence of a Deity, for though much paganism is to be discovered in the Middle Ages, it was the paganism of the

---

1 Cf. Cl. Baeumker, *Witelo*, BGPM. iii. Heft 2, 1908, p. 287.

2 Rhabanus, *de Universo*, i. 1, PL. 111, col. 13 D; Erigena, *de Div. Nat.* 1. PL. 122, col. 411.

3 *Policrat.* vii. 7, col. 649, and *Metal.* iv. 41, col. 944; cf. William of Conches, *Philos. Mundi*, 1. 4, PL. 172, col. 44 D.

4 Viz.: Deinde viderint omne quod mutabile est non posse nisi ab illo qui incommutabiliter et simpliciter est. *Sentent.* 1. dist. 3. 3. See Baeumker, *op. cit.* p. 288.

5 In his proof of the procedure of the Many from the One (*Monologium*, 18, PL. 158, col. 167) he employed the Platonic theories of ἀφαιρεῖν and χωρισμός. His statement, *necesse est ut omnia sint per aliquid bona* (*ibid.* 1, col. 145 c), ultimately comes from Cicero, *de Officiis*, iii. 8. See Baeumker, *op. cit.* p. 296.

natural man, and not that of the modern agnostic.[1] And so there was no incentive from outside to force men to draw up carefully considered theistic proofs. The Aristotelian doctrines of the Prime Mover and the First Cause, so frequently utilized by later scholastics, were as yet unknown, and could not therefore supply thinkers with ready proofs of the existence of God. In general, men were far more interested in the dogmas of the Trinity and of the Eucharist than in the truth of a belief which, since none doubted it, provoked no necessary discussion.

Abailard himself did not strike out along any new lines, save in his attempt to quote from pre-Christian writers proofs in support of the Christian doctrine of God. He takes but little pains to prove the existence of God; so convinced is he of the truth of theism that he begins both the *Introductio* and the *Theologia Christiana* with a categorical assertion that there is a God and that the Godhead is triune, and it is only much later that he discusses the problem of God's existence. The false trinitarian theories of Roscelin occupy his attention far more than any possible atheistic attitude; his subject in his theological books is *de unitate et trinitate Dei*, and not *utrum Deus est?*

It is the cosmological proof of God that Abailard uses, but he destroys its validity by his assumption that man possesses an inborn, spermatic reason. Like so many of his contemporaries, he follows closely in the footsteps of St Augustine, holding that the world of sense is not regarded as supplying the thinker with data which compel him to posit the existence of a God; the world is rather a looking-glass in which the nature of God is clearly mirrored.[2] We have already seen how he thought that the property of human reason is to transcend the senses and to investigate the things to which they cannot attain, and that human reason is also the sign by which man is especially likened unto his Creator. Passing from the things that are visible to those that are not, Abailard claims

1 Cf. F. M. Powicke, in the *Legacy of the Middle Ages*, Oxford, 1926, p. 25.
2 Augustine, *de Trinitate*, xv. 4, PL. 42, col. 1061.

that all men can easily see that "God, the excellent creator and disposer of all, proclaims his nature by his creation, through those things which he makes and ordains, for we judge the activity of an artist by the effects which we see".[1] That is why St Paul, writing to the Romans, held that men were inexcusable and guilty of contempt for God, since even without the aid of Scripture Natural Law, which resides in the human reason, makes known the existence of God by the display of his works.[2] The verse, "the invisible things of him from creation are clearly seen, being understood from the things that are made",[3] was quoted again and again in Christian philosophy as a proof that God's existence was patent in his creation.[4] The cosmos was, indeed, a book which bears the impress of its maker. But his very quotation stultifies Abailard's attempted proof; in the *Expositio ad Romanos* he distinctly claims that men's knowledge of their Creator from the world depends upon their use of the reason which God has given them.[5] True to his character as an apologist, Abailard is not really proving the existence of God, but is shewing how a belief in the existence of a God is consistent with a rational enquiry into the ordered nature of the world. Abailard could never forget the story of man's creation in the image of God, for upon it depended his defence of reason's validity, and he always remained the Christian philosopher, unable to build up a system of natural theology independent of the Christian belief in God, the creator both of man and of the world. The Aristotelian progression from effect to cause, without the prior assumption that the cause existed, was foreign to his thought. The Platonism which he imbibed from traditional Western philosophy, posited the existence of the world of Ideas without which the world of Appearance was inexplicable.

1 Facile etiam erat, ut omnium optimus conditor atque dispensator Deus, per ea quae tam mirabiliter et facit et ordinat, ex ipsis suis quantus sit operibus indicaret, quia et per qualitatem operum quae videntur, absentis artificis industriam dijudicamus. *Introd.* III. col. 1086 D; *Theol. Christ.* v. col. 1316 A.
2 *Introd.* III. col. 1087 A; *Theol. Christ.* v. col. 1316 AB.   3 Rom. i. 20.
4 Cf. Augustine, *de Trinitate*, xv. 4, PL. 42, col. 1061.   5 I. 1, col. 803.

The reason for Abailard's quotations from classical philosophers is evidently the same as that which led him to seek in pre-Christian writers for indications of their belief in the Trinity. If the existence of God is accessible to human reason, then the non-Christian has no more excuse than the Christian for disbelief; the acceptance of a belief in God among the classical thinkers is an additional argument against any contemporary that might deny the being of God. Abailard cites from Cicero[1] and Plato[2] to prove that the cosmos is not governed by chance, but by reason. All the philosophers held that the world was made and ordered by a *summum bonum*, though they called it by various names, God, Nature, the Mind or the Soul of the world. But chief of all these thinkers, Anaxagoras, taught that the divine mind was the author of all nature,[3] for

it is easy to be convinced by reason that neither the world nor the things it contains are either self-existent or self-subsistent, but that they were made and are ruled by something far more excellent than themselves. That which is of itself (*a se ipso*) is certainly in nature more worthy than that which is from another. Now, as everything that is capable of reason and intelligence is without a doubt more excellent than anything else, we cannot allow that a rational substance is derived from another, if we consider that a thing which lacks reason is derived from itself. We all know that we are produced (*gigni*), not from ourselves, but from some other source, how can we then say that the world of irrational things is self-existent?[4]

Further, it is generally agreed that the parts of the universe which were made before man, were indeed created, and therefore that the world was begun and made by some external agent. Since the world was so plainly made for man, we should do mankind an injustice, unless we held also that both the human race and the world were equally created. To suppose that rational and irrational beings are alike dependent upon

1 *Introd.* III. col. 1087–8; *Theol. Christ.* v. coll. 1316–17.
2 Plato, *Timaeus*, 28 A, Chalcidius, ed. Wrobel, p. 23.
3 *Introd.* III. col. 1088 A; *Theol. Christ.* v. col. 1317 D, from Augustine, *de Civit. Dei*, VIII. 2, PL. 41, col. 226. Cf. Cicero, *de Nat. Deor.* I. II. 26.
4 *Introd.* III. col. 1088 CD; *Theol. Christ.* v. col. 1318 A.

their own government is impossible, for "in the sea of this life" not even man can order himself as he wishes. Much less then can we think of the universe as governing itself, since it is plain that it does not possess the necessary rationality. And so we must postulate the existence of a creator and ruler of the entire universe, and to him we give the name of God.[1]

By elaborating his cosmological proof of God's existence and by weaving into it the typically Platonic idea that perfection and unity are equivalent, Abailard comes to the conclusion that God must be one. "It is certain", he says,[2] "that everything is governed with greater order in proportion to the fewness of the rulers." As there is nothing which is ruled with more order than the universe, it follows that there is but one God. In addition, all are agreed that God is rightly called the *Summum Bonum*, and as such he must surpass all else and be unique, for unless we consider the Highest Good to be single, this uniqueness is impossible. Again, God in himself is perfect, and he is alone sufficient for all that he does. He can, therefore, have no compeer, as the existence of an equal would be superfluous and, according to Platonic standards, anything that is superfluous is the negation of good. The opponents of monotheism might well argue that the good becomes better when it is multiplied and, thus, that many Gods are better than one, but such an argument is fallacious. To preserve the essential infinite character of the divine glory we should have to posit an infinite number of Gods. The result of this would be that our knowledge of God would become impossible, for there would be no limit to his number, while not even God would be able to know himself, since he cannot know things which are not comprehended by a natural limit. Moreover, if many Gods existed, none could be called the *Summum Bonum*, for any one would be surpassed in goodness by a couple of his compeers. Lastly, polytheism means that the Godhead would be a collection, and as such it would be as a whole necessarily pos-

1 *Introd.* and *Theol. Christ. locc. citt.*   2 *Ibid.*

terior to its parts; but such temporal factor in the formation of the Godhead is unthinkable. In a composite body, too, the essential characteristic of God as eternal could not exist, for a collection is always subject to decay through the disintegration of its parts.[1]

These proofs of God's existence and his unity, Abailard maintains, are sufficient to disarm any criticism; those who will not accept them have no reason for their refusal. That the whole of creation points to the being of a single creator and disposer no man of good conscience will deny, for, otherwise, what is the use of our good works, if we say that he whom we now venerate with love and fear is not God?[2] The existence of such a God can be established by many arguments; his non-existence is proved by none. Those who would deny God are exercising the grossest impudence in rejecting every reason and authority. Why, he asks,[3] do they spurn the authority of men, when they themselves are prepared to accept the same human authority in matters regarding astronomy and the hidden secrets of Nature, matters, indeed, where no human experiment is possible? With that, Abailard dismisses the objections of possible atheists in a somewhat arbitrary fashion. Either his proofs must be accepted, or the task of persuading his opponents is to be discontinued. The obstinate cannot be persuaded, since there are no arguments that can silence their foolishness.

In his account of God's being, Abailard followed in the tradition of St Augustine, and thereby ignored the negative theology of the Hellenistic neo-Platonists.[4] Like Anselm of Canterbury he pictured God as the *Summum Bonum*, and not like Erigena as the above-good, the ὑπεράγαθος.[5] We have

---

1 *Introd.* III. 2, coll. 1088–91; *Theol. Christ.* v. coll. 1318–20. Roland follows Abailard in proving the unity of God from the idea that many Gods would involve superfluity, and from the idea that perfection is a sign of unity. See *Sentenzen*, pp. 16–17.

2 *Introd.* III. 2, col. 1090 D; *Theol. Christ.* v. col. 1320 C.

3 *Introd.* III. 2. col. 1091 A; *Theol. Christ. loc. cit.*   4 Seeberg, III. p. 165.

5 Anselm, *Monol.* 16, PL. 158, col. 165 C; Erigena, *de Divisione Nat.* I. 15, PL. 122, col. 464 A, from pseudo-Dionysius, *de Div. Nomin.* 5, *ibid.* coll. 1147–8.

already seen that Abailard employed analogies to express the truths of the infinite in finite, human language; the difficulty of discovering suitable analogies was very present to him, for "the farther the excellence of the divine nature departs from the other natures which it has founded, the more difficult it is to find in those natures satisfactory analogies" to express the being of God.[1] Hence it is that many of the philosophers have said that no man can know the quiddity of God,[2] and that they could not even make mention of his name,[3] while other thinkers have called God nothing. Each art, each teaching and science possesses its proper terminology, and so when we employ human words to express the ineffable divinity, we must recognize that such words can only be used of God if we use them with a special meaning; for, although man has found a language in which he can express his own understandings (*intellectus*), that language is entirely insufficient for the understanding of divine matters, and therefore man does not dare to mention the unspeakable goodness of God.[4] Hence, when we say that God is a substance, we employ that term in a special way. Substance according to human experience implies the capability of sustaining one or more of the possible accidents which may be attached to the being or thing in question. Since God can suffer no change neither in quantity nor in number,[5] substance cannot be used of him according to the ordinary connotation of the word. Everything, indeed, that can be predicated of God must be predicated of him substantially (*secundum substantiam*);[6] there can be no accidents in God, and

1 Quanto autem excellentia divinae naturae a caeteris quas condidit naturis, longius abscedit, tanto minus congruas similitudines in illis reperimus, quibus satisfacere de ista valeamus. *Introd.* II. 10, col. 1059 D.

2 *Ibid.* col. 1061 B. Cf. Augustine, *de Trin.* VII. 5, col. 942.

3 *Ibid.* col. 1062 C.

4 *Ibid.* coll. 1063–4.

5 *Ibid.* col. 1062 C, and *Theol. Christ.* IV. col. 1243. Cf. Boethius: Ita ut neque accidens sine substantia neque sine accidenti substantia esse posset. *In Isagogen Porph. Comment.* I. 2, PL. 64, col. 10 B, and ed. S. Brandt, CSEL. XLVIII. p. 6.

6 Cf. Si quidquid de Deo dicitur, secundum substantiam dicitur. Augustine, *de Trin.* v. 3. 4, col. 913.

his substance is of a different order than that implied by every-day human terminology.

It was inevitable that the problem of the omnipotence of God should have been fully discussed in the Middle Ages; the problem was not so simple as the casual observer might perhaps expect. The question at issue was largely whether the fact that God does not perform certain acts, either because they are inconsistent with his nature or because they do not agree with his will, may justifiably be taken as a proof that his power is restricted. Again, is it correct to say that God is omnipotent, not indeed because he has the ability to do everything, but because he can do all that he wishes? An earlier writer, Peter Damiani, had insisted so much upon the fullness of divine omnipotence that he taught that God even had the power to make an unchaste woman pure.[1] Abailard, however, mainly as the result of his own inability to distinguish adequately between God's will and his power, placed unwarrantable restrictions upon the power of God. Anxious to preserve intact both the rationality and the absolute goodness of everything that God accomplishes, he denied that God can act in any other way than he actually does. For the Creator—the *Summum Bonum*—there has only been one course of action which is both entirely good and rational. Abailard's argument roused a storm of bitter criticism;[2] the anonymous abbot, who was especially vocal in his condemnation, demanding, "What Augustine, what Gregory has hurled you into the stupidity of such rubbish?"[3]

When he tells us that we must not imagine that God is limited because he cannot perform things which men can do, Abailard was orthodox enough. Certainly God cannot walk, speak, and feel; but, since he is an incorporeal being, lacking

1 *De divina Omnipotentia*, 8, PL. 145, coll. 607-8.
2 Cf. Bernard, *Tract. de error. Abael.* 3, PL. 182, col. 1049 D; *Disp. anon. abbatis*, 3, PL. 180, coll. 315 ff.; Roland, *Sentenzen*, pp. 63 ff.; Gandulph, *Sentent.* 1. 42, ed. J. Walther, p. 31.
3 Quis Augustinus, quis Gregorius...talium in horum ruderum horrendam spissitudinem te projecit? *Loc. cit.* col. 317 A.

the physical faculties of man, the possession of such human
abilities would be foreign to his nature. We have indeed to
remember that many of our so-called powers are but in-
firmities consequent upon our fallen state. Thus, we may not
say that God is not omnipotent because he has not the power
of sinning, for that "power" is really a weakness in man.[1]
Walking, on the other hand, is a truly human power which
suits our needs and does not impair our dignity; yet, to God,
who can effect all things through his will alone, the ability
to walk would be superfluous. And so, what is our necessity
would be a defect in God. We are told by St Paul to attribute
to God all that we possess, since it is in him that we live and
move and have our being.[2] God, indeed, has the power to
work through others, and this ability to effect his will through
the agency of his creation as well as through his own activity
is a sign of his might. He uses us to build whatever he desires just as if we were tools, and in this way he may be said
to do whatever we do, just as a rich man is said to build
a tower, although the actual work is performed by the
labourers whom he employs. And though he cannot walk,
God can compel others to do so; the powers which he does
not possess because they are inconsistent with his nature, he
is at least able to exercise through the creatures he has made.
Since none can resist his wishes, God may therefore rightly
be called omnipotent.[3]

Yet, we have to recognize that divine omnipotence is
limited by our possession of free will. Abailard firmly rejects
the theory of the absolute determinist who holds that all
things have been foreseen and predestined by God from the
beginning so that they can only happen in the way that they
actually do. The maintenance of such a theory would make
God the author of our evil actions as well as of our good
deeds.[4] Our free will, the ability to decide whether or not a
thing ought to be done,[5] provides us with a certain freedom

1 *Logica*, p. 230. 2 Acts xvii. 28.
3 *Introd.* III. 4, coll. 1091–2; *Theol. Christ.* v. coll. 1321–2.
4 *Logica*, p. 426.
5 *Introd.* III. col. 1110 A; *Logica*, p. 425.

of action in which the responsibility is ours alone. Hence Abailard reproduces the traditional distinction between the *dispositio* and the *praeceptum* of God,[1] the one being the ordering of creation against which no man is able to rebel, the second, the rules which God would have us observe, but which, since we possess free will, he does not compel us to obey. Thus, by his very nature, God is anxious for the salvation of the whole world, but, if we held that this and every wish of God will some day be actualized, we should fall into the "detestable heresy" of Origen, and believe that in the end even the devils are saved. Our salvation therefore is not a matter of God's *dispositio*, for salvation is only gained by our free will co-operating with the necessary grace and observing the precepts of God,[2] and those whose actions make them unworthy of salvation cannot be saved.

But when Abailard proceeds to argue that God cannot act otherwise than he does, his logic leads him astray at the expense of his orthodoxy. He was certainly on safe ground when he held that all the actions of God must of necessity be dictated by the exigencies of reason, and that he cannot act irrationally, leaving undone the things which he ought to accomplish. Since God is incapable of breaking the laws of rational behaviour, there must always be some satisfactory explanation to shew why he has rejected a possible course of action; our failure to understand his deeds does not prove that he works in an arbitrary fashion.[3] Nor can God accomplish things which are inconsistent with his nature; he cannot save those who ought to be damned. But when Abailard declares that God is impelled to act by a kind of necessity proper to his own nature rather than by a free volition,[4] his nature allowing him no choice between alternative courses of action since the one adopted is the only one consistent with his divinity, his views are certainly strange. He was in-

---

1 Cf. Augustine, *Enchiridion*, 100, PL. 40, col. 279.
2 *Introd.* III. 4, col. 1093; *Theol. Christ.* v. col. 1323.
3 Cf. Augustine, *de Gen. c. Manich.* I. 4. 7, PL. 34, col. 177.
4 *Introd.* III. 3, col. 1097 B; cf. *Theol. Christ.* v. col. 1326.

deed totally incapable of understanding that of several possible modes of action two or more may be equally rational, and that the course which God adopts is not necessarily the only one he can choose, but is one which God selects by his own free will. But for Abailard God can only act as he actually does. Nor is he shaken from his position by the statement of Jesus that he could have asked and obtained from the Father twelve legions of angels. Those words, we are told,[1] are to be interpreted conditionally, and in no absolute sense; had Jesus asked for aid against the Jews, he would have obtained his request, but in point of fact he could never have made such a request. And the same blind force of his logic drives Abailard to infer that God's rationality and his character as the *Summum Bonum* mean that God can make nothing better or in greater quantity than he actually does.

If we suppose that he can make more or fewer things than he does, or that he is able to cease from the things which he is doing, we should then certainly detract from his extreme goodness. It is clear then that he can do nothing but what is good. And, if he does not do the good things which he has the ability to accomplish, and if he withholds from effecting what ought to be done, who would not then account God to be both grudging and unrighteous?[2]

And so we must conclude that God does everything that he can and as well as he is able.[3] He cannot improve upon the world which he has created; for, if we held that he possessed that power, we should be forced to say that the present world is inconsistent with his character as a rational and supremely good being.[4] The quality and quantity of his creative work as well as the time of its creation are determined by the nature of God. Thus, Abailard could not contemplate the

1 Matt. xxvi. 53; *Introd.* III. 3, col. 1097 B.
2 Si enim ponamus ut plura vel pauciora facere possit, vel ab eis quae facit cessare, profecto multum summae ejus bonitati derogabimus. Constat quippe eum non nisi bona facere posse; si autem bona, cum possit, non faciat, et ab aliquibus quae facienda essent, se retrahat, quis eum tanquam aemulum vel iniquum non arguat? *Introd.* III. 5, col. 1094 A; *Theol. Christ.* v. col. 1324 B.
3 Facit itaque omnia quae potest Deus, et tantum bene quantum potest. *Theol. Christ.* col. 1325 B.
4 *Introd.* col. 1098 A; *Theol. Christ.* col. 1326.

possibility of there being many worlds which God could have made, a possibility which intrigued many later scholastics; nor could he allow the claim of his predecessor, Damiani, that God has the power to make an unchaste woman pure. The latter power, if it belonged to God, would derogate from his essential goodness.[1]

In his discussion of divine immutability, Abailard warns his readers against the acceptance of anthropomorphic ideas. God's movements, his rest upon the seventh day of creation, are not to be interpreted literally, for, unlike ourselves, God is neither restricted spatially, nor does he change or communicate himself in his creative activity.[2] Since he is Spirit, he cannot be moved and be locally anywhere.[3] Just as the sun suffers no change either in itself or in its heat when it warms the earth, although the things it warms are indeed changed, God remains immutable despite the presence of alteration in the universe.[4] He is, in short, the being whom Boethius describes as:

> ...stabilisque manens das cuncta moveri.[5]

His actions imply no movement or exertion, since they are accomplished by the exercise of his will alone. He is said to be everywhere through his substance because of his power and operation, and when we speak of his whole presence in a place, we mean that he never ceases to work something everywhere and that his power is nowhere inactive. No places, and nothing which they contain, can endure unless they are conserved by him; he is said to be in them through his substance, for in them he never ceases from doing something through the virtue of his proper substance, either by conserving them or by executing something in them.[6] By

1 *Introd.* III. 5, col. 1096 A.   2 *Introd.* III. 6, coll. 1104 B–1105 D.
3 Nullum igitur incorporeum localiter moveri potest, quia nec localiter alicubi esse potest. *Ibid.* col. 1105 C; cf. *Dial.* coll. 1666–7.
4 *Introd. ibid.* col. 1105 B.
5 *De Consolatione Phil.* III. metre 9; *Introd. ibid.* col. 1104 D.
6 Quod tamen ubique esse per substantiam dicitur, juxta ejus potentiam vel operationem dici arbitror, ac si videlicet diceretur ita ei cuncta loco esse praesentia, ut in eis aliquid operari nunquam cesset, nec ejus potentia sit

thus insisting upon God's immutability and essential separateness from creation, Abailard guards his theology from any charge of pantheism.

It is by his Wisdom that God directs all the universe, and this Wisdom has been called by various names, his Word, his Reason, and his Mind.[1] By its power God knows everything, discerning all things truly, so that he can neither err, nor can anything obstruct his knowledge.[2] And his knowledge comprehends the future as well as the present and the past, and without his ordinance nothing can happen; for, just as he cannot be ignorant of what he has ordained for the future, so he is also able to foreknow what will be its outcome.[3] Certainly, men often speak of chance, but that is because they are ignorant of the providence of God. Though we perhaps consider them contingent, the eclipses of the sun and the moon are governed by the divine reason. To Abailard, as to St Augustine,[4] knowing nothing of deistic or modern scientific notions, the laws of Nature were the laws of God. Since it is his creature Nature cannot be hostile to God and, accordingly, cannot restrict his omnipotence. To speak of miracles as being contrary to Nature is therefore incorrect. That a virgin should bear or that the blind should see is certainly against Nature, but in whatever way he wishes, God can change the very character of things even against their customary habits. The universe is, therefore, governed by and depends upon the reason of God. When we say that by its nature a thing is either possible or impossible, we are measuring its possibility by the standard of Nature and not,

alicubi otiosa. Nam et ipsa loca, et quidquid est in eis, nisi per ipsum conserventur, manere non possunt; et per substantiam in eis esse dicitur, ubi per propriae virtutem substantiae aliquid nunquam operari cesset, vel ea ipsa, ut dictum est, servando, vel aliquid in eis per seipsum ministrando. *Ibid.* col. 1106.   1 *Introd.* III. 7, col. 1109 A.

2 ...ea vis divinae potentiae, qua cuncta sapit hoc est veraciter discernit, ut in nullo errare possit, nec quidquam ejus obsistere queat cognitioni. *Loc. cit.*

3 Sicut ergo Deus quod de futuro praeordinat, ignorare non potest, ita nec eorum eventum potest non praescire. *Ibid.*

4 Cf. *Quaest. lxxxiii.* 24, PL. 40, col. 17, quoted *Introd.* III. 7, col. 1111 B.

as we should, by the might of God's power.[1] To God all things are possible, save only those things, the performance of which would be inconsistent with his divinity.

Just as God can do no more than he does, so his foreknowledge and providence are fixed from eternity by the immutability of his being.[2] Whatever he has foreknown and predestined must necessarily happen, and it is impossible for anything which has thus been predestined to perish; it is certain that all things before they are done are foreseen by God in the way that they will happen, and in nothing can his providence be deceived.[3] But as in the case of divine omnipotence, the immutability of God's foreknowledge does not imply that human activity is determined without the action of free will. If God foresees that a man who is perchance about to commit adultery will indeed do so, that does not mean that his commission of that sin is due to necessity; that would be to make God responsible for all human guilt. To extricate himself from any such difficulty Abailard states that neither God's providence nor his predestination confers necessity on events.[4] All sin is a matter of the will and not of necessity, and its commission is not due to any element of compulsion either on the part of Nature or of God.[5] God only foresees that an event will take place, though he does not override man's free will to ensure its occurrence. To be

1 Unde cum aliquid possibile vel impossibile, id est naturae consentire vel repugnare dicunt, juxta solam creaturarum facultatem, non divinae potentiae virtutem haec metiuntur. *Introd.* III. 7, col. 1112 A.

2 Roland, *Sentenzen*, p. 71, Omnibene, p. 172 and the *Epitome*, 21, coll. 1728–9 deduce from this that God can foreknow no more and no less than he actually does.

3 ...cum omnia videlicet sicut a Deo praevisa sunt, necesse sit evenire, nec aliquem praedestinatum possibile sit perire. Certum quippe est omnia antequam fiant eo modo quo futura sunt, a Deo esse praevisa, sive bona sint sive mala, nec in aliquo providentiam ejus posse falli. *Epist. ad Romanos*, III. 8, col. 907 B.

4 *Logica*, pp. 428–9. It may be remarked that the *Summa Sentent.* I. 12, col. 61, will not allow that foreknowledge is applicable to God, in whom there is no future.

5 ...et omne peccatum magis voluntarium quam necessarium sit, et ex libero procedens arbitrio, non ex aliqua coactione naturae vel divinae providentiae compulsione. Non enim providentia, hoc est praescientia Dei,

sure, he often condemns to eternal damnation unbaptized children who have committed no sin, but their sentence is due to God's foreknowledge that, had they been allowed to live, the character of their lives would have qualified them for such punishment.[1] Although his foreknowledge would in no way have determined the conduct of these children if they had been permitted to live, God yet could know what their conduct would have been. And, in the case of the man about to commit adultery, God does not compel him to do so; he only foreknows that he will commit that crime.[2] Nor will Abailard allow that there is such a thing as fate which can be distinguished from divine providence, as Boethius in one place would appear to do.[3] Opposed to, though dependent upon, providence, fate is that which God establishes and disposes in creation.[4] We may only speak of fate being attached to things, as indeed Boethius does when he describes fate as "a disposition inherent in changeable things", if we treat fate passively, as *fatatio*, as that which is ordained and established in God's providence.[5] And there is this further distinction between the foreknowledge and predestination of God; his foreknowledge covers both good and evil, while his predestination is alone concerned with good, and more particularly with the gift of grace through which a man's salvation is effected.[6]

Now Joscelin, one of the four masters who are attacked in the *Introductio* for holding "chairs of pestilence" around

necessitatem rebus infert magis quam nostra praescientia sive scientia. *Opp.* ed. Cousin, ii. p. 145. Cf. Quod autem videtur posse probari omnia necessario evenire per providentiam, ad hoc videtur: nullam necessitatem infert providentia Dei magis quam providentia alicujus hominis. *Sentent. Florian. ed. cit.* p. 12.

1 *Epist. ad Romanos*, ii. 5, col. 870 B.
2 *Ibid.* iii. 8, col. 907 B.
3 *Logica*, p. 427; Boethius, *de Consol. Phil.* iv. prose 6.
4 Et fatum (*scil.* dicitur) ex eo quod stabilit atque disponit in creaturis. *Logica*, p. 428.
5 *Ibid.* and Boethius, *loc. cit.*
6 *Logica*, p. 427. Cf. *praedestinavit*, id est donis gratiae suae praeparavit, *Epist. ad Romanos*, iii. 8, col. 906 C. See also Augustine, *de Dono Persev.* 14. 35 (PL. 45, col. 1014), and *de Praed. Sanct.* 10. 19 (PL. 44, col. 974), quoted *Logica, loc. cit.*

Abailard, was then teaching that, as events can happen otherwise than God foresees, it is therefore possible for God to
be mistaken.[1] Abailard, accordingly, discusses his theory at
length. In the *Logica* he traces the doctrine held by Joscelin
to the teaching of Cicero described in the *de Civitate Dei*,[2] and
summarizes it by the following proposition: If it is possible
for an event to happen otherwise than it does, then it is
possible for it to happen otherwise than God foresaw that it
would.[3] Now the proposition—it is possible for an event to
happen otherwise than it does—may be understood in two
ways, of which the first is true and the second false. We can
say that it is possible for a thing to happen otherwise than it
actually does and otherwise than its occurrence was foreseen
by God, who only foresaw that it would happen; and we can
also say that a thing can happen otherwise than it has happened and so otherwise than God foresaw. This latter interpretation is patently impossible. But in the first interpretation of our proposition, we allow that God only foresaw the
occurrence of the event, and that the event itself could
possibly have happened in some other way than God foresaw. Although this may appear sound, it is yet unsatisfactory;
it does not fulfil the requirements of a rule of logic which
demands that the supposition of possibility in an antecedent
must equally be supposed in the consequence. Thus, in the
proposition: If *A* is, then *B* is, if only the possibility of *A*'s
existence is granted, then we may only infer from it the
possibility of *B*'s existence.[4] To be strictly logical, therefore,
we should have to alter our original proposition to: If it is
possible for an event to happen otherwise than it does, then
it is possible for it to happen otherwise than God *possibly*

1 Quartus autem in tantam prorupit insaniam, ut quia res aliter evenire
possunt quam Deus providerat, Deum posse falli concedat. *Introd.* II. 9,
col. 1057 B. See *infra*, p. 265.

2 v. 9, PL. 41, coll. 148 ff., and Cicero, *de Fato*, 10; *de Divinatione*, II. 3.

3 Si possibile est, rem aliter evenire, quam evenit, possibile est aliter
evenire quam Deus eventurum esse providit. *Logica*, p. 429.

4 Cujuscunque possibile est antecedens, esset et consequens, ut si vera
haec consequentia: si est homo, est animal, vera est et ista: si possibile est esse
hominem, et animal. *Ibid.* p. 429, and *Opp.* II. p. 146.

foresaw that it would. As the truth of this can in no way be proved, we are not forced to conclude that it is possible for God to be mistaken.[1] Joscelin's theory is unsound, for he applies an element of possibility only to the antecedent of his proposition. Further, we may say that an event may possibly happen otherwise than it does and otherwise than God foresaw, without necessarily impugning the infallibility of God's foreknowledge; for when we say that an event can happen otherwise than God foresaw and not in the way in which he foresaw, it does not follow either that he foresaw its occurrence in another way or that he was mistaken in his foreknowledge.[2] Again, since the content of God's foreknowledge can change without impairing his immutability, it is also possible for events to take place otherwise than they have done and still to have happened in accordance with the divine providence, because that foreknowledge can be changed.[3]

Such a doctrine of God aroused a great deal of criticism among Abailard's contemporaries and immediate successors. Only the writers of the *Epitome* and of the St Florian *Sentences* accepted his theory that God can do nothing or better than he actually does;[4] Roland definitely rejected the teaching of Abailard upon divine omnipotence.[5] Without mentioning any names, both Hugh of St Victor and Peter Lombard at-

1 Ad quod quidem respondemus, quod haec propositio: Possibile est rem evenire aliter quam Deus providit, habet duos sensus: unum quidem verum, si istud 'aliter quam Deus providit' referamus ad possibile; alium falsum, si ad evenire conjungamus. Si enim dicamus, quia rem evenire aliter quam Deus providit, hoc totum est possibile, falsum est, sicut et rem evenire aliter quam evenit, hoc totum falsum est. Si vero ita dicamus, quod illud quod evenit est possibile aliter quam Deus habuit in sua providentia, vel quam evenerit, profecto verum est, sed nihil ad supradictam regulam cum videlicet possibile non referatur ad totum antecedens praemissae consequentiae illius: Si res evenit aliter quam Deus providit, Deus fallitur. Sin autem toti applicetur antecedenti possibile, ut supramemorata regula servetur, falsum est, ut diximus, quod possibile sit hoc totum, quod res evenit aliter quam evenit. Unde cum hoc nullatenus probari possit, nequaquam recipere cogimur quod possibile sit Deus falli. *Opp.* II. p. 146; cf. *Logica*, pp. 429–30.

2 *Logica*, p. 430. 3 *Dialectica*, pp. 289–90.
4 *Epitome*, 20, coll. 1724 ff., and *Sentent. Florian.* p. 11.
5 *Sentent.* pp. 49 ff.

tacked doctrines similar to those taught by Abailard, and
may thus be considered to have been directly answering his
theology. Hugh maintains that God can do all things, save
those alone which he could not do without injury to himself.
This restriction in no way limits his omnipotence, since the
power to do himself any injury is but the mark of impotence.
God can do all things, but he cannot destroy himself, for
that ability would be a weakness, and not a power.[1] Like
Abailard, both Hugh and the Lombard reproduce the traditional theory that divine omnipotence is not lessened by
the lack of those typically human powers which would be
inconsistent with the nature of God.[2] But in contradistinction to Abailard, our two theologians followed St Augustine
more closely in emphasizing God's will rather than his
ability to perform any deed as the mark of his omnipotence.
Since God never wishes anything that he cannot do, and thus
his omnipotence is assured, "for God does not wish to perform anything that he cannot do either by his own direct
action or through that of his creatures, and he does not desire to do anything that he is unable to accomplish".[3] Thus
Hugh and Peter Lombard are saved by their insistence upon
the nature of God's volition from the unsatisfactory character of Abailard's theodicy. Nor would they allow that the
passage in St Matthew, in which Jesus says that he could
summon twelve legions of angels, may be taken to mean that
because of his divine nature Jesus could not really have made
the request, although, had he been able to do so, his prayer
would have been answered. That Jesus did not call upon the
Father for aid was not due to any restriction imposed upon

1 Omnia quippe facere potest, praeter id solum quod sine ejus laesione fieri
non potest; in quo tamen non minus omnipotens est, quia si id posset,
omnipotens non esset. Dico ergo quod Deus omnia potest; et tamen se
ipsum destruere non potest. Hoc enim posse posse non esset, sed non posse.
Itaque omnia potest Deus, quae posse potentia est. *De Sacrament.* I. 2. 22,
col. 214 B.

2 Peter Lombard, *Sentent.* I. dist. 42. 1–5 and 7. Cf. *Summa Sentent.* I. 24,
PL. 176, col. 68 B.

3 Lombard, I. dist. 42. 8. Cf. Augustinus: "id solum potest Deus, quod
vult"; si id solum potest, quod vult: ergo non potest facere, quod non vult.
Roland, p. 50, from Augustine, *Sermo ad Catechum.* I. 2, PL. 40, col. 627.

him by his divinity, but to the ordinance of God that the sacrifice on Calvary should take place. If Jesus had wished, he could have made the request, but he did not so wish.[1] The same Jesus who had raised up Lazarus in the flesh could also have raised up Judas in the spirit.[2] Further, although God always acts rationally, we may not suppose that he cannot act otherwise than he actually does,[3] for any alteration in his will would not entail a new will in God; both now and from eternity he has the ability to change his volition, even if the action which would be altered had originally been fixed *ab aeterno*.[4] By doing something different God does not himself suffer change; whether he does the same thing or another, he remains in himself always the same.[5] And God can do better than he does, if he so desires, for he could have made man in such a way that he would be unable to sin, nor would he have wished to sin.[6] But this does not mean that God can make anything better than he is himself, nor that he can do better in the sense that he can act more wisely than he does,[7] two obvious impossibilities. Still, he has the power of making the good into the better.[8]

From these criticisms we can understand how Abailard came to formulate his unsatisfactory doctrine of God. His error proceeds from a false identification of the will of God with his power, while his orthodox contemporaries carefully separated the two by declaring that, although God can do all things, there are yet many things which he does not wish to perform. That he leaves many things undone does not imply that their performance would conflict with his rationality; God indeed cannot perform things which his own righteousness demands that he should not do, and so he cannot effect anything which would be inconvenient to his own

1 Roland, p. 52; *Summa Sentent*. I. 24, col. 68 C; Lombard, I. dist. 43. 4.
2 *Loc. cit.*; cf. Augustine, *de Natura et Gratia*, 7. 8, PL. 44, col. 250.
3 Lombard, I. dist. 43. 4.   4 *Ibid.* 5.
5 Hugh of St Victor, *de Sacrament*. I. 2. 22, col. 215 C.
6 *Summa Sentent*. I. 24, col. 70 A; Lombard, I. dist. 44. 1–3; cf. Augustine, *de Genesi ad Litt*. XI. 7. 9, PL. 34, col. 433.
7 *Summa Sentent. loc. cit.*
8 Hugh of St Victor, *de Sacrament*. I. 2. 22, col. 214.

justice.[1] But Abailard failed to understand that of two alternatives both may be equally possible for a rational being to do, and that that being can choose between these alternatives without doing injury to himself. Because it is his will, and not his nature, that is the primary regulative principle of his activities, God can choose the less good of two possible actions without damaging his own essential rationality.

II

Abailard's account of the six days of the creation—his *Expositio in Hexaemeron*—must now engage our attention. In its compilation the chief sources which he used were the *de Genesi ad Litteram* of St Augustine, and Bede's *Hexaemeron* and *Commentary on the Pentateuch*. There is also strong evidence to shew that he was familiar with the *Exameron* of St Ambrose, while for the elucidation of the original Hebrew names he was dependent upon St Jerome.

His reason for writing the book was the importunity of Héloise, who had written to him for aid in difficulties which she found in attempting to understand the first chapter of Genesis.[2] St Augustine had himself realized that his commentary raised more difficulties than it answered,[3] and Héloise naturally looked to Abailard for further aid. His own method of exposition was to follow the usual lines; it was to be historical, moral, and mystical,[4] for all these three methods of exegesis were then applied to the explanation of a biblical text. Abailard takes the historical approach first, telling his readers that it was the intention of the author of Genesis to bring men to the worship of God by describing the creation and the government of the world. The invisible

1 Non potest facere quod sua justitia exigit ut non faciat, id est, non potest facere id quod ipse, qui est summa justitia, non vult facere, falsum est. Si autem his verbis intelligas eum non posse facere id quod justitiae ejus convenire non potest, verum dicis. Lombard, 1. dist. 44. 3. See also Gandulph's criticism of Abailard in *Sentent.* 1. 42, pp. 31–2.

2 *Hexaem.* Praef. coll. 731 C, 732 BC.

3 Augustine, *Retract.* 24. 1, PL. 32, col. 640.

4 *Hexaem.* col. 731 D.

and incomprehensible Godhead cannot be known in itself, but it can be understood through the things it has made.[1] Further, from an account of their creation in the likeness of God and from the favours extended to them both in Eden and after the Fall, men ought to realize how great an obedience they owe to the God who created them.[2] Unlike St Augustine, Abailard does not carry his commentary beyond the account of the six days of creation; he makes no attempt to explain the entire book of Genesis, nor does he expound the story and consequences of the Fall. His book is not, like the *Exameron* of St Ambrose, a collection of addresses, and he does not instance the moral lessons which we may learn from the different animals of creation, as Ambrose with his deep knowledge of Pliny had already done. Abailard set out to write a commentary upon traditional lines, like that of Bede; he was not composing sermons for the people of Milan, in which he would naturally have been forced to keep always before him the homiletic value of his text.

In his account of the method of creation, Abailard accepted the Platonic theory of pre-existent ideas in the mind of God, the archetypes of the things which are to be made.[3] This theory is further discussed in the *Logica*, where Abailard compares God to an artist about to compose something, and therefore preconceiving in his mind the exemplary form of the thing which he is about to make. God, indeed, works to a likeness of this form, which is said to "go into" the body when the thing itself is made in that likeness.[4] This method of procedure only applies to the general works or the special states of nature which are made by God, and not to any creative activity on the part of a human artificer; that is, to the creation of a soul or of a stone, and not to the building of a house or to the making of a sword.[5] Further, Abailard reproduces the current theory, drawn from Greek philo-

---

1 *Ibid.* coll. 732–3, quoting Rom. i. 20.   2 *Ibid.* col. 733 B.
3 Cf. *Introd.* I. 9, col. 991 B, and *Theol. Christ.* IV. col. 1307.
4 P. 22. Cf. Anselm's comparison of God to a smith in *Monol.* 11, PL. 158, col. 160, where he also treats of the divine ideas.
5 *Logica*, p. 23; cf. *Dial.* p. 377.

sophy, that the universe is constituted of four elements, fire, air, earth and water. Since the first two are by nature the lighter, God called them the heavens, while the other two he called the earth.[1] These elements, he says,[2] have well been termed the materials of the universe, for it is from them that all created things derive their being, just in the same way as every living thing takes its food and subsistence from the things which it eats.[3] But he will not allow that the materials of creation were in any way pre-existent; the world itself was created *ex nihilo*. He holds that the creation of the universe must be sharply distinguished from the creation of man, for the world was not made of any pre-existent material, while man was formed from the dust.[4]

As yet the earth was "without form, and void", with no inhabitants, and neither the sea nor the earth contained any living thing. The heavens, on the other hand, were not devoid of inhabitants; either before their creation or else at the time when they were made, the heavens were peopled with the angels.[5] But the universe was still confused and indistinct, while the face of the waters was shrouded in darkness. Following Plato, Abailard calls this confusion chaos, but by this term he does not mean that creation was the ordering of a mass of pre-existent, whirling matter, but that for the first period of its existence the world was an unordered congeries of the elements. Any knowledge of these elements was at the time impossible, for, even if man had then existed, they could neither have been seen nor known.[6] In his statement, however, that the universe was at one time in a state of chaos, Abailard was at variance with many Christian writers; William of Conches, for example, com-

1 *Hexaem.* col. 733 CD.   2 *Ibid.* col. 734 AB.
3 *Ibid.* col. 734 B.
4 *Ibid.* col. 734 BC. The distinction is made to depend on the difference between *creavit* in Gen. i. 1, and *formavit*, used of man's creation, in Gen. ii. 7. Cf. De nihilo mundum, et angelos, et animam; ex aliquo, hominem et pecora, et caeteras creaturas, Bede, *in Genes.* 1, PL. 91, col. 191 B.
5 *Hexaem.* col. 734 B; cf. Bede, *Hexaem.* 1. col. 14 A.
6 *Hexaem.* col. 735 AB; cf. Ambrose, *Exameron*, 1. 7. 26, ed. Schenkl, CSEL. XXXII. p. 25.

bating the Platonic theory, definitely states that the elements were created in the places which they now occupy.[1]

Over this confusion the Spirit of God was moving to bring to it the order that was necessary. But, since the Spirit had not yet effected its work, we may with propriety say that the Spirit was moving *upon* the face of the waters. In the place of *ferebatur*, one translation reads *fovebat*,[2] and this variant had already introduced into Christian exegesis the comparison of the beginning of the world to the hatching of an egg, a comparison sufficiently familiar to anthropologists.[3] Abailard expands this conception with obvious pleasure, stating that the confused mass of the elements may well be compared to an egg from which the chick has not yet come. Its yolk represents the earth in the midst of the universe; the white is the water adhering to the earth; the skin beneath the shell is the air, and the shell itself fire. Just as the chick is formed out of the yolk and the white, the whole of animate creation is formed out of earth and water, and as the bird broods over the egg, so the Spirit of God brooded over the waters to produce and quicken man together with the rest of the animate world.[4] Again, for *ferebatur*, we may read *volitabat*, and this suggested to Abailard a connexion between *spiritus* or πνεῦμα, and breath or wind.[5] Literally taken, the passage then would mean, Abailard tells us,[6] that a wind was sent forth from God and drove up the topmost part of the waters —which is always held to be the lightest—so that it remained afterwards suspended in the sky. Mystically, this wind re-

---

1 William, *de Phil. Mundi*, I. 21, PL. 172, coll. 53–4. .

2 *Hexaem.* col. 735 B. Cf. Ambrose, I. 8. 29, p. 29; Augustine, *de Genesi ad Litt.* I. 18. 36, col. 260, both from a Syriac version; see Basil, *Homil. in Hex.* II. 6, PG. 29, col. 44 B. Bede (*Hexaem.* I. col. 15) has *superferebatur*, which he interprets as a sign both of the Spirit's power to illumine the waters and to bring them together into one place, and of the pre-eminence of his power. See also his *Comment. in Genes.* col. 193.

3 In similitudinem volucris, ova calore animantis. Jerome, *Quaest. in Genesim*, I. PL. 23, col. 939 A.

4 *Hexaem.* coll. 735–6.

5 *Ibid.* col. 736 B; cf. Deut. xxxii. 11, where the same Hebrew word is used.

6 *Ibid.* col. 736 BC. Abailard instances the action of God's breath in driving back the Red Sea when the Hebrews crossed it; Exod. xv. 8, 10.

presents the resurrection of mankind through water and the Spirit.[1]

The phrase, "God spake", is not to be interpreted literally; like St Augustine, Abailard makes the expression refer to the Word of God, the coeternal Wisdom in whom all things are determined before they are made.[2] Creation is thus a double activity; things are first settled in the ordinance of divine providence, and then they are put into operation. The light which God commanded to be made must be taken to mean the separation by which the confused mass which could not yet be seen, and which appeared to be unfit for any use or purpose, could now be seen and be recognized as something which had been created for some purpose and use.[3] And through this light men were to be given the power of understanding God from his creation.[4]

We must regard the days of creation only as divisions of God's work, for the six days are not to be measured by the present standard of time given us by the alternation of day and night.[5] On the first day, then, God created the elements, the material of the world; the work of the second day was the division of the waters by the creation of the firmament. Here, Abailard was faced with a problem which had quite obviously troubled previous exegetes: How can such light elements as fire and air in the heavens uphold the water which is by nature heavier than they are? The suspension of the waters above the firmament, he says,[6] was rendered possible by the fact that their texture can be so rare and their subtlety so great, that the mass of fire and air can sustain them, just as a piece of water or a stone can be supported by a volume of water. The waters, too, are held up in the same way as the bodies of birds and dragons are supported in the air. Moreover, some writers have held that the upper waters were

1 *Hexaem*. col. 736 D.
2 *Ibid*. col. 738 BC; cf. Augustine, *de Genesi*, I. 2. 6, col. 248, and Bede, *Hexaem*. I. coll. 16–17.   3 *Hexaem*. col. 738 D.   4 *Ibid*. col. 738 A.
5 *Ibid*. col. 745 CD; Bede (*Hexaem*. I. col. 17 CD) adds that God caused the day and night to be named, whether in Hebrew, Greek, or any other tongue.
6 *Ibid*.; cf. Augustine, *op. cit*. II. 4. 7–8, coll. 265–6.

solidified by a glacial or crystalline process, and have thus
been hardened,[1] this glacial process being effected through
the action of the wind moving over the face of the waters.[2]
And, if this interpretation is correct, Abailard proceeds to say
that, since the more solid the waters become, the more
powerfully they are sustained by fire and air, it is then not
perhaps necessary for them to be upheld at all, for they are
no longer fluid, but have been hardened into a crystal.[3] It is
true that all this was done against Nature, but Nature is the
power conferred upon creation from the first preparation of
things, by which it is sufficient to produce things.[4] No one
would, therefore, ask by what power of Nature God placed
the upper waters above fire, and hardened them into crystal,
for all this was done by his will alone. Finally, Abailard refuses to accept the teaching of some writers who held that
the water for the Flood came from the waters above the
firmament; since these waters are crystalline, they could not
have descended upon the earth, and therefore the Flood must
have been caused by waters from below the firmament.[5]

The work of the third day was the formation of the dry
land on which God was to create and place mankind. The
waters beneath the firmament were gathered into one place
so that the ball of the earth sat in the waters. Not only did
the sea border the dry land, but Abailard holds that the water
penetrated through the earth by means of veins, from which
our rivers and springs came to be born.[6] The water of the sea

1 Josephus, *Antiq. Judaeorum*, I. 1 (ed. B. Niese, 1. Berlin, 1887, p. 9) is
quoted by Abailard. Cf. Jerome, *Ep.* LXIX. 6, PL. 22, col. 659. The same idea
is to be found in Bede (*Hexaem*. 1. col. 18 D), but there the Clementine *Recog-
nitions*, I. 27 is quoted.

2 *Hexaem*. col. 747 A.   3 *Ibid*. col. 743 B.

4 Naturam itaque dicimus vim rerum ex illa praeparatione illis collatam ad
aliquid inde nascendum, hoc est efficiendum sufficientem. *Ibid*. col. 746 D.

5 *Ibid*. col. 743 D.

6 Ita ille globus terrae in aquis insedit, ut ex una parte eum mare con-
tingeret, et per venas ejus se infunderet, unde nobis fontes vel flumina nas-
cerentur. *Ibid*. col. 748 B. See Augustine, *de Genesi*, v. 10. 25, coll. 329–30;
Ambrose, *Exameron*, III. 3. 8, p. 64. Ambrose (*ibid*. 3. 12, pp. 67 ff.) and Bede
(*Hexaem*. 1. col. 20 BC) point to the fact that all the seas are joined together.
Bede also notes that in Hebrew the word for 'water' and 'the sea' is the same,
in Genes. col. 196.

was in consequence made deeper than it had previously been, in order that our springs should never fail.[1] Then, as the waters fell back, the earth dried, conceiving and bringing forth its vegetation. At this point, another difficulty had to be met. At what season of the year was the world created? Like St Ambrose and Bede, Abailard declares that the creation took place in the spring,[2] or at least its equivalent. Still, the sun had not been created to warm the soil. By taking refuge behind his earlier statement that the world had been miraculously made against Nature by the will of God alone, and by supposing that the newness of the earth gave it greater powers of production than it afterwards possessed, he sought to explain how plants grew at a time when the sun was not yet in existence. And the growth of the plants was doubtlessly aided by the abundance of the waters which had covered the world, and which were conserved through the creation of the sun on the following day.[3] But since the seasons differ in the various parts of the world, spring was not present in every region of the earth at the time of creation. Although the Scriptures do not mention the simultaneous creation of the fruits with the trees which bear them, yet we must believe that the fruits were produced at the same time as the trees, for when man was placed in Paradise, he found all that was necessary for his sustenance.[4] Poisonous and unfruitful trees, however, were not made as such until after the Fall, and thorns and brambles were either not created with the other trees and plants, or else they were originally harmless and fruitful, and then degenerated on account of man's sin.[5] Till the Fall indeed everything in the whole world was good.

1 *Hexaem.* col. 748 c.
2 *Ibid.* col. 749; cf. Ambrose, *Exameron*, 1. 4. 13, p. 11, and Bede, *Hexaem.* col. 21 b.
3 *Hexaem.* col. 749.
4 *Ibid.* col. 750 A.
5 *Ibid.* coll. 750 B, 766 D. This notion was not shared by Bede who taught that, although the earth did not produce harmful and unfruitful trees before the Fall, the earth did not produce them as a direct consequence of the Fall, for the earth did not feel man's guilt. They were produced so that men should

The creation of the stars, the sun, and the moon on the fourth day leads Abailard to discuss the problem whether the planets are animate and are governed by spirits, or whether their movements are solely to be attributed to the will of God. From St Augustine,[1] he knew that the Greek philosophers—and among them Plato—had taught that the planets were immortal, rational, and impassible beings. The planets indeed, more excellent than the other stars, have a greater influence upon the creation of men. Abailard does not commit himself to a solution of the time-honoured problem whether the stellar system is in character animate; since the Fathers have never actually condemned the theory, he considers that it is at least possible for a Christian to hold that the stars may possess reason. Certainly, on the supposition that they are moved and controlled by spirits, it is easy to explain their movements; but, if we find it necessary to seek elsewhere for another explanation why the stars move, then it is enough to say that they are moved by the will of God alone.[2] And, coupled with this problem, comes the question whether the stars enable us to foretell the events of the future, a question which the Middle Ages had inherited from classical times when it was very often held that the affairs of the world were controlled by the heavenly bodies. In the *City of God*,[3] St Augustine had fulminated against the idea that a man's life could be known in advance from the position of the stars at the time of his birth, and, despite this criticism, mediaeval thinkers continually coquetted with theories of astrology. In his own discussion, Abailard distinguishes between natural and contingent occurrences in the future, and refuses to deny that natural events may be known beforehand in precisely the same way as many things in a sick man

always have pain, see *in Genes.* col. 196 c. St Ambrose, with a clearer idea that what is harmful to man is meat for animals, states (*Exameron*, III. 9. 38, pp. 84–5) that poisonous and unfruitful trees were created at the beginning.

1 *De Civitate Dei*, VIII. 14 ff., PL. 41, coll. 238–41, quoted *Hexaem.* col. 752.
2 *Hexaem.* col. 753 D.
3 v. 8, PL. 41, col. 148; cf. *de Genesi ad Litt.* III. 17, col. 278, and Ambrose, *Exameron*, IV. 4. 13, pp. 118 ff.

can be predicted by medical men through a diagnosis of the state of his body. Those, indeed, who are skilled in astronomy, can tell us much concerning the weather we are to expect, whether it will be warm or cold, wet or dry.[1] But though many astronomers claim for themselves the ability to read the heavens, they can predicate nothing about the nature of future contingent events. Their pretended divination of such happenings is devilish, and their practices have nothing in common with the honourable science of weather prophecy.[2]

His account of the creation of the animals on the fifth day reveals little of interest. Abailard held that, as the fish and the birds were created from water and not from earth, their flesh was accordingly permitted to Benedictine monks by their rule, which only forbade them the meat of four-footed animals, for these were created out of earth and water.[3] The action of God in blessing the waters and those beings which the waters produced, again signifies the regeneration of mankind by means of the water of baptism.[4] The animals, however, were created out of the earth, and this fact explains why their movements are slower than those of birds and of fish. The life-giving spirit of the beasts was not formed out of the earth, but out of the water.[5]

The creation of man was the end for which the entire universe was made, and to his rule every created thing was subjected. Man himself was made in the image, woman only in the similitude of God, and thus man must be considered the

1 Hexaem. coll. 754-5; Bede (Hexaem. col. 22 c) does not discuss the question. He points to the stars as guides for sailors, and for the Ethiopians wandering in the desert.

2 Hexaem. coll. 755-6. The same differentiation is to be found in Aquinas, Summa Theol. II a. 2 ae, quaest. 95, art. 1. Cf. the attack on astrologers in John of Salisbury, Polycr. 1. 9, PL. 199, col. 406 ff.

3 Hexaem. col. 756 c. The same theory is found in Rhabanus Maurus, de Instit. Cleric. II. 27, PL. 107, col. 339 D, and Hildegarde, Exposit. regulae S. Benedicti, PL. 197, col. 1053 c. Bede (in Genes. col. 199 A) compares reptiles and birds to evil and to good thoughts, and later (col. 201 CD) says that cattle signify the Jews, reptiles the Gentiles, and fish, Christ.

4 Hexaem. col. 758 c.

5 Ibid. col. 759 CD.

more worthy of the two.[1] Abailard here instances the parallel
of the relationship which exists within the Godhead; as
Christ is of the Father only, so man alone was made after the
image of God, while, like the Holy Spirit which proceeds
from both the Father and the Son, the woman was formed
not only in the image of God, but also from the rib of Adam.[2]
Man is the only part of creation which is endowed with
reason and wisdom, and participates in the love of God; but
here again, although reason, wisdom, and the love of God
belong to both sexes, man is the more gifted, for his nearer
creation in the image of God makes that image the more
easily discoverable in him than in womankind.[3] In this connexion, Abailard strangely does not refer to the identification
of human reason with the divine Λόγος. He does, indeed,
mention the corresponding triune nature of the Godhead and
the human mind, though the reader might well have expected that he would have dwelt at greater length upon the
aetiological validity of human logic. It must be remembered,
however, that the *Hexaemeron* was written for Héloise, and
not in defence of his theological method. She would never
have questioned the use which he made of dialectic.

We have already seen how God's rest upon the seventh
day is not to be regarded literally.[4] God ceased from cre-
ating any new species, but he did not cease from multiplying
the numbers contained in the species which had already been
created, nor did he stop from his activity in governing the
universe. Although the mule and many of the worms which
are born out of corruption were not made during the six
days, the seed of their creation was contained in the things
which had been made.[5] Further, God continues to create

1 Intelligimus virum ad imaginem Dei creatum, feminam vero ad similitudinem.... Distat autem inter imaginem et similitudinem quod similitudo
rei potest dici quod convenientiam aliquam habet cum ipsa, unde simile illi
dici queat. Imago vero expressa tantum similitudo dicitur, sicut figurae
hominum quae singula membra perfectius eos repraesentant. *Ibid*. col. 760 D.
2 *Ibid*. coll. 763–4.   3 *Ibid*. col. 761 CD.
4 See *supra*, p. 136; cf. Augustine, *de Genesi*, IV. 8. 15–16, coll. 301–2, and
Bede, *Hexaem*. col. 35 D.
5 *Hexaem*. coll. 760–70.

fresh souls.[1] Abailard, it will be seen, did not believe in Traducianism.

Abailard's moral and allegorical exposition of the Genesis story must now be studied. The confusion of earth and heaven represents for him the dualistic nature of man, caused by his possession of a body as well as a soul. At the start every man is unformed and uncontrolled by moral considerations; his body is not yet subject to the rule of spiritual things, and he is himself a brute animal. The Spirit of God, however, brooding over the waters of his desires, makes him spiritual and, cherishing him as a bird cherishes its young, re-forms the old man into the new. Then comes the light of faith, followed by those of hope and charity.[2] The creation of the physical light signifies the illumination of faith which the Holy Spirit infuses into our hearts and without which we are unable to please God; after faith, hope comes to lead us from earthly to celestial desires. Like an anchor of a ship, hope preserves man against the storms of the world, and, implanting in him a longing for spiritual things, strengthens him to endure whatever trials may come. Then, as the waters fall back and as some are submerged underground to irrigate the earth which has now been dried and drained, charity approaches, and subjects the body to the spirit until, drained from the desires of carnal lusts by the warmth of charity, the soul itself is made dry. In those places where the waters of concupiscence no longer exist, the devil cannot find rest, nor does he entice a soul which has thus been dried to consent to evil desires. And, like the earth, the soul brings forth its plants by shewing the charity with which it burns, and by the production of good works. If a soul grows to such perfection that it can further edify others by its preaching, it then becomes the "lights in the firmament of heaven", and like them it illuminates the world. Since weak men need preaching if they are not to be broken by misfortune or puffed up

1 *Hexaem*. col. 770 A.
2 *Ibid*. col. 770 CD. To Bede, the sun and the moon signified Christ and the church, *in Genes*. col. 197 B.

by success, these "lights" shine by night and day, just as do their counterparts in the heavens.[1] The birds, the moving and the creeping things represent the various kinds of faithful, the celibate, the "rulers" (*rectores*), and the married. Lastly, the creation of man outside Paradise and his subsequent removal thither indicate the manner in which he will be brought through grace from his exile on earth to his home in heaven.[2]

With their great interest in the allegorical it was natural for most patristic and mediaeval writers to infer that the six days of creation meant the existence of six ages in the history of the world. Numbers exercised a fascinating influence over men as they emerged from primitive religion to philosophy, and this fascination, present in classical thought—notably in Pythagoreanism—was copied by early Christian exegetes, and became traditional in theology. Six had long been regarded as a sacred number, since it is formed of the first three integers in various combinations; it is both twice three and three times two, while it is also the sum of one, two, and three.[3] The numerical correspondence of ages in the history of the world to the days of creation formed Abailard's allegorical interpretation of the *Hexaemeron*. The first age, the infancy of the world, lasted from the time of Adam to that of Noah, and corresponded at once to the inability of infants to articulate and to the undifferentiated chaos of the elements, for then it was that mankind lacked the Law of God. This age was blotted out by the Flood, just as the memories of infancy are erased from the minds of men. This second age, from the time of Abraham, was the boyhood of the world. Since men can recall to mind the deeds of their own boyhood, this age was not destroyed, but was saved through the ark. The adolescence of the world, from Abraham to David, marks the third age, when the Law was given to restrain men from the flux of carnal desires, just as on the third day the earth was freed from the waters and brought forth its fruit. But, like the earth, men of that age,

1 *Hexaem.* col. 771 B.   2 *Ibid.* col. 771 CD.
3 *Ibid.* coll. 768–9; cf. Augustine, *de Genesi ad Litt.* IV. 2, coll. 296 ff.

still adhering to mundane desires, gave birth only to worldly desires. The manhood of the world, lasting from David to the Babylonish exile, was the age when the prophets, the great lights of the heavens, lighted the human race. From then till the time of Christ came the fifth age, the senility of the world, when the patriarchs and prophets had died and the people of God no longer worshipped at Jerusalem. To this age Christ came to make the old man new, and to preach baptism to a world that had grown weary. The sixth age is when the renewed man is placed in the Paradise which has been opened by the Passion of Christ.[1]

1 *Hexaem.* coll. 771–3. The same division of world-history is to be found in Augustine, *de Trin.* IV. 4. 7, PL. 42, col. 892.

Chapter vii

THE TRINITY AND
THE PERSON OF CHRIST

I

WE have already noted that Abailard regarded the doctrine of the Trinity as the basis of all Christian truth, a foundation indeed which, if it were once disturbed, would bring the entire edifice of Christian theology tumbling to the ground. This emphasis upon the outstanding importance of a single dogma was not wholly due to any particular choice on the part of Abailard, although his special interest indicates the character of his intellectualist approach to the problems of theology. Coupled with many Christological difficulties, the doctrine of the Trinity was one of the chief questions which the theologians of the early Middle Ages set themselves to solve, the numerous trinitarian heresies of the eleventh and twelfth centuries shewing how great an interest was taken in the task of explaining the nature of the triune Godhead.

In one way, the special interest in a single dogma was dictated by historical reasons. The teaching of Photius upon the *Filioque* clause and the schism between the churches of Rome and Constantinople necessitated further investigation into the catholicity of the Double Procession of the Holy Spirit, so that the Latin theologians could persuade the Greeks of their error. But this widespread concern for a deeper treatment of the dogma of the Trinity was more especially an inheritance from patristic times. The *de Trinitate* and the various theological writings of Boethius had done much to elucidate the doctrine, but despite their metaphysical grandeur they were not entirely satisfactory. While the great contribution of St Augustine had been his insistence upon the relations of *ingenitus*, *genitus*, and *procedens* within the Godhead, his thought needed further clarification and development, and this need was increased when the logicians of the eleventh and twelfth centuries began to apply their science to theology. Although Boethius had provided the mediaeval philosopher with his standard definition of a person as "an individual substance of rational nature",[1] the meaning of personality was a problem which then as now required much investigation.

We have already seen that Abailard's theological work was dominated by a double aim; he sought to instruct his pupils and to disprove the teaching of contemporary heretical professors. This same double aim moulded the character of his discussion upon the doctrine of the Trinity. He wished to shew the reasonableness of that dogma to his students, and at the same time to demonstrate how unsound were the opinions of men like Roscelin and Gilbert Porrée. Abailard's first theological essay, the *de Unitate et Trinitate Divina*, had been, as we have already shewn, directed against the errors of Roscelin, and this animus against his former master is to be traced throughout all his definitely theological writings. But, so far as we know, Roscelin does not seem to have followed out to the full the metaphysical and theological consequences of his logical theory that universals are but *flatus vocis*; this was done for him by his first great opponent, Anselm of Canterbury. That scholar shewed that his Nominalism made it impossible for Roscelin to understand that the three Persons of the Godhead were one by virtue of their common substance. In his theology the Persons became similar to three angels or three souls, and were in consequence three things, for a Nominalist logic cannot recognize the unity of the Persons in the single really existent divine substance. On the other hand, if the single substance is emphasized as the unity, then Nominalism leads to Patripassianism with its theory that the Father and the Holy Spirit became incarnate

---

1 Persona vero, rationabilis naturae individua substantia. *De Persona et duabus Naturis*, 4, PL. 64, col. 1345 c.

with the Son.[1] Anxious at all costs to avoid this latter pitfall, Roscelin himself fell into the snare of tri-theism. Again, his inability to grasp the reality of the divine substance common to the three Persons led him to regard the various attributes of divinity, goodness, wisdom, and the like, as personal pro-perties which are proper to the persons only in so far as each is a member of the single undivided Godhead.[2] Lastly, his logic again brought him into difficulties; he found himself totally unable to distinguish between the two natures, human and divine, in the person of the incarnate Christ.[3]

Gilbert Porrée was a far deeper thinker than Roscelin, and although his theories were censured at the council of Rheims (1148), his opinions were quoted with respect by later scholastics.[4] His logical doctrines have already been de-scribed; it remains here to shew how their acceptance led him to a view of the dogma of the Trinity which was fiercely criticized. When applied to theology, his distinction between *substantia* and *subsistentia* was thought to imply a distinction between *deus* and *divinitas*, that is, between God and the divinity from which each of the three Persons draws his individual, special and general attributes. But since his in-composite nature prevents the existence of any distinction in God,[5] his essence must be both *quod est* and *a quo est*. Gilbert's differentiation between God as *subsistens* and divinity as *sub-sistentia* was therefore one of logic and not of metaphysics.[6] Accordingly, the three Persons do not owe their separate existences to any distinction in the divine substance, nor to the presence therein of any accident; the Father, the Son, and the Holy Spirit are the same through the singleness of their

1 Si tres personae sunt una tantum res, et non sunt tres res, unaquaeque per se separatim, sicut tres angeli aut tres animae; ita tamen ut voluntate et potentia omnino sint idem, ergo Pater et Spiritus sanctus cum Filio incarnatus est. *De Fide Trin.* 3, PL. 158, col. 266 A.

2 *Ibid.* col. 268 B.   3 *Ibid.* 6, coll. 278 ff.

4 Cf. Albert the Great, *Liber de sex principiis*, tr. 1, c. 1, *Opera omnia*, 1. Paris, 1890, p. 305, quoted A. Heysse, *Liber de sex princ. G. Porretano ascriptus*, Münster, 1929, p. 6.

5 *In Librum de Trin. Comment.* coll. 1269, 1283.

6 Cf. Seeberg, III. p. 243.

essence and subsistence, their "otherness" being not an
alteritas rerum, but a difference of relationship. The three
Persons are three separate existences which are yet one
through their one *subsistentia*, their divinity; yet this subsistence is also the basis of both their unity and their diversity.
"Each one of the three Persons by reason of that singular,
individual, and simple οὐσία, that is essence, is that which
he is; by that essence too he is other, being one, simple,
undivided and without participation in a different essence
God, so that the three are one through the propriety of
essence".[1] Here there is a distinct, but certainly unintentional,
differentiation between the divine substance and the subsisting Persons, but, as we have said, it is really one of logic,
not of metaphysics. Although Gilbert energetically defended
his orthodoxy, it was argued that his logic substituted a
quaternitas for the *trinitas* of Christian belief.[2] That he was
charged with believing in a Godhead composed of three
Persons with the addition of the divine substance was hardly
his fault; such a doctrine certainly does not represent his
views. Gilbert was also criticized for holding that the Person
of Christ alone, and not his Godhead, became incarnate,[3] a
belief which again he did not hold.

To disprove the trinitarian errors of Roscelin Abailard
had to shew how it was possible to distinguish between the
Persons without endangering their unity; while to combat
the supposed heterodoxy of Gilbert he was compelled to
demonstrate the unsoundness of the distinction between *id
quod est* and *id quo est*, between *deus* and *divinitas*. Since both
his opponents were logicians, Abailard used his own logic
to disprove their teaching, applying his own rule that the
enemies of catholic truth must be silenced by the employ-

1 Unusquisque horum trium est illa singulari ac simplici et individua et
sola οὐσία, id est essentia, hoc quod est, qua alius est, unus et simplex, et in-
dividuus, et absque diversae essentiae consortio deus, ita quod ipsi tres simul
sunt unus essentiae proprietate. *In Librum de Trin. Comment.* col. 1295 c.
2 Geoffrey of Auxerre, *c. Gilbert. Porret.* 3. 40, col. 609.
3 *Ibid.* 3. 54, col. 614. See also Otto of Freising, *Gesta Fred.* 1. 52 ff., *ed.
cit.* pp. 74 ff., and John of Salisbury, *Hist. Pontif.* 8-10, pp. 16-41.

ment of their own weapons. And as a logician, Abailard considered the clear differentiation between identity and dissimilarity to be his chief problem. Once that distinction was made, it would be comparatively easy to shew wherein lay the unity and the "otherness" of the three Persons. Analogies were also to be used to indicate the reasonableness of the orthodox view.

Like all his contemporaries, Abailard founded his discussion of the doctrine of the Trinity upon the *de Trinitate* of St Augustine, but, unlike many of his fellow-writers of the time, he failed to reproduce much of the metaphysical greatness of that book. Following St Augustine, however, he based much of his theology upon the three special properties of the three Persons, the attribution of *ingenitus* to the Father alone, of *genitus* only to the Son, and of *procedens* only to the Spirit.[1] But he recognized that these special properties are only those of relationship within the Godhead;[2] they do not say whether the three Persons are identical or not in substance and essence. While these special properties belong only to the several Persons, all other predications must be predicated of the three Persons alike, *secundum divinae naturae dignitatem*. Thus, each Person is equally omnipotent, eternal, and immeasurable.[3] The difference between the Persons is neither one of nature nor of number, but of person alone; since they cannot alternate, these special properties, *ingenitus*, *genitus*, and *procedens*, are alone indicative of the personal distinction between the Father, the Son, and the Holy Spirit. In that they both share a common humanity Socrates and Plato are not different things; but through the numerical separation of their special substance they are none the less different as persons.[4] Much less are the three Persons of the Trinity three different things, for in the Godhead there can be no parts or divisions. Further, as the divine substance in which the three Persons exist together is indivisible and uniform, the Persons must again be less different one from the

1 *Theol. Christ.* III. col. 1230 AB. 2 *Ibid.* coll. 1231–2.
3 *Ibid.* col. 1232 D. 4 *Ibid.* col. 1232 C.

other than are Plato and Socrates; while Plato and Socrates
are not of the same essence, the essence of the Father is the
same as the essence of both the Son and the Holy Spirit.[1] And
so, before we can arrive at any satisfactory account of the
doctrine of the Trinity, a minute investigation into the meaning of identity and dissimilarity must be entered upon, and
this can only be accomplished through the aid of logic.

One preliminary must, however, be noted; does the distinction of the person lie in names (*in vocabulis*), in reality
(*in re*), or in them both? Now if we hold that the distinction
between the persons is purely that of name, unsatisfactory
conclusions inevitably follow. Since the predication of
epithets is only a human activity, the Trinity cannot be regarded as eternal, for the separate existence of the Persons
would then depend upon human predication. And as many
names can rightly be applied to the divine substance, should
we not be forced to hypostatize all the possible predications,
making thereby the number of the Persons more than three?
But, on the other hand, if we refer the distinction of the
Persons to a distinction in the substance of God, should we
not then be saying that God is triune both in substance as
well as in person?[2] Again, we know that in God there is nothing save "the unique essence of the simple and wholly indivisible substance", and that God generates God; unless we
are careful to distinguish the Persons from the substance, we
shall be compelled to say that as substance generates substance so the Father generates himself, an opinion held by
Alberic of Rheims, a follower of Gilbert Porrée. Abailard
replies that it is untrue to hold that anything generates itself,
and that Alberic's doctrine was sufficiently disproved by St
Augustine.[3]

In discussing the various meanings which may be attached
to identity and dissimilarity, we must always remember that
the divine substance is spiritual, and therefore beyond our

1 *Theol. Christ.* III. col. 1236 CD.
2 See further, *de Unit.* II. 2, p. 37; *Theol. Christ.* III. coll. 1237–41.
3 *Ibid.* col. 1240 A; Augustine, *de Trin.* I. 1, PL. 42, col. 820.

comprehension; in consequence our terms must be employed with special connotations. Now identity and dissimilarity may be understood in many ways. We can speak of difference in form; but there is no accidental form in God, and thus that mode of diversity is inapplicable to our subject.[1] Identity may then be referred to essence and number, as in the case of sword and blade (*ensis* and *mucro*), and of animal and man, where the essences of each pair are identical, and there is no separation of things (*discretio rerum*) to give numerical distinction.[2] There is again identity and diversity of property, as in a wax figure where there is the material and the thing fashioned from it. As regards their properties, the wax and the object fashioned are different; although they are one, the material and the thing made are not numerically identical, as not all the material is necessarily employed, while the material is by property always anterior in time to the thing formed from it.[3] Further, there is identity through definition, when two things are not only the same but have also an identical origin, as for example Marcus and Tullius, *ensis* and *mucro*.[4] Here, however, the pronoun, *idem*, may be understood in two ways; both in accordance with the identity of number and the identity of definition. Thus, when we say that a woman brought damnation to the world and the same saved it, we should be wrong if we implied that the two were numerically the same, but we should be correct if we held that the identity stated was one of definition. Eve and Mary were separate in number, but identical in their womanhood.[5] Again, things are the same through likeness, as species are the same as their *genera*, or as through participation many men are one.[6] Lastly, there comes identity through incommunicability, according to which God is always the same since he does not change,

1 *De Unit.* II. 3, p. 50; *Theol. Christ.* III. col. 1247 c.
2 *De Unit.* p. 51; *Theol. Christ.* coll. 1247–8.
3 *De Unit.* p. 51; *Theol. Christ.* col. 1248 BD.
4 *De Unit.* p. 52; *Theol. Christ.* col. 1249 AB.
5 *Theol. Christ.* coll. 1249 D–1250 A; cf. *Logica*, p. 397.
6 *De Unit.* pp. 53–4; *Theol. Christ.* col. 1251 A, quoting Porphyry, *Isagoge*, ed. A Busse, Berlin, 1887, p. 6. Cf. Boethius, *in Porhyrium Comment.* III. 9, PL. 64, col. 111 c, and ed. S. Brandt, p. 228.

enlarge or decrease.[1] Corresponding to these five types of identity there are five kinds of dissimilarity. Some things differ in essence, as do Socrates and Plato; others only in number, when, although they are of the same essence, they are none the less separate, both because the one is not the other and because the one does not even share a part with the other. Things, too, differ by definition, when they cannot be covered by the same term, although indeed they may be the same thing, as, for instance, substance and body, hard or white. Finally, when one thing becomes another through change—when Socrates now stands, and now sits—the difference is said to be one of mutation.[2]

We are now in a position to see how the Persons in the Godhead may be distinguished without destroying the unity of the one substance in which they participate. It is naturally impossible to say that they differ in essence, definition, likeness, or by mutation, for then the identity of their substance would be lost. But the three Persons of the Godhead may be said to be identical in both essence and number, as the substance of sword and blade is the same,[3] although in definition and property the Persons differ from each other. Thus, as we have said, the Father alone is *ingenitus*, the Son alone *genitus*, and only the Holy Spirit may be called *procedens*.[4] And these properties cannot be called either names or forms. If we adopted the Nominalist view and regarded them as names, we should then have to conclude that the distinction between the Persons was merely nominal, and we should thus be driven to accept either a Sabellian or a Patripassian theology. And if we held that these three distinctive properties were

---

1 *De Unit.* p. 54; *Theol. Christ.* col. 1250 AB.

2 *De Unit.* pp. 55–9; *Theol. Christ.* coll. 1250–53.

3 Eadem, inquam, essentialiter ac numero, sicut eadem est substantia ensis et gladii, vel hujus hominis et hujus animalis. *Theol. Christ.* col. 1253 D. The words *ac numero* are omitted in *de Unit.* p. 60.

4 Quod quamvis eadem penitus essentia sit Deus Pater quae Deus Filius, seu Deus Spiritus sanctus, aliud tamen proprium est Dei Patris, in eo scilicet quod Pater est, et aliud Spiritus sancti. Patris quidem proprium est...non ab alio, et coaeternum sibi Filium aeternaliter gignere. Filio vero gigni a solo Patre, Spiritus sancti procedere ab utroque. *Theol. Christ.* coll. 1253–4.

forms, the essential simplicity of the divine substance would be destroyed. The properties, however, denote subsistencies (ὑποστάσεις), each of the same substance, yet distinct from each other by reason of their special characteristics of *ingenitus*, *genitus*, and *procedens*.

At this point Abailard turns to attack the theories of Gilbert Porrée, whose pupils are charged with making a distinction between the Persons and the divine substance, that is, between *deus* and *divinitas*, and with holding that the very properties of the Persons are things other than either God or the Persons themselves.[1] Hence they cannot account for the distinction of Persons whose essence is wholly the same without positing that the properties through which the Persons differ are different things from the substance of God.[2] Gilbert's allowance that in God there is something other than God astonished Abailard; it is, he says, a doctrine which not even an infidel would hold. If, indeed, the paternity which is in God is other than God, does not the Father then consist of two essences, God and paternity? And since God is called Lord relatively to his creation and as his lordship is other than his substance, it follows that God suffered a change when he began to be Lord at the moment of creation.[3]

Rejecting Gilbert's theory that the properties are different from the divine substance, Abailard follows St Augustine in maintaining that they are merely relations,[4] inseparable from the divine substance. Thus through the individuality of their properties the three Persons are distinct in such a way that the Father is not the Son, nor the Son the Holy Spirit. But care has to be exercised in applying the term "person" to the Godhead; the vocabulary of one science does not suit the needs of another branch of learning. When employed by the

---

1 *Theol. Christ.* col. 1254 D.
2 In hanc haeresim ex hoc maxime sunt inducti, quod nisi proprietates istas, per quas scilicet personae differunt, diversas res ab ipsa substantia divina ponant, nullo modo assignare valent, in quo sit personarum diversitas, quarum eadem penitus est essentia. *Ibid.* coll. 1254 D–1255 A.
3 *Ibid.* coll. 1255–6; cf. Augustine, *de Trin.* v. 16. 17, col. 922.
4 *Theol. Christ.* col. 1256 C.

theologian the word "person" only denotes the difference between the three hypostases which are distinct through their mutual relationships, although in substance they are identical.[1] But the word "person" is not used with the orator and the theologian with precisely the same connotation. Hence, we cannot apply to the divine Persons the rhetorical definition of a person as "an individual substance of rational nature"; if we accepted the Boethian definition, we should imply that the Godhead is composed of three individual substances. Nor can we accept the meaning attached to *persona* by the dramatists; since the divine Persons are not representatives of anything or of any quality, they cannot be regarded as characters such as those of a play.[2] The unity of the divine substance must at all events be assured; the discreteness of the Persons can only be explained through their mutual relationships. And to illustrate the meaning of this substantial unity Abailard puts forward an analogy from the three persons of grammar. A man remains the same when he speaks, when he is spoken to, and when he is spoken about; thus, the substances of both the persons in grammar and of the three Persons of the Godhead are identical each to each, although they can be distinguished through their special properties.[3]

This relational distinction between the Persons brings Abailard back again to face the problem whether the Trinity exists *in re* or *in vocabulis*. His Platonism as well as his concern for his orthodoxy compelled him to decide in favour of the first alternative against the Nominalism of Roscelin.[4] From eternity, he declares, God's substance is one and indivisible, the Persons being three only in number, but not in property or in definition. Although according to our grammatical illustration Socrates may be said to be three, he remains in fact but one; in the same way God cannot be regarded as three things. Nor is there multitude in the Godhead.

1 *Theol. Christ.* col. 1257 B.   2 *Ibid.* col. 1258 CD.
3 *Ibid.* coll. 1257–8; *Introd.* II. 12, col. 1067 BC.
4 *De Unit.* III. p. 68; *Theol. Christ.* IV. coll. 1259 ff.

Number requires the priority of the parts over the whole, and thus if multitude were posited, we should be forced to say that the Godhead was subsequent to the Persons.[1] And Abailard refused to allow that the Trinity may be called three-fold (*trina*), an epithet applied to it by Gottschalk and much criticized by Hincmar.[2] The Trinity is to be referred to the Persons alone, not to the substance; the term *deus* again, since it covers the identity of the Persons, is to be regarded as being more general than particular.[3]

In the *Introductio* there occurs an analogical description of the Trinity which has become famous. By Abailard's own contemporaries, it was considered as heretical. In it Abailard compares the Trinity to a copper seal like those used by kings for the purpose of sealing their letters. In such a seal there is the material of which it is made, and the figure of the king which gives the copper its form, while the act of sealing proceeds from both the copper and the image of the king. Moreover, in the seal there is nothing else save the sculptured copper.[4] Amongst others, William of St Thierry vehemently attacked this analogy. Involving the existence of degrees within the Godhead, it was Arian; the seal is formed only out of a certain quantity of copper, and in the actual process of sealing no material is used, and so, when applied to the Trinity, the analogy makes the Son a kind of power (*quaedam potentia*), while the Spirit, represented by the act of sealing, is no power (*nulla potentia*).[5] This criticism was also reproduced by St Bernard and by the anonymous abbot who wrote an attack upon Abailard.[6] Yet, it is abundantly evident that

1 *De Unit.* III. p. 72; *Theol. Christ.* IV. coll. 1262–5.
2 *De Una et non Trina Deitate*, PL. 125, coll. 473 ff.
3 De eo etiam arbitror esse discussum quod dictum est hoc nomen Deus magis universale quam singulare dicendum esse, cum de diversis personis dicatur. *De Unit.* III. 9, p. 84; *Theol. Christ.* col. 1270 C.
4 Est igitur in sigillo illo ipsum aes materia, ex quo factum est, figura vero ipsa imaginis regiae, forma ejus; ipsum vero sigillum ex his duobus materiatum atque formatum dicitur, quibus videlicet sibi convenientibus ipsum est compositum atque perfectum. Nil quippe est sigillum quam aes ita formatum. I. 13, col. 1068 D.   5 *Disp. adv. Abael.* 3–4, PL. 180, coll. 254–5, 259.
6 *Ep.* CXC. 3–6, PL. 182, col. 1059 C; *Disp. anonymi abbatis*, I. PL. 180, col. 285 C.

these critics missed the real object of Abailard's analogy. It is indeed unfair to judge the orthodoxy of any theologian by the analogies which he employs to express matters lying beyond the scope of human language to discuss; to take an analogy in a different way from that in which it was intended is equally unjust. No doubt, according to strict logic, William was correct in his assertion that the picture of the copper seal led to Arianism, for by it an obvious distinction was made between the persons. But Abailard was not so foolish as to think that the analogy illustrated the one substance of the three Persons; his aim was to shew the relationships of generation and procession within the Godhead, and for this the analogy was perfectly suitable and theologically correct. That he had no desire to differentiate between the Persons is adequately shewn by his emphasis here and elsewhere upon the one substance of the Godhead. Only the hypercritical fussiness of William and Bernard can convict Abailard of holding Arian doctrines. We must ourselves take this analogy with another which occurs in the *Theologia Christiana*, clearly the original form of the illustration. There the relationship of the Father and the Son is compared to an image made of wax. Both the image and the wax are of the same substance; the generation of the Son is shewn by the fact that the wax is not of the image, but the image of the wax.[1]

The relationship of generation between the Father and the Son is mainly founded upon the attribution of a set of special attributes to the three Persons. The Father is said to be Power, the Son Wisdom, and the Holy Spirit Goodness. Abailard was by no means the only mediaeval writer to refer to these attributes; it has been shewn that they were used by many theologians both before and after the publication of Abailard's writings,[2] and, although some theologians who

1 IV. col. 1288 D.

2 See references given in R. M. Martin, "Pro Petro Abaelardo", in *Revue des Sciences philosophiques et théologiques*, XII. 1923, p. 311 note, and M. Grabmann, *Note sur la Somme théologique de magister Humbertus, Recherches de Théologie*, I. 1929, pp. 229 ff.

criticized their applicability were disinclined to admit it, these attributes were ascribed to the three Persons by no less an authority than St Augustine. St Bernard, William of St Thierry, and Walter of Mortagne all held that these special attributes of Power, Wisdom, and Goodness created a distinction in the Godhead, making the Father alone powerful.[1] Such criticism would be sound enough, if it fairly represented Abailard's position. Power is a general term, denoting the ability to know, to will, to create and the like; wisdom can only be knowledge. Hence, if we say that the Father is Power and the Son Wisdom, the absolute equality of the two Persons cannot be maintained. Even when hypostatized, power and wisdom are not distinct. Not only does power include wisdom, but as power is the wider term, its ascription as the special property of the Father would make him unequal to the Son. But Abailard disclaims that such a distinction was made in his theology. To be sure, Abailard states that wisdom is a kind of power (*quaedam potentia*), the power, that is, of discernment.[2] The Son is of the Father, and is therefore a kind of power and a certain portion of that divine omnipotence which is the Father, as a child is said to be part of his parents.[3] But we have to remember that in the Godhead there can exist no division. Thus, we call the Son as it were a part of divine omnipotence only because it is from his wisdom alone that God knows what he does, although his omnipotence gives God the power of doing infinite things. And, although we speak of the omnipotence of God as if we meant all his power, in a way we are speaking of his many powers in reference to their effect, that is, in regard to the diversity of the things which he can do. Despite the multiplicity of his activity God remains in substance always the same. In like

1 St Bernard and William, *locc. citt.*; Walter of Mortagne, *Epistola*, ed. Ostlender, p. 35.

2 *Introd.* I. 10, col. 994 B; *Theol. Christ.* IV. col. 1288 D.

3 Est itaque Filium gigni a Patre divinam Sapientiam ita, ut determinatum est, ex divina Potentia esse, cum ipsa, ut dictum est, Sapientia quaedam sit potentia atque ipsius Potentiae Dei, quae est omnipotentia, quasi portio quaedam ipsa sit Sapientia, quomodo et quislibet filius portio quaedam parentum quodammodo dicitur. *Ibid.* col. 1289 B.

manner we speak of the Spirit as seven-fold, not because he is seven-fold in substance, but on account of his seven-fold gifts.[1] As the image is from the wax and not from itself, so the Son is from the Father, being of the same substance but possessing different properties.[2] Further, the special attribute of power well describes the Father as the one Person who is *ingenitus*. If power is referred both to the nature of his subsistence and to the efficacy of his operation, it will be seen that omnipotence properly and specially suits the Person of the Father; not only can he do all things with the other two Persons, but he derives his existence from himself alone, having his power from himself and not from another. As they derive their being from the Father, the other two Persons have also from him the power to effect whatever they wish.[3]

Abailard denies that he ever held that the Father was full Power, the Son a kind of power, and the Spirit no power.[4] In his *Apologia* he reiterates his belief that the special attribute of power well suits the Father, who can accomplish whatever he wishes to do. Wisdom is indeed the special mark of the Son who as the Word of God can never be deceived, while the Spirit has the property of goodness because he wishes all things to be made and to be disposed in the best manner.[5] And divine wisdom is a kind of power through

1 In eo tamen quasi partem quamdam Omnipotentiae dicimus Sapientiam, quod cum ipse Deus ex omnipotentia sua ad infinita agenda se habeat, ex Sapientia ad discernendum tantum se habet; et cum dicamus omnipotentiam Dei quasi omnem potentiam ejus, plures ejus potentias quodammodo dicimus, quantum ad effecta scilicet, hoc est diversitatem eorum quae agere potest, secundum quod dicimus eum diversa agere cum unus atque idem omnino perseveret. *Theol. Christ.* IV. col. 1289 BC and *Introd.* I. col. 992 D.

2 *Theol. Christ.* col. 1290 B.

3 Si itaque potentiam tam ad naturam subsistendi quam ad efficaciam operationis referamus, inveniemus ad proprietatem personae Patris proprie vel specialiter omnipotentiam attinere, qui non solum cum caeteris duabus personis Deus omnia efficere potest, verum etiam ipse solus a se, non ab alio existere habet, et sicut ex se habet existere, ita etiam ex se habet posse. Caeterae vero personae, sicut ab ipso habent esse, ita et ab ipso habent posse, quod volunt, efficere. *Introd.* I. col. 993 D. Cf. ps.-Ambrose, *in Ephesios*, 4. 6, PL. 17, col. 386 B.

4 *Apologia*, ed. Ruf, pp. 12–13.   5 *Introd.* I. col. 989 C.

which God can discern and know all things perfectly.[1] He recognizes that the love and the goodness of God cannot be called power; whether in God or in us love and goodness do not represent ability, for many a well-wisher cannot put his good intentions into effect.[2] And it is quite evident that in saying that the Son is a kind of power, Abailard did not intend to impair the omnipotence of Christ; all he meant is that the Son is endowed with the special property of discernment. His critics, he maintains, had grossly misunderstood his position. St Bernard, to whom the *Apologia* is addressed, is to learn what he has never learnt, to know what he has never known. To say that the Wisdom of God is the Son and that the Goodness of God is the Holy Spirit is not the same as to say that the Son of God is a kind of power of God or that the Holy Spirit is no power.[3] Care has to be employed in the use of words. Often it happens that words taken by themselves do not have the same meaning as when they are used in connexion with others. Abailard was here bringing his heaviest batteries to bear upon his critic; knowledge, whether of philosophy or of theology, must begin with a study of words, the *Sprachlogik* of which we have spoken. God is nothing else save divinity; the word *deus* denotes *divinitas* alone. But if I say that divinity became incarnate, I shall be incorrect; I shall only be right if I state that God became man. Again, God means nothing else save the divine substance or the substance of God, but that does permit us to state that the divine substance of God was crucified, suffered, died, or was born of the Virgin.[4] And so, when we say that the Wisdom of God is a kind of power of him, that is, the faculty of discerning everything, we are not forced to concede also that the Son of God is a kind of power; nor does the fact that the Spirit is the Love and the Goodness of God necessarily imply that the Spirit is no power.[5] As the three Persons are of the same substance and power, so are they also equal in

1 *Ibid.* col. 994 B. 2 *Apologia*, p. 14.
3 *Ibid.* pp. 14-15. 4 *Ibid.* p. 16.
5 *Ibid.* p. 16.

essence and dignity, and each is equally omnipotent.[1] When
we say that the Wisdom of God is a kind ôf power, that is,
the power of discernment, we simply mean that he is God,
and wise, and that God has this faculty of discernment—a
statement which is eminently correct. To maintain that the
Wisdom of God is a kind of power because he can do certain
things, but not all, is patently false.[2] The power of the Son
can accomplish everything just as the power of the Father can
do all things, and the knowledge of the Father and the Son is
equal. Neither in God nor in us can love be called a power;
to love is not the ability to accomplish anything, but is rather
a good desire to possess something. The Spirit must be regarded as equally powerful with the Father and the Son, for
the power of the Holy Spirit is no less able to do whatever
he wishes.[3]

The importance of the newly-discovered *Apologia* is that
it shews how St Bernard misunderstood Abailard's discussion of the dogma of the Trinity.[4] Nowhere in his work
does Abailard state that the Father is *plena potentia*, the Son
quaedam potentia, and the Spirit *nulla potentia*, as the worthy
Saint averred. His attribution of the traditional attributes of
Wisdom to the Son and of Goodness to the Holy Spirit did
not imply that the Son and the Spirit are inferior to the
Father in power. Their power is an attribute of their divine
substance—of their *divinitas*—and the fact that the Son receives his power from the Father and the Spirit his from them
both does not make either the Son or the Holy Spirit less
powerful than the Father who is the sole source of his omnipotence. The operation of the three Persons cannot be separated; yet to each may be attributed certain special attributes
which do not intrude any element of inequality into the
Godhead. Thus, the Son is specially designated as the
Wisdom of God; the Spirit as the Goodness of God. There
is, of course, as his adversaries were all too ready to point

---

1 *Apologia*, p. 16, and *Introd.* 1. col. 988 CD.
2 *Apologia*, p. 17.   3 *Ibid.* pp. 17–18.
4 See Grabmann's paper in Ruf's edition of the *Apologia*, pp. 19–41.

out, a danger in attributing to the Father alone the power which belongs to the three Persons. Provided, however, that it is sufficiently made clear that this power belongs equally to them all, orthodoxy should be satisfied. It should perhaps be added that there is one somewhat unsatisfactory verbal addition in Abailard's statement of these three attributes; as we shall see, a later thinker, active in the defence of Abailard, was prepared to omit the word "special", as being unfortunate in that it may lead the reader to think that Power is the attribute of the Father alone. But it should be clear that his attribution of these special attributes was purely notional; it did not mean that in power the Father is superior to the other two Persons. These three personal attributes of Power, Wisdom, and Goodness well suited Abailard's insistence upon the fact that the being of a triune Godhead was within the cognizance of philosophers before the birth of Christ. Since these are the necessary attributes of God, these philosophers perforce came to the conclusion that the Godhead must be triune.[1] There is, however, no clear distinction between the properties, *ingenitus*, *genitus*, and *procedens*, on the one side, and the personal attributes, Power, Wisdom, and Goodness, on the other. This omission certainly gave a handle to the critics who wished to convict Abailard of heterodoxy.

The *Apologia* reflects in miniature a fierce discussion between rival twelfth-century theologians over the question whether the attributes of Power, Wisdom, and Goodness may rightly be applied to the Persons. We have already noted that the application of these attributes was made by several writers. We find it in the *Epitome*, in the *Sentences* of Roland and of St Florian, in William of Conches, and in Hugh of St Victor.[2] The opposite view of the propriety of the attribution was taken by St Bernard, William of St Thierry, and the

1 Cf. *Introd.* 1. coll. 989 ff.; and see Thomas Aquinas, *Summa Theol.* 1. quaest. 32, art. 1.

2 *Epitome*, 5–9, coll. 1699–1707; Roland, p. 21; St Florian, pp. 4, 6; William of Conches, *Philosophia Mundi*, 1. 5, PL. 172, col. 44 D; Hugh of St Victor, *de Sacrament.* 1. 3. 26, col. 227 C. Cf. Augustine, *de Trin.* VII. 2. 3, PL. 42, col. 936, and 3. 4, col. 937; Aquinas, *c. Gent.* IV. 11.

anonymous abbot in passages to which reference has been made. One defender of Abailard's position in the matter must be noticed at length, and that is Robert of Melun, *natione Angligena*. Robert prefaces his defence with a catena of quotations from the Scriptures and the Fathers permitting the application of these properties to the several Persons.[1] He concedes, however, one thing to his adversaries; he was prepared to drop the awkward point "special" applied to the attributes. In his more reasoned defence of their applicability, he maintains that the attributes guard the dogma of the Trinity against a possible misconception. Men are accustomed to regard fathers as wiser than their sons, and in their turn sons as being physically more powerful than their fathers. If we say that Power designates the Father and Wisdom the Son, the equality of these two persons is sufficiently assured.[2] Robert then reproduces the argument which we have already found in Abailard, citing, however, as his authorities the pseudo-Jerome and St John Chrysostom. The Father, he says, is the beginning of the Trinity, and the other persons have their being from him, although he has his from himself alone. The Father may therefore rightly be designated by the attribute Power, not because he alone is powerful, but because the Son and the Holy Spirit, being equally powerful with the Father, have their power from him.[3] The opponents of Abailard had declared that the attribution to the Father of this underived power makes him superior in power to both the Son and the Holy Spirit.[4] Robert replies that the fact that Power designates the Father does not make him more powerful than either the Son or the Spirit, while the power of the Spirit comes from both the other two Persons of the Trinity. The Father is indeed no more powerful than the entire Trinity; the Generation of the Son and the Double Procession of the Spirit does not render them any the less

---

1 *Sentent.* I. 3. 17–23, in R. M. Martin, *loc. cit.* pp. 320–28.
2 *Ibid.* 24, pp. 328–9.
3 *Ibid.* 25, p. 329; pseudo-Jerome, *Regulae definitionum*, PL. 17, col. 511 B, and John Chrysostom, *in Johann.* 14. 29, *Homil.* 75, PG. 59, col. 408.
4 *Disp. anonymi abbatis*, col. 288.

omnipotent than the Father. The attribution of the three attributes of Power, Wisdom, and Goodness does not impair the equality of the Persons. When it is said that the Son is powerful because he is of the Father alone, a distinction is not being made between the power of the Father and the power of the Son, for all the three Persons are equally powerful. Our sole object in attributing these properties to the Persons is to shew that the person of the Son is not that of the Father nor that of the Holy Spirit.[1] And Robert of Melun was seeking to accomplish precisely the same thing that Abailard had attempted to do; that is, to demonstrate the distinction of the three Persons who are yet of the same substance and essence.

But to return to Abailard. It must not be thought that he considered the Son in any way posterior to the Father in point of time, and it was on this account that he attacked a traditional analogy which he found reproduced by St Anselm. By this illustration the Trinity was compared to a spring issuing into a pool, both the spring and the pool then becoming a river. Such an analogy, he argued,[2] perhaps over-critically, leads one to suppose that an element of time is involved in the Generation of the Son and the Procession of the Spirit; although the spring, the pool, and the river are undoubtedly of the same substance, the spring does not become either the pool or the river without some passage of time. And with regard to his own analogy of the copper seal, Abailard refuses to allow that the Father may be called the material of the Son as the copper is the material of the seal. If, indeed, the Father could be regarded as the material of which the Son is formed, Abailard would certainly not have escaped a charge of Arianism, for he would have been echoing the cry of the porters on the quays of Alexandria, "there was a time when he was not". Further, the statement that the Father is the material of the Son would imply the

1 Martin, *loc. cit.* p. 331.
2 *Theol. Christ.* IV. col. 1287 BC; *Introd.* II. col. 1071 AB. Cf. Anselm, *de Fide Trinitatis*, 8, col. 280.

existence of a subject-form within the Godhead—an impossible implication.[1] But, can we say that the Father is either the cause or the beginning of the Son? Strictly speaking, the Father cannot so be called; a cause necessarily presupposes an effect, and in the Godhead nothing was made. And, as the three Persons are equally eternal, the Father cannot be regarded as the beginning of the Son. Yet, in one sense the Father may be considered the beginning of the Word, as well as of the Spirit, though in no temporal sense; both the Son and the Spirit take their origin from the Father, the one by generation, the other through procession.[2]

The coeternal character of the three Persons is indeed a very necessary consequence of their mutual relationship, for, as the logicians tell us, no two things related through their nature can exist, the one without the other.[3] And so, in Abailard's opinion the Son is always being generated, and he has always been generated. In this any element of time is completely removed; hence the Generation of the Son was perfect before time and is so now, for in eternity there is no imperfection, no cessation, and no change. That this opinion had been rejected by some writers Abailard was well aware, but he argues that St Augustine had objected to the phrase, "the Son is always being generated", only because the verb *nasci* in the present tense implies a birth which is not completed, although it has been begun.[4]

In discussing the Double Procession of the Holy Spirit Abailard had naturally to bear in mind the denial by the Greek theologians of the catholicity of the *Filioque* clause. It was then generally considered that the breach between the Eastern and Western churches was a political affair, due to the political ambitions of the patriarchs of Constantinople; once the theological errors of the Greeks were made evident, men thought that re-union could easily be effected. In consequence, all the theologians of the time felt themselves to be

1 *Theol. Christ.* IV. col. 1290 D.   2 *Ibid.* coll. 1290–91.
3 *Ibid.* col. 1293 C.
4 *Ibid.* col. 1297; cf. I. 5, col. 1135, and Augustine, *LXXXIII Quaest.* 37, PL. 40, col. 27.

under an obligation to write *contra errores Graecorum*. The form of these controversial treatises had been set by Alcuin of York when he propounded a catena of patristic quotations to shew for how long and to what extent the doctrine of the Double Procession had been accepted by canonical authority. Alcuin's example was followed by Abailard in his main treatment of the question,[1] but he attempted as well to illustrate the reasonableness of the doctrine by the use of his dialectic. The Spirit, as we have seen, is the Goodness of God, and as such it must be thought of as proceeding rather than as being born.[2] But as the good disposition (*affectus*) of God comes from both his power and his wisdom, we are compelled to conclude that the Holy Spirit proceeds *ab utroque*.[3] And the truth of the Double Procession must be accepted if with Abailard we accept the identification of the Holy Spirit with the third Person of the Platonic trinity. Like the World-Soul, the Spirit is the life of all creation, but creation was made by the Father through the Son.[4] This Procession is both temporal and eternal; the connexion of the Spirit with the universe was made in time, when the universe was created, while the processional relationship of the Spirit with the two other divine Persons is eternal.[5] The Procession of the Spirit within the Godhead is naturally timeless and, as the substance, the splendour, and the illumination of the sun are contemporary, so the three Persons of the Godhead are absolutely coeternal.[6] And Abailard was very definite in his assertion that he had always considered the Spirit as being of the same substance as the Father and the Son.[7]

From our discussion of his theology it should be evident that Abailard denied with some truth that his theology was guilty of the Sabellian and Arian doctrines attributed to him

1 *Theol. Christ.* coll. 1300 D–1306; *Introd.* I. 15, coll. 1075 ff.
2 *Theol. Christ.* col. 1299 C.
3 *Ibid.* col. 1300 D.   4 *Ibid.* coll. 1307–9.
5 Quid mirum cum duobis modis Spiritum procedere dicamus, si secundum alterum processionis modum dicatur Spiritus a nobis, et secundum alterum vocetur anima a philosophis. Illud ergo Spiritus aeternaliter, hoc temporaliter habet. *Ibid.* col. 1309 D.
6 *Ibid.* col. 1306 CD.   7 *Apologia*, p. 18.

by contemporary and by modern writers. It seems, however, certain that the charge of Sabellianism preferred against him at Soissons was based upon some sure foundation of fact. Unfortunately, the proceedings of that council are no longer extant, while the passage to which, according to the account of Otto of Freising, exception was taken, cannot be identified in any of his writings. But one passage in the *de Unitate* is Sabellian, and may have been the one referred to by Otto. There Abailard says that "God is three persons in such a way as if we said that the divine substance is powerful, wise, and good".[1] That this passage from the *de Unitate* was not repeated in the subsequent recensions of the books suggests that Abailard well realized its heretical nature. Similar Sabellian opinions can also be found elsewhere in his books.[2] To me it seems clear that the main cause of any unorthodox views upon the dogma of the Trinity held by Abailard was due to his desire to refute the Nominalistic tri-theism taught by Roscelin. His own concern to emphasize the oneness of the substance inclined him to lay insufficient stress upon the discreteness of the Persons, and in this his attribution of the special attributes of Power, Wisdom, and Goodness to the Persons obscured his attempt to shew how indeed the Persons were three in number. Had he made some clear connexion between the attributes of Power, Wisdom, and Goodness and the properties of *ingenitus*, *genitus*, and *procedens*, his position, as we have said, would have been made clearer and his orthodoxy more evident. There is, indeed, much truth in the statement of Otto of Freising that Abailard mixed logic and theology incautiously.[3] Abailard, it is certain, did not see what unfortunate conclusions his dialectic ability and his zeal to rebut the opinions of Roscelin were leading him to adopt. In the main, he must be acquitted of Sabellianism,

1 Tale est ergo Deum esse tres personas..., ac si dicamus divinam substantiam esse potentem, sapientem, benignam. 1. 3, p. 3.
2 Cf. *Theol. Christ.* 1. 2, col. 1124 A.
3 Sententiam ergo vocum seu nominum in naturali tenens facultate non caute theologiae admiscuit. *Gesta Fred.* 1. 49, *ed. cit.* p. 69; cf. Geyer-Ueberweg, pp. 222–3.

although in certain places, notably in the passage in the *de Unitate* which was afterwards retracted, his skill in logic as opposed to his insufficient training in theology induced him to make careless statements which were charged with unorthodoxy. As an illustration solely of the Generation of the Son and of the Procession of the Holy Spirit, the analogy of the copper seal was sound; a little more care in its use would probably have saved him from the criticism of his opponents.

II

Abailard's intellectualist conception of faith provides us with the main clue to his Christological ideas. His dialectical approach to matters of theology made him regard Christ almost exclusively as the Wisdom of God, the eternal Λόγος rather than as the Incarnate Jesus who died upon the Cross. In this he stood far apart from his two chief opponents, St Bernard and William of St Thierry. Both these men centred their religion upon mystical contemplation, regarding Jesus as the Saviour who suffered on Calvary and who extends to his followers that gracious kindliness which he shewed during his incarnate life. It was not because Jesus was the divine Λόγος, but because he exhibited such great love and humility in becoming man that these two men regarded Jesus as the Lord of the world. And so, in the words of St Bernard, Jesus was "honey in the mouth, melody to the ear, and joy to the heart".[1] The hymn:

Jesu dulcis memoria	Nil canitur suavius,
Sed super mel et omnia	Nil cogitatur dulcius,
Dans vera cordi gaudia;	Nil auditur jucundius
Ejus dulcis praesentia.	Quam Jesus Dei filius

was certainly not composed by St Bernard, yet it reflects his Christology with his deep longing for a personal experience with the Jesus of Nazareth, the divine Bridegroom of the soul. For Abailard, however, Christ was primarily the

---

[1] Jesus mel in ore, in aure melos, in corde jubilus. *In Cant. Cant.* 15. 6, PL. 183, col. 847 A.

Word of God, in whom all things were created, the Master (διδάσκαλος) who became incarnate in order to teach the world. To be sure, he did not neglect either the importance or the greatness of the ministry in Galilee. As we shall see, Abailard dwelt in his sermons upon the Gospel story, explaining the miracle of the Virgin Birth and recounting the history of both the Passion and the Crucifixion; but his main preoccupation lay with the λόγος theology, while with his unaccommodating theory of the immutability of God he never succeeded in picturing Jesus with the full panoply of manhood. He was indeed unaffected by the mysticism of the Benedictines who loved to dwell upon the historical scenes of the Gospel, elaborating and deepening their meaning for men. The Christ of Abailard's theology is the eternal Λόγος of the Father, who lived on earth, residing in human flesh, making his wisdom known to the world, and not the Jesus who emptied himself of his glory and became a servant. Nor was the Incarnation the cataclysmic event such as it had been described in St Bernard's writings. Both Bernard and Abailard indeed held, as did other theologians, that some of the great Hebrew saints were justified, but Abailard alone believed that through the operation of their reason, men before the Incarnation accepted the Christian doctrine of the Trinity and so were numbered among the blessed. In Abailard's outlook there is something of the spirit of Greek theology. Like the Eastern writers, he insisted upon the essential Christ who has always been present in men's souls, the fountain-head of all wisdom. Whence this influence came it is difficult to explain; if he had read Erigena that writer's views may have shaped his thought. Or perhaps his almost Gnostic spirit was more the result of his interest in logic with its natural emphasis upon man's reasoning abilities and of his attempt to discover in the divine Word the justification for man's use of his reason in matters of theology.

The divine Wisdom, we are told,[1] is called the Word because it is by a man's speech that his wisdom is known.

[1] *Theol. Christ.* I. 4, col. 1129 A.

Care, however, must be taken in translating λόγος; although of course the word has that meaning, it may not here be rendered "pronouncement of the voice".[1] It means rather the thought reasoning of the mind.[2] Nor has the phrase, *conceptus mentis*, which he applies to the Word, any logical connotation; Abailard employs it as a synonym for *cogitatio*, a term used by Boethius in the passage referred to as an alternative translation of λόγος when that Greek word does not mean *oratio*. And Christ is the Word and the Wisdom of God because the operation and ordering of all things dwell in his providence, established there from eternity, for it was in the Word that God founded everything according to his wisdom and reason.[3] The phrase, *conceptus mentis*, indeed, means the concepts of the divine mind, the Ideas after which the things of appearance were created, these Ideas being situated in Christ as the Wisdom and the Word of God.[4]

We come now to Abailard's account of the Incarnation. As we should expect, he was definite in his assertion that Jesus was born of a virgin and that he was without sin and guilt. Like most of his contemporaries, he held that Mary herself had been conceived in sin, thus rejecting the doctrine of the Immaculate Conception which was then making its appearance.[5] The doctrine had already been championed by the canons of Lyons and by Anselm, abbot of Bury St Edmunds, the nephew of the archbishop of the same name, but both Anselm of Canterbury and St Bernard wrote against its reception,[6] the latter on the ground that the doctrine was

1 Abailard's source for the meaning of λόγος is Boethius, *in Categ.* II. PL. 64, col. 204 A. The opposition of the two meanings of the word comes from the Stoic distinction between λόγος προφορικός and λόγος ἐνδιάθετος, for which see R. P. Casey, JTS. xxv. 1923, p. 48.

2 Logos itaque Filius Dei cum dicitur, id est Verbum, secundum illam significationem sumitur, secundum quam λόγος apud Graecos ipsum etiam mentis conceptum seu rationem mentis significat, non vocis prolationem. *Introd.* I. 11, col. 995 D.

3 *Theol. Christ.* I. 4, coll. 1129–30; *Introd.* I. 11, col. 996 D.

4 See *supra*, p. 133.   5 *Epist. ad Romanos*, I. 1, col. 795 C.

6 For Anselm of Bury see E. M. Williamson, *Letters of Osbert of Clare*, Oxford, 1929; Anselm, *Cur Deus Homo?* II. 16, col. 416; Bernard, *Ep.* CLXXIV. col. 332, to the canons of Lyons.

unknown to the liturgy, unacceptable to common sense, and unrecommended by authority. The Birth of Christ of a mother without a father was as miraculous as his Generation from a Father without a mother.[1] He was born in no natural fashion, but was conceived of the Holy Spirit, a fact which does not mean that the Spirit himself became man or that the Spirit was the father of the incarnate Word, but only that Christ alone of the three Persons took upon himself our human form.[2] From the Virgin as his mother Jesus took his flesh; from God the Father he received his divinity.[3] His flesh was woven out of the substance of the Virgin, and it was not therefore created out of nothing;[4] it was both passible and mortal.[5] Both the human and the divine natures of Christ were born of Mary; thus Abailard was not guilty of the Nestorian denial that the Virgin was θεοτόκος.[6] And while Abailard does not describe the mode of the relationship between the two natures, he maintains none the less that Christ was one, as indeed every individual man is one, although he has two natures, the body and the soul, of which the one is corporeal and the other incorporeal.[7] That Jesus was crucified, died, and was buried is a sure proof that the two natures were one; had not Christ been human as well as divine, these events should have been impossible.[8] To express this unity, which is naturally beyond human experience, Abailard resorted to his favourite method of analogy. Alloy, he says,[9] made as it is from gold and silver,

---

1 Cf. *Sermo* II. col. 388 D.
2 *Theol. Christ.* IV. col. 1279 C; *Exposit. Symboli.* col. 624 A.
3 *Ibid.* col. 624 B.   4 *Sermo* II. col. 389 B and v. col. 419 B.
5 *Sermo* XII. col. 487 B.
6 William of St Thierry charged Abailard with Nestorianism, see *Disput.* 8, col. 276 ff.
7 *Exposit. Symboli.* col. 624 C.   8 *Ibid.*
9 Electrum quippe est metallum ex auro simul et argento commistum. In qua quidem mistura argentum ad claritatem proficit, aurum vero a suo temperatur fulgore. Electrum igitur istud ipse intelligitur Christus, in cujus una persona divinitatis et humanitatis duae naturae ita sibi ad invicem sunt unitae, ut inferior natura, quae per argentum exprimitur, sese visibilem praebeat, et divinae majestatis splendor carnis velamine obumbratus qui per aurum figuratur, invisibilis persistat. *Sermo* I. coll. 385–6.

THE TRINITY AND THE PERSON OF CHRIST 171

typifies Christ "in whose person the two natures of divinity
and humanity were united each to each, so that the lower—
expressed by the silver—shews itself visible, while the gold—
the splendour of the divine majesty—is shrouded by the flesh
and therefore continues unseen". The union of the natures
is again compared with the product of botanical grafting. If
a sprig of oak is grafted into a fig-tree, the whole tree is not
therefore called a fig, but it takes its name from its more
noble part, as can well be seen by the fruit it bears. At the
Incarnation "an insertion of divinity was grafted into
humanity", the two natures coming together into the one
person of Christ.[1]

In his attempt to explain how God could have become
man in the womb of the Virgin, Abailard encountered some
difficulty, and this was largely due to his zeal to preserve intact the immutability of God. His difficulty was that at the
Incarnation some change, wholly incompatible with his
theory of the unchangeability of God, seemed to have taken
place, while the Incarnation itself appeared to imply the
temporary localization of Christ. In his solution of the
problem, however, he was aided by two considerations.
When he effects anything God cannot be regarded as chang-
ing, for it is by his will alone that he moves the universe;[2]
nor can he move from place to place, since he is by his very
nature omnipresent. When Christ entered the womb of
Mary, we cannot think that he suffered any local change; he
was only present there through the efficacy of his operation,
and his descent was but an act of self-humiliation.[3] After as
well as before the Incarnation he still remained omnipresent.
When he became incarnate, "his spiritual substance was not
changed into anything corporeal, for he remained what he
had been before, and thus he did not put off his own divine
nature to take upon himself our own, for change can only be
produced when something ceases to be what it had formerly

1 *Ibid*. col. 386 C.   2 *Introd*. III. 6, col. 1104 CD.
3 Cum itaque Deus in Virginem venire, aut aliquo dicitur descendere,
secundum aequam suae operationis efficaciam, non secundum localem ac-
cessionem intelligi debet. *Ibid*. col. 1105 D.

been".[1] And so when God became man, he united his divine substance, which is spirit, to a human corporeal frame, not in the sense that things spiritual can become corporeal, but in that the two became united in the person of Christ. In Jesus there dwelt together the divinity of the Word, soul, and human flesh, joined but not transmuted the one into the other.[2] The two natures indeed remained distinct; though we sometimes call the whole now the Word, now soul, or now flesh, we must never ascribe to his humanity those things which properly belong to his divine nature.[3] Thus the chief difficulty with which Abailard had to contend was not the distinction of the natures, but the unity of the single person.[4] Though he does not give a full explanation of the mode in which he considered that their union was effected, being content with analogies by which he tried to shew the reasonableness of the doctrine of the two natures, he did not reproduce, as Deutsch shews, the Nestorian συνάφεια.[5] All our evidence goes to prove that, despite the incompleteness of his Christology, Abailard was not heretical, as many of his contemporaries insisted that he was. He did not unite the two natures merely by conjunction, as Nestorius is reported to have done; for Abailard the natures were one in the unity of a single person. Nor is his statement that the human Jesus was a man *assumptus a Deo* unorthodox;[6] that phrase had already been used by St Augustine,[7] and Abailard himself was careful to reject any theory of the Incarnation which did not allow that both the natures were born of the Virgin. All that Abailard intended the words, *homo assumptus a Deo*, to convey was that the Man Jesus was a vehicle through which

1 *Introd.* III. 6, col. 1107 B.
2 Quid est enim dicere Deum fieri hominem, nisi divinam substantiam quae spiritualis est, humanam quae corporea est, sibi unire personam in unam? Non enim quod spirituale corporeum fieri potest, sed in illa unione personae Christi in quo simul divinitas Verbi, et anima, et caro. *Ibid.* col. 1106 C.
3 *Exposit. Symb. Apostol.* coll. 624–5.
4 Cf. O. Baltzer, *Die Sentenzen des Petrus Lombardus*, Leipzig, 1902, p. 100.
5 P. 303.   6 *Epist. ad Romanos*, I. 1, col. 795 C.
7 *Enchiridion*, 12. 40–41, PL. 40, col. 252; *de Agone Christi*, 20. 22, PL. 40, col. 301.

the eternal Word was made known to the world. This is amply brought out by the writer of the *Epitome*, who declares that "just as the flesh which is subjected to the soul, cannot have any motion or operation save that which it has from the soul, in the same way that soul which had been subjected to the Word could give no movement to the body except in so far as it was inspired by the Word".[1]

Gerhoh of Reichersberg was certainly attacking Abailard himself when he said that his pupils taught that God was not taken from the Virgin, but that the human Jesus was only the dwelling-place in which the full plenitude of divinity resided.[2] A somewhat cursory perusal of his treatment of Christological problems perhaps might convince a critic—especially if he were none too well disposed—that Abailard regarded the human Jesus solely as a medium through which the eternal Word was made apparent to mankind, and that, in consequence, the two natures were not united. But, as we have pointed out, such criticism is unjust. John of Cornwall, again, maintained that according to Abailard Christ was neither *proprie* nor *essentialiter* man; Christ had indeed put on man like a garment.[3] John further asserts that Abailard was the originator of that "depraved doctrine" held by Peter Lombard, according to which the human Jesus was considered to have been nothing.[4] Certainly, it is true that his statement that Christ could not properly have been either man or flesh was incautious, but by it Abailard had no intention of separating the divine and the human in the incarnate Lord. He states quite definitely that the two natures were joined together (*sociari*) in the one person.[5] But John was correct in his belief that the Christology of the Lombard was influenced by the teaching of Abailard, although, it must

---

1 Sicut caro animae subjecta est, quod nullum motum, nullam operationem nisi ab anima habere potest, sic anima illa Verbo subjecta erat, quod nullum motum illi corpori attribuere poterat, nisi quantum Verbum inspirabat. *Epitome*, 24, col. 1733 A.

2 *Liber de Novitatibus*, 4, MGH. *Libelli de Lite*, III. p. 292.

3 *Eulogium ad Alexandrum III*, 3, PL. 199, col. 1052 C.

4 *Ibid.* col. 1052 D. 5 *Introd.* III. col. 1107 CD.

be added, he over-estimated that influence. The Master of the
Sentences was faced with the choice of three interpretations
of the phrase, "God became man".[1] Either he could follow
the view of Cyril of Alexandria that in Christ humanity was
transfused into, though without perishing in, the being of
God, and thus that divinity appropriated humanity to itself,
making it an integral element of its own being; or he could
adopt the theory of John Damascene whereby divinity was
held to have been substantially united in one compound personality. Lastly, the Lombard could have accepted a third
doctrine, largely based upon the words we have quoted from
the *Introductio*, which taught that the Word was clothed as it
were with a garment (*indumentum*), formed of flesh and soul,
but that the human body and soul of Christ were not the
substantial reality of the incarnate Word. According to this
latter doctrine, no nature nor person was made or composed
out of the two or three parts, the Word, soul, or body.[2]
Apparently aware of the danger of this teaching, the Lombard did not actually make the choice, but that he was strongly
inclined to adopt this third interpretation of the mode of the
Incarnation seems evident. And so, the Word is thought of
as assuming manhood only as a *habitus*, an accidental addition which made no alteration to the thing to which it was
joined. Hence in becoming man, Christ did not become anything.[3] This so-called "Nihilism" Alexander III commanded
William, archbishop of Sens, to condemn at Paris,[4] and
anathematized it himself at the third Lateran Council (1179).
Although Abailard's words were partly responsible for the

[1] See J. A. Dorner, *History of the Doctrine of Christ*, E.T. ii. 1, pp. 310–19;
Lombard, *Sentent.* iii. dist. 6.
[2] Sed sic illa duo, scilicet animam et carnem, Verbi personae vel naturae
unita esse aiunt, ut non ex illis duobus, vel ex his tribus aliqua natura vel
persona fieret sive componeretur, sed illis duobus velut indumento Verbum
vestiretur, ut mortalium oculis congruenter appareret. *Ibid.* dist. 6. 6.
[3] Christum secundum hominem non esse personam nec aliquid, nisi forte
"secundum" sit expressivum personae. *Ibid.* 10. 1. Cf. (Christus) aliquid esse
incoepit, Hugh of St Victor, *de Sacrament.* ii. 1. 9, col. 397, and Roland,
Sentent. p. 178.
[4] Denifle-Chatelain, *Chartul. Univ. Paris*, i. p. 4.

Nihilism held by the Lombard, it will be noted that his own words guarding and emphasizing the unity of the two natures in Christ make it impossible for a critic to charge Abailard with the heresy taught by his pupil. The "Nihilism" of Peter Lombard is, however, latent in the Christology of Abailard.

In his *Exposition of Romans* Abailard turns to discuss the question whether Christ had during his life on earth the power of sinning. His negative answer is largely due to his emphasis upon the indwelling of the Λόγος in the incarnate Christ. Had Jesus been purely human, he would have possessed all the attributes natural to man, and amongst them free will which, as it is the power to choose between good and evil, implies also the ability to sin. Consequently, like all men Jesus would have been dependent upon the gift of God's grace if he was to avoid wrongdoing. But as in him the divine Word was united to man, Jesus possessed the ability not to sin through the property of his own nature alone (*ex naturae suae proprietate*), and not from any gift received from outside.[1] Yet, purely as a matter of speculation, he maintains that we must enquire whether the man to whom the divine Word was united had the power to sin. He comes to the conclusion that by itself Christ's human nature had that power, but once the two natures were associated, and as long as their union lasted, the human nature of Jesus could not possibly commit a sin.[2] It must be fully understood that this discussion is purely an academic one, advanced to satisfy our author's delight in logical precision.

I turn now to the difficult problem of the suffering and volition of Christ. The *Epitome* contains a passage dealing with this question, which may fairly be taken as representing Abailard's own theories. Further, the various patristic statements relative to the question are set out in the *Sic et Non*.[3]

1 I. 3, coll. 823-4.
2 Sic et fortasse non est absurdum nos concedere simpliciter, quod cum hominem qui Deo unitus est, possibile sit peccare, non tamen postquam unitus vel dum unitus est. *Ibid.* col. 824 C.
3 *Epitome*, 25, col. 1734; *Sic et Non*, 80, coll. 1457 ff.

The prayer in which Jesus begged the Father to take away
the cup had always proved impatient of interpretation. St
Augustine had maintained that it came from "the lower
members" of Christ's nature; his divinity had reasserted
itself when he declared that he would do the will of the
Father.[1] Abailard further quotes St Augustine's opinion that
Christ took our entire human will and sorrow and that in his
person these were very real, and in no way illusory.[2] Hilary
of Poitiers had taken the opposite view; Jesus, he held,[3] had
not felt the nails driven into his hands; they might as well
have been driven into wax.

Faced by these contradictory opinions, Abailard followed
St Augustine more closely than he did Hilary of Poitiers.
Christ, he says,[4] suffered all the more on account of his
divinity. "As we only will things which please us and abhor
the reverse", volition can never exist unaccompanied by desire, and so we are forced to conclude that "Christ suffered
those pains and sorrows against his will. He suffered indeed,
not because he wished to taste the death which he dreaded so
greatly, but because he loved the Father and he knew that the
Father desired him to die. And in addition, he died because
he wished his death to bring salvation to his neighbour".[5]
Christ's consent to suffer death may be compared to the
dread of a sick man for an operation that impends; since he
knows that the operation alone can restore him to health,
he is willing to undergo it despite the pain.[6] Accordingly, we
may say that no difference exists between Christ's wish to die
and that of the martyrs to suffer torture. The martyrs did not
desire pain, and they fled from their persecutors as long as they
could; in the end, however, their love for Christ made them
willing to endure their fate. The same views are given in the

1 Cf. *Sermo* 344. 3, PL. 39, col. 1519.
2 *Epitome*, 25, col. 1734 C.
3 *De Trinitate*, x. 45, PL. 10, col. 296.   4 *Sermo* xi. col. 469.
5 Passus est ergo, non quod vellet pati in morte [quam] formidabat, sed
quia Patrem diligebat, quem hoc velle sciebat, et quia per mortem suam
salutem proximi fieri cupiebat. *Epitome*, 25, col. 1734 D.
6 *Ibid*. col. 1735 A.

Exposition of Romans, where Abailard declares that "the mind of Jesus desired our salvation which, as he knew, entailed his own death. On that account he consented to die, just as a sick man is prepared to endure many bitter things for the sake of the health he desires, suffering them indeed because he is compelled to do so, and not of his own accord, for through them he thinks that he will regain his health".[1]

Abailard also states that "as Jesus was one with the Father according to his Godhead, he was also one with him as regards his will. Accordingly, he could say of himself, 'No man taketh my life from me, but I lay it down of myself'".[2] In all this there is no suggestion that Christ did not actually wish to die for the sake of mankind; the distinction which Abailard intends to make is between the inclination and the will of Christ. As God, Christ's will was naturally one with the will of the Father; in all that they do, the three Persons of the Trinity act in complete unison. Consequently, although his human inclination made Jesus unwilling to die, his will in obedience to the commands of the Father made him prepared to suffer on man's behalf. Thus, the prayer in Gethsemane must be taken to mean that "if the human race can be saved without my death, then I will not die, because I cannot wish to die; but if on the other hand mankind can only be saved through my death, then I will resign my will to yours".[3] Abailard's account of the will of Christ is not so exhaustive as that of Hugh of St Victor, who held that Jesus possessed four wills. Of these one belonged to his divine nature and by it he desired only what was just, as the leper

[1] Desideravit quidem anima hominis illius salutem nostram quam in morte sua consistere sciebat et propter illam quam desiderabat hanc tolerabat, sicut infirmus vel sauciatus aliquis propter sanitatem quam desiderat, multa tolerat aspera, coactus non spontaneus, per quae sanitatem se adepturum existimat *Epist. ad Romanos*, ii. 6, col. 876 c.
[2] Secundum divinitatem vero sicut unum est cum Patre ita et unius voluntatis et juxta quod ipse de se ait, "Nemo tollit animam meam a me, sed ego pono eam...". *Ibid.* 876 BC.
[3] Si genus humanum sine morte mea salvari potest, non moriar, quia non possum velle mori; sin autem, voluntatem meam tuae postpono. *Epitome*, 25, col. 1734 B.

confessed when he begged the Lord to make him clean;[1] another was his rational will by which he approved only of what was just. A third was the will of his flesh which inclined him to hold back from the pain of the Cross, while the fourth was his will of pity through which he pitied all men and desired the ill of none.[2]

[1] Cf. Luke v. 12.
[2] *De quatuor voluntatibus in Christo*, PL. 176, coll. 841–6, especially coll. 841–2.

Chapter viii

HIS ETHICAL THEORIES, AND THE DOCTRINE OF THE ATONEMENT

I

WE must now turn to discuss Abailard's ethical theories and his doctrine of the Atonement, and in many ways we touch here upon the very centre of his theology. It is of course generally impossible to determine the order in which any thinker arrived at the various doctrines associated with his name; yet in the case of a theologian the problems of soteriology are usually found to be the basis from which he built up his other doctrinal views. Abailard's own soteriological ideas, however, cannot be properly understood without a prior knowledge both of the emphasis which he laid upon the incarnation of the Word who came to teach men and to draw them away from their love of themselves, and of his theories upon the character of sin and merit. His predominating interest in Christ as the Word made flesh, and not as the Man of Sorrows, led him to minimize the effect of the Fall upon the human race, and, in consequence, to work out his own conception of the nature of Original Sin; his exemplarist theory of Christ's ministry, excluding as it did the sacrificial aspect of Calvary, is intimately connected with his account of the atoning work of Jesus.

Our knowledge of Abailard's ethical theories is mainly derived from his book, the *Scito teipsum*. The portion of the *Introductio* in which he intended to discuss moral and ethical questions is not at present available, while his Dialogue between a Jew, a Christian, and a Philosopher was never finished and lacks the judgement which Abailard was to pass upon the arguments of the three participants. The Dialogue is mainly concerned with the problem of the nature of the Highest Good. Whatever originality we may find in his work was in no way due to the discovery of new literary sources which supplied Abailard with novel theories. Certainly, many of the problems to which he gave his attention were dictated by the discussions of his time, and the question of confession was perhaps the most notable of these. But any novelty which may be found to exist in his teaching was the product of his own analytical ingenuity and dialectical acumen alone. In this Abailard was entirely different from the ethical writers of the thirteenth century, such as Thomas Aquinas, who were acquainted with the *Nicomachaean Ethics* in translation. All that Abailard knew of the ethical theories of Aristotle was derived from allusions which he found in the pages of Boethius.[1]

To understand Abailard's ethical theories we must enquire into those held by some of his contemporaries. The current ethical ideas of the twelfth century were, as we should expect, based upon those of St Augustine, and were objective in character. Augustine himself had founded his doctrines upon a voluntarist psychology in which the will was regarded as the principle by which we act.[2] Our will is free, single and God-given, for Augustine refused to accept the Manichaean theory that men have two wills, one derived from God, and the other from the principle of evil.[3] His neo-Platonist studies had taught him that being and goodness are identical, and therefore that evil has no existence; the will is accordingly good and knows only of evil because it knows the *Summum Bonum*, which is God.[4] And so he defined sin as the will to retain or to pursue that which justice forbids.[5] The lusts of the flesh are in themselves neither good nor bad; they only become sinful when our will consents to their incitements. Thus, in a sense, all sin must be regarded as negative;

1 E.g. *Nich. Ethics*, VI. 1144 b from Boethius, *in Categ.* IV. col. 277, quoted *Dialogus*, col. 1651 C.
2 Cf. *de lib. Arb.* III. 1. 3, PL. 32, col. 1272.
3 *De duabus Animis*, 12. 16, PL. 42, coll. 105–6.
4 *Ibid.* 8. 10, coll. 101–2.   5 *Ibid.* 11. 15, col. 105.

it is the desertion of the good and not the pursuit after evil.[1] The highest end of mankind is the ability *non posse peccare*, and the aim of all men should be to subject their volition to the decrees of God; it was pride—the desire to be more than they should—that led to the fall of Satan and his angels.

This same theory of the nature of sin is to be found in Anselm of Canterbury. For him as for St Augustine the will is the mainspring of all human activity, the God-given principle which is to control our bodies, and by it we are judged.[2] Again, the mere appetites of the flesh are not considered to be in themselves sinful;[3] it is only when we wish what we ought not to wish that we desert justice and commit a sin.[4] To God we owe a debt of obedience, and this debt is a right will by which men are made just.[5] This emphasis upon the purely voluntarist character of all sin is also to be met with in St Bernard, who tells us that through our evil will we belong to the Devil, while it is by a good will that we belong to God.[6] In all these three writers there is the same insistence upon an objective standard of just action and merit, fixed by the decrees of God and called by Augustine the *lex aeterna*.[7] Yet, despite their acceptance of Augustinian theories, both St Anselm and St Bernard betray a certain tendency towards a more subjective conception of wrongdoing. Thus, Anselm allows that their ignorance made the sin of those who crucified Christ venial, whilst St Bernard reckoned the same men as *magni quidem peccatores sed pusilli aestimatores*, allowing that their ignorance of Christ's true character lessened the gravity of their sin.[8]

Original Sin was regarded by Augustine as the sin of Adam which is also the sin of the whole human race. Its outward form is concupiscence, and it is inherited from

1 *De Natura Boni*, 34, PL. 42, col. 562.
2 *De Conceptu Virginis*, 4, PL. 158, col. 438.
3 *Ibid.* col. 437.
4 *De Casu Diaboli*, 4, col. 332.
5 *Cur Deus Homo?* I. 11, col. 376.
6 *De Gratia et lib. Arbitrio*, 6. 18, PL. 182, col. 1011.
7 *De lib. Arb.* I. 6 ff., PL. 32, coll. 1228 ff.
8 *Cur Deus Homo?* II. 15, col. 415; Bernard, *de Praecept.* 9. 20, coll. 872–3.

generation to generation through the act of procreation, so that the entire human stock is *sub obligatione peccati*,[1] while the chain of sin by which we are bound can only be unloosed through baptism.[2] Anselm again reproduced the theories of St Augustine, elaborating them by the aid of the Platonism which he imbibed from traditional theology. His ultra-Realism, aided by the Platonic doctrine of the plurality of forms, enabled him to distinguish clearly between the general and the individual in man, the one giving him his human qualities, the other his accidental characteristics as an individual.[3] With our human nature we inherit the sin of Adam, and it is through this inheritance that the race of mankind has become corrupt.[4] To this sin are added those which we commit ourselves, together with the sins of our immediate forebears which, according to the exegesis of Gregory the Great, are visited upon their children unto the fourth generation alone.[5] Greatly influenced by the renaissance of legal studies in the Northern Italy of his day, Anselm speaks of Original Sin as a debt which all men owe to God,[6] and not for one moment would he agree with those who refused to believe that infants who die unbaptized are therefore to be counted amongst the damned. To the argument that since no man holds that it is right for unbaptized infants to suffer for the sins committed by others, God cannot therefore be considered as judging more severely than do men,[7] Anselm replies that children inherit the sin of Adam because they are in him *causaliter sive materialiter velut in semine*.[8] Yet, as the volitional character of all sin presupposes the possession of Reason, the blemish of Original Sin can only be dated from the time when the foetus is quickened in the womb.[9]

Abailard himself accepted the theory that the appetites of the flesh do not of themselves constitute a sin, but he parted company with his contemporaries both in his attitude toward

1 *Sermo* 27. 2, PL. 38, col. 179.
2 *Op. Imp.* IV. 29.
3 *De Conceptu Virg.* 1, PL. 158, coll. 433–4.
4 *Ibid.*
5 *Ibid.* 2, col. 435.
6 *Ibid.* 3, coll. 435–6.
7 *Ibid.* 28, col. 461.
8 *Ibid.* 23, col. 454.
9 *Ibid.* 3, col. 435; 27, col. 461.

the actual part played by the will in the commission of a guilty act and in the general subjectivism of his ethical theories. We have, he says,[1] weaknesses of the mind (*vitia animi*) similar to those of the body, for foolishness and injustice correspond to bodily sloth and lack of sight. These weaknesses of the mind are present in us all, and they may not therefore be thought of as affecting our conduct any more than do the natural appetites of the flesh. If, indeed, these weaknesses constituted sin, no one, neither saint nor sinner, could be regarded as free from guilt. Anger, for example, is potentially in our minds, whether or not it impels us to perform an angry deed, just as a man is lame both when he is seated and when he moves about. We may ourselves compare these weaknesses of the mind to the germs of modern pathology which, although they are always in our systems, do not thereby necessarily injure our health. And these weaknesses can never be eradicated; they are part of our natural constitution as men, and, if they did not exist, the character of the Christian life as a war against the devil would lose its meaning.[2] All that the weaknesses can accomplish is to make us prone to sin; but we incur no guilt, unless we consent to their promptings. To sin, therefore, is to be a slave of these weaknesses. While lust is in itself ethically neutral, we become guilty once we surrender to its suggestion and perform an adulterous act.[3]

We have to remember, however, that all wrongdoing is ultimately directed against God. Yet, Abailard reminds us, if we think of sin in terms of violation of God's commandments, we must not forget that the divine majesty can in no way be lessened by anything that we may do. And so, since our evil deeds do not injure the majesty of God, some definition of the act of sinning must be discovered which will make clear the fact that in committing a sin we alter our relationship with God without inflicting upon him any injury, and this definition Abailard found in his statement that sin must

1 *Scito teipsum*, 1, coll. 634–5.   2 *Ibid.* 2, col. 635, quoting II Tim. ii. 5.
3 *Ibid.* 3, coll. 635, 638, 639; cf. *Problemata*, 24, col. 710 D.

be regarded as contempt for the wishes of God. It is, indeed, the non-performance of those things which we believe God would have us do, and the performance of acts which we believe that he would not wish us to perform. In consequence, we may say that sinning is negative; it is "not-doing" and "leaving undone", and it possesses no reality, for, as darkness is the absence of light, so sin is the absence of light where light should be.[1]

His emphasis upon consent as alone constituting a guilty act and his definition of sin as contempt for what we believe to be the will of God form the two chief bases of Abailard's ethical theories. He refused to accept the doctrine of his contemporaries that the will to effect an evil deed is the sin which makes men guilty in the sight of God. Will for him was desire (*desiderium*) and concupiscence (*concupiscentia*) and is not identical with consent (*consensus*).[2] Not only, he argued, does it often happen that men sin without willing to do so, but equally as often they commit no sin although they do not entirely suppress the desires which prompt them to perform some sinful action. Only when a definite consent has been made to a desire does a man become guilty; and it does not matter whether or not the incitements due to our weaknesses are wholly extinguished, provided that an actual consent has been refused. To make his position clear, Abailard gives two examples which may well be summarized here. The first is the case of a servant running away from his master who is threatening him with death; much against his will, however, he turns and kills his master in self-defence.[3]

1 Peccatum itaque nostrum contemptus Creatoris est et peccare est Creatorem contemnere, hoc est id nequaquam facere propter ipsum, quod credimus propter ipsum a nobis esse faciendum: vel non dimittere propter ipsum quod credimus esse dimittendum. Cum itaque peccatum diffinimus abnegative, dicentes scilicet: *non facere*, vel *non dimittere quod convenit*, patenter ostendimus nullam esse substantiam peccati, quod in *non esse* potius quam in *esse* substitit, velut si tenebras diffinientes dicamus: *absentiam lucis, ut lux habuit esse. Scito teipsum*, 3, col. 636 A.

2 Cf. Th. Ziegler, "Abälards Ethik", in *Strassb. Abhandlung. zur Philos.* Ed. Zeller zu seinem 70 Geburtstag, 1884, p. 205.

3 Abailard seems to be arguing against Augustine, *de lib. Arb.* 1. 4. 9–10, PL. 32, coll. 1226 ff.

Can the servant rightly be said to be guilty of murder? Upon the theory that the mere possession of an evil will constitutes guilt, the servant must be accounted blameless, for he did not wish to slay his master. All that he actually wished to accomplish was to escape death himself. Such a solution of the problem, however, did not satisfy Abailard; he maintained that, since the servant assented to the impulse to commit murder, laying his hand to his sword, he must be held to be guilty.[1] And to illustrate his thesis that men can often escape guilt despite the fact that they feel the promptings of evil lusts, Abailard pictures a group of men passing the garden of a neighbour and coveting the fruit it contains. Although they continue to desire the fruit, they repress their feelings of covetousness and go on their way. In the eyes of those who hold that evil desire alone condemns a man, these wayfarers must be considered as guilty; but Abailard contends that, even if they did not entirely suppress their desire to steal, they did not accede to its instigation, and therefore that they cannot be held to have been guilty. Indeed, he found it impossible to hold that sin can be thought merely to be voluntary, for we do not wish to contemn God, nor to consent to leave undone what we believe he would have us do.

Since he maintained that sin is not evil will, but the consent we give to an impulse which bids us perform what we know to be against the wishes of God, Abailard had to withstand the criticism of some of his contemporaries, who taught that the measure of a man's guilt is increased by the enjoyment proceeding from the completion of an evil deed. Such criticism, he allows, would carry weight, if it were conceded that pleasures are in themselves sinful, but that concession Abailard was not prepared to make. He took the view that pleasures are natural to man and, because we are human, we cannot but enjoy them. Moreover, if we were to allow that the enjoyment of natural pleasures is sinful, we should then have to condemn all married couples who are not living in strict celibacy, as well as the sick who take during their con-

[1] *Scito teipsum*, 3, coll. 636–7.

valescence more pleasant food than usual, and enjoy it.[1] Knowing, as we do, that the world was made for mankind, how can we say that we may not eat of its good things, for if we deny ourselves that pleasure, would we not be attributing guilt to the Creator who made them for our use?[2] "If cohabitation with a wife and the enjoyment of pleasant things were allowed us in Paradise from the first day of our creation without guilt being incurred, who may argue that these things are now sinful, provided only that we do not exceed the limits of our permission?"[3] Certainly, Abailard did not disregard the Pauline preference for the celibate state. While allowing that celibacy is indeed the Christian ideal, he followed the Apostle in maintaining that a less rigid form of conduct is permissible, not as a permission to sin, but that fornication may be avoided.[4] Nor will Abailard allow that guilt is increased by the pleasure which follows the completion of a sinful act. The soul cannot be contaminated by pleasurable feelings which are due entirely to the sensations of the body and, as the soul is the source whence all our motives spring, both our merit and our guilt must be judged by standards which are consistent with those of the spirit. Again, since actual sin is committed by our consent to an evil impulse, the perpetration of the deed intended can add nothing to our guilt. Our intentions in short are the criterion by which our guilt and merit must be judged, and it is of no consequence whether or not our intentions are carried into effect. A man is good, not because he does a good deed (*bonum facit*), but because he acts well (*bene facit*),[5] that is, because his intentions are meritorious. The inability to perform some intended evil deed does cancel the guilt which has already been incurred through a consent to an evil impulse, nor is merit lost if your purse does not allow you to give the

---

1 *Scito teipsum,* col. 640 BC.   2 *Ibid.* col. 640 D.

3 Si ergo concubitus cum uxore vel esus etiam delectabilis cibi a primo die nostrae creationis, quo in Paradiso sine peccato vivebatur, nobis concessus est, quis nos in hoc peccato arguat, si concessionis metam non excedamus? *Ibid.* coll. 640–41.

4 *Ibid.* col. 642 AB.   5 *Dialogus,* col. 1676 C.

alms that you desire to pay.¹ Such an attitude towards
pleasure is quite different from the strict asceticism of St
Bernard with his assertion that bread is pleasing only to the
hungry and drink only to those who thirst, and with his fear
that pleasure may be quickly turned into loathing and
vexation.²

Now in his definition of sin Abailard clearly infers that the
nature of God's will must first be known before it can be
spurned. Such is indeed the obvious deduction from his
theory, but it leads to somewhat surprising results. Evil
deeds which men commit in ignorance cannot, according to
his view, be counted as conferring guilt; guilt can only come
from the commission of an act which men know to be sinful.
In consequence, Abailard went further than either Anselm
or Bernard in his lenient attitude towards the Jews who
crucified Christ. Those two writers had declared that the sin
of the Jews was venial; Abailard states that, as their intention
was sound and since they believed that they were doing the
will of God, neither those who crucified Christ nor those who
persecuted the early Christians can be reckoned as sinful, and
to support his contention he quotes the prayer of Christ upon
the Cross for the forgiveness of those who crucified him "not
knowing what they did". It was Chorazin and Bethsaida,
not Tyre and Sidon, that were guilty, for in the two latter
cities Jesus had never preached.³ Yet, although sins committed in ignorance may not properly be called sins, Abailard
did allow that those who persecuted Christ and his followers
did commit a sin; by their actions they harmed themselves,
although in ignorance, by doing what they did.⁴ But since
a man can be saved only through his belief in the Gospel,
through his knowledge of Christ and his use of the sacraments, ignorance of Christianity does not exempt him from
damnation.⁵

As sins are not all of the same magnitude, a distinction be-

1 *Scito teipsum*, col. 643 D.
2 *De Gratia et lib. Arbitrio*, 5. 14, col. 1009 C.
3 *Scito teipsum*, 13 ff., coll. 653 ff.
4 *Ibid.* 14, col. 657 D.   5 *Ibid.* col. 656 A.

tween those which are venial and those that are mortal has
to be made. Venial sins are those to which we consent knowing that we ought not to do so, yet for the moment forgetting
that our consent should be withheld. In idle talking or in our
cups we do things which we know ought not to be done,
although at the time we do not remember our duty. Such
sins are light and are not to be remedied by a large satisfaction, either by exclusion from the church or by much abstinence, but by daily confession, a means of correction that
is not permissible in the case of mortal sins. But mortal sins
are those which we do not commit in forgetfulness, but in
deliberation; they are those sins which are far more dis-
pleasing to God, for God is more offended by perjury, homi-
cide, adultery and the like than by our greed.[1] The character
of venial sins is further discussed in the *Epitome* in a passage
which may be taken to reflect the opinions expressed in the
portion of the *Introductio* which is no longer accessible. There
we are told that if a man who is by nature easily angered, or
has some sure reason for his anger, attacks a fellow in anger,
his sin is to be regarded as venial. Further, he adds that a sin
which is venial in character becomes mortal when it is done
either in pleasure or by design.[2] In this latter statement
Abailard shews himself far more stringent than any of his
contemporaries, and in this our author stands midway between the rigorism of ascetics like St Bernard and the laxity
of many men of his day. Abailard was far more lenient towards those who had some physical disability which made
them all the more prone to commit acts of guilt, and he was
less rigorous in denouncing the inherent sinfulness of guilty
passions. Yet his emphasis upon the fact that demerit must
be gauged by intention, and so upon the theory that a venial
sin committed intentionally and with delight becomes mortal,
shews how firmly he withstood the lax morals which were

1 *Scito teipsum,* 15, coll. 658–9.
2 Quantumcunque igitur, ut ait Augustinus, in se leve sit peccatum, dum
placet et ex industria perpetratur, mortale est. *Epitome,* 33, col. 1754 A. I cannot discover the passage in Augustine.

prevalent not only in the monastery of St Gildas, but throughout mediaeval Europe.

There are, accordingly, three factors which constitute a guilty act. First, there is the weakness of the mind which renders us liable to sin; then the consent which we give to an evil suggestion, spurning thereby what we know to be the will of God. Lastly comes the evil deed itself. In themselves the weaknesses of the mind do not confer guilt, for they are no more than the potentialities of the commission of a sin, while the actual performance or non-performance of the deed which is contemplated neither alters nor increases the guilt incurred by our consent. It is, in short, one thing to desire, another to fulfil our wishes; one thing to sin, but quite another to bring our sinful desires to fruition.[1] And, had not Abailard believed that devils, wise in their long experience, were continually suggesting evil actions to men, he would have scarcely been a mediaeval. Devils represent the outward forces against which the Christian has to contend, just as the weaknesses of the mind are the foes from within. The question how the devils are to be defeated is not discussed, though we are told that in our struggle against temptation there are many herbs and seeds, trees and stones, which if we are but familiar with their use can stimulate our minds to action and soothe our passions.[2] Abailard further bids us take comfort in God's promise that he will not permit us to be tempted more than we can bear.[3]

Such a conception of sin naturally shaped Abailard's theory of punishment. To the astonishment of his critics he denied the existence of any real relationship between the enormity of the crime and the punishment which it requires. His theory of intention as the source of all our guilt forced

1 Quattuor sunt quae praesumimus, ut ab invicem ipsa diligenter distingueremus: vitium scilicet animi, quod ad peccatum pronos efficit; ac postmodum ipsum peccatum, quod in consensu mali vel contemptu Dei statuimus; deinde mali voluntatem malique operationem. Sicut autem non idem est velle, quod voluntatem implere, ita non idem est peccare, et peccatum perficere. *Scito teipsum*, 3, col. 645 C.

2 *Ibid.* 4, col. 647 C.   3 *Ibid.* col. 646 D.

him to conclude that the heinousness of a deed cannot be judged by the character of the act committed. Certainly, with their limited knowledge men are compelled to apportion their punishment in accordance with the magnitude of the offence and, since they are unable to gauge the intention of the criminal, they must take into account the preventative aspect of their sentence. Thus, even when the guilt is small, a relatively heavy sentence may be a necessity. Again, because of the office they enjoy, the clergy are judged more severely than laymen.[1] But God does not punish men for what they do; rightly called the inspector of the heart and reins, he judges motives alone and gauges punishment in strict accordance with the guilty nature of men's intentions.[2] Nor, like human judges, does he punish the body, for it is the soul that is responsible for our guilty assent.[3]

We come now to Abailard's teaching upon penance and confession. During the twelfth century theologians were subjecting the current theories of repentance to a thorough investigation, and in this enquiry Abailard played no little part. The division of penance into compunction, confession, and satisfaction dates from patristic times, and has been accepted ever since;[4] the necessity of confession as the sole means whereby guilt may be removed had been recognized by the church in its earliest days. Ambrose, Augustine, and Gregory the Great all based their doctrine of confession upon scriptural authority, chiefly upon the raising of Lazarus from the dead. We are told that Lazarus was commanded to come forth in order that he should confess his sins;[5] that he was bound as men are bound by their guilt when they do penance

---

1 *Scito teipsum,* col. 647 CD.
2 *Ibid.* col. 648 A.
3 *Epist. ad Romanos,* I. I, col. 812 B, quoting Augustine, *de Civitate Dei,* XXI. 3. 2, PL. 41, col. 711.
4 Cf. Gregory, *In I Regum Exposit.* VI. 2. 33, PL. 79, col. 349 A; see also P. P. Schmoll, *Die Busslehre der Frühscholastik,* Munich, 1909, to which I am much indebted. Also H. C. Lea, *History of Auricular Confession,* Philadelphia, 1896; O. D. Watkins, *A History of Penance,* London, 1920.
5 Gregory, *Homil. in Evang.* 26. 6, PL. 76, col. 1200; Radulfus Ardens, *Homil.* I. 40, PL. 155, col. 1810 A.

for their sins;[1] and that the disciples unloosed him as a sign that the pastors of the church ought to free men from their guilt when they are not ashamed to confess what they have done.[2] It is indeed the duty of every sinner to bring to the light the guilt which lies hidden within his conscience. Again and again, writers insisted upon the propriety of and need for confession as the method by which men are set free from their sins.[3] During the Carolingian period vigorous attempts were made to popularize the practice of confession, despite the strong opposition of certain laymen who held that confession should only be made to God.[4] Nevertheless, councils at Châlons (813) and at Paris (829) emphasized both the catholicity and the usefulness of confession, while at the latter council bishops were ordered to instruct their priests in the duties of a confessor.[5] Hitherto, the power of the Keys had been generally regarded as belonging to bishops alone.[6] Attempts were also made to insure that priests were equipped with up-to-date penitentials, although it was not until the end of the twelfth century that Alan of Lille (ab Insulis) wrote the first real handbook for the use of confessors. Both in his letters and books Alcuin was especially active in advocating the use of the confessional. Commenting upon Leviticus v. 12, he states that our confession is the offering which we make corresponding to the sin-offering of the Jews.[7] Elsewhere, he asks how a doctor can cure a wound which the sick man is ashamed to shew. "God indeed desires our confession so that he may have just cause for pardon. Our confession justifies and gives remission for sin; in confession rests all our hope of obtaining pardon."[8] The opposition of many men to confession is clearly reflected in the treatise, *de Vera et Falsa Poenitentia*, which was attributed to St Augustine

1 Augustine, *loc. cit.*   2 Gregory, *loc. cit.*
3 Rhabanus Maurus, *de Cleric. Instit.* II. 14, coll. 331–2; Radulfus Ardens, I. 40, PL. 155, col. 1810 D.
4 Council of Châlons, canon 33, Mansi, XIV. p. 100.
5 Liber I, canon 32, Mansi, XIV. pp. 558–60.
6 Cf. Gregory, *Homil. in Evang.* 26. 5, col. 1200 A.
7 *Ep.* CXII. PL. 100, col. 3380 D.
8 *De Virtutibus et Vitiis*, 12, PL. 101, col. 622 A.

during the Middle Ages, but which certainly dates from the
ninth century. Its author is at pains to convince his opponents that a second repentance is possible after baptism.[1]
Indeed, so far from it being impossible for men to do penance
and obtain forgiveness after they have once been baptized,
penance is to be regarded as the necessary completion of
baptism, and it can be repeated many times.[2]

Two events, however, aided the spread of the confessional:
the appearance of the Cathari, and the Crusades. First known
to Western Europe through the council of Arras (1025)[3]
summoned to rebut their heresies, the Cathari held that
penance, whether in this world or in Purgatory, was unnecessary, since souls either enter into bliss directly after the
death of the body, or pass to eternal punishment whence there
is no remission.[4] And so, those who wrote against the
Cathari took especial pains to defend penance as the means
whereby men can obtain forgiveness in this world, those who
are unable to complete their penitence being purified in
Purgatory.[5] The later Waldenses, also, taught ideas upon
the uselessness of penance, similar to those of the Cathari.
Religious fervour provided one of the motives which led
men to the Crusades, and this again brought men in greater
numbers to the confessional, while to take the Cross was a
very common method of performing satisfaction. In addition, the period from the eighth century onwards saw the
supersession of the old public form by the private or
auricular confession.[6]

But yet there remained several important problems which
demanded solution. The Fathers, as we have seen, regarded
repentance as three-fold and were tireless in pointing out the
utility of confession, but it still was necessary to decide

1 3. 5, PL. 40, coll. 1114–15.   2 5. 11, col. 1116.
3 See Leclercq-Hefele, *Hist. des Conciles*, IV. 2, pp. 924 ff.
4 Cf. Eckbert (d. 1182), *adversus Catharos*, Sermo 9, *Max. Bibl. Patrum*,
Lyons, XXIV. p. 620.
5 *Ibid*. pp. 619, 620.
6 A description of public penance will be found in *Sent. Divinitatis*,
pp. 143–4.

whether repentance was to be considered as a sacrament of
the church, and to determine the precise relationship between
the subjective act performed by the penitent in confessing
his sins and the objective act of the priest in giving absolution.[1] Further, although Carolingian and other councils had
recommended the practice of confession, could sin be forgiven by penitence without the obligatory recourse to the
confessional? Naturally, mortal sins stood on a different
level; confession, public or private, had always been necessary for their forgiveness. Though they followed the Fathers
in their attitude towards penance and confession, early
writers such as Anselm of Canterbury and St Bernard make
no reference to the need for solving these problems. Anselm
taught that no grievous sin could be forgiven without penitence, and that in true confession all sinful stains are removed.[2] That confession should be made to a priest is shewn
by the words "Go shew yourselves unto the priests".[3]
St Bernard speaks of the confessionis sacramentum et sacerdoti-
alis ministerii mysterium,[4] and insists upon confession and
obedience as the two principal roads of a monk's life;[5] but,
although he made much of the reality of the power of the
Keys,[6] he did not attempt to solve the problem of the relationship between the subjective and objective elements in
confession.

Abailard was the first theologian to make penance a part
of theology.[7] Discarding the definition of Isidore with its
supposed etymological connexion between poenitere and
punire, a definition that had been accepted as authoritative by
previous theologians, he defines penance as Dolor animi super
eo in quo deliquit, cum aliquem scilicet piget in aliquo excessisse.[8]

1 Cf. Schmoll, p. 13.   2 Meditatio, 6, PL. 158, coll. 737–8.
3 Homil. 13, col. 662 B; Luke xvii. 14.
4 Ad Milites Templi, 12, PL. 182, col. 938 A.
5 Sermo de div. 40. 2, PL. 183, col. 647 C.
6 Sermo in festo SS. Petri et Pauli, 1. PL. 183, col. 406 D.
7 Introd. 1. 2, col. 984; Schmoll, p. 28.
8 Scito teipsum, 18, col. 661 A; Isidore, Etym. VI. 19. 71, PL. 82, col.
258 C; eo quod ipse homo in se puniat poenitendo quod male admisit. For
the influence of this definition, see Seeberg, III. p. 83.

Penance, he says, receives its validity from the infinite patience and loving-kindness of God, and is inspired by him. Unlike the princes of this world, God does not punish us immediately for our sins, but he allows us time for repentance, although the longer he has to exercise his patience, the stricter he becomes in apportioning our punishment.[1] In our dealings with our fellow-men, we seek to hide our misdeeds; from the omniscient God and his angels no sin can be concealed and, because our repentance is a debt which we owe to God, we shall some time have to repent. Our penance, however, must not be an annual or even a daily affair; it should take place immediately we have committed a sin. And when we are truly penitent, we are sorry for all the misdeeds which we can recall to memory, for it is impossible to repent for a single misdeed to the exclusion of the others which we may have committed, and for each we must be prepared to render due penance.[2] But whereas other previous theologians had allowed for a necessary motive of fear among those which prompt us to repent,[3] or at least had stressed the love of God shewn in his forgiveness, almost if not entirely omitting our love for God as an element in our repentance,[4] Abailard declares that our repentance must spring from our love for God alone.[5] Since the cause of our sin is always subjective, in that our sin is due to the consent we give, repentance must be subjective as well. Fear, especially the spirit of bondage, can never be the pure motive of love.[6]

Yet Abailard will not allow that confession should be made to God alone, for as all our sins are known to him, such confession would not profit us.[7] Confession is indeed the means

1 *Scito teipsum*, 19, col. 664 B.
2 *Ibid.* 19, col. 664 D. The problem whether a man can repent for one sin alone was much discussed by the scholastics; cf. Roland, *Sentent.* pp. 240–41; Omnibene, pp. 204 ff.; *Summa Sentent.* IV. 13, col. 151; Peter Lombard, IV. dist. 15. 1–3; Aquinas, *Summa Theol.* III. quaest. 86, art. 3, all of whom held the same views as Abailard.
3 Cf. Bernard, *de diligendo Deo*, 14. 38, col. 998 A.
4 Anselm, *Medit.* 6, col. 738 D.   5 *Scito teipsum*, 19, col. 664 D.
6 *Exposit. ad Romanos*, III. 8, col. 902 D; cf. Rom. viii. 15, and Schmoll, pp. 30–31.
7 *Sermo* VIII. coll. 440–43.

whereby our repentance is shewn, and Abailard gives three reasons why we should confess our sins to our fellow-men. First we receive aid from the prayers of those in whom we confide;[1] then, through the humility which is entailed in the recital of our misdeeds, we accomplish a great portion of the satisfaction which our sins require; lastly, there is the benefit obtained by confession to a priest, for priests have the charge of the souls of the faithful and possess the ability of enjoining the necessary satisfaction by which our guilt may be removed. Thus, through the aid of a priest, those who have used their free will to spurn God's will can be corrected by the authority of another's power, while satisfaction is the better effected when a sinner follows the direction of a priest rather than that of his own inclination.[2] Abailard, however, was very careful to guard the penitent against any possible error on the part of the confessor in determining the nature of the requisite penance. Should the prescribed means whereby satisfaction is to be obtained prove to be either too severe or too lenient, the responsibility rests with the priest alone. Here it seems that Abailard may well have been echoing the canon of the council of Rouen (1048) by which confessors were forbidden to aggravate or lessen a penance which they had already prescribed.[3] He well understood the difficulties which a would-be penitent had then to encounter, especially as priests were neither too well-trained nor too scrupulous in their methods. Drawing the usual comparison between confessors and physicians, he declares that, as there were many doctors who were unskilled in their art, so there existed many a prelate to whom it would have been even dangerous to confess, both because his advice would do harm rather than good and because he could not be trusted to keep the secrecy of the confessional.[4] When a priest re-

1 *Scito teipsum*, 24, col. 668 c; James v. 16.   2 *Ibid.* col. 668 c.
3 Ut poenitentes occasione avaritiae gravare aut levare nemo praesumat; sed juxta modum culpae vel possibilitatem naturae moderetur poenitentia. Mansi, xix. p. 753; see N. Paulus, *Gesch. des Ablasses im Mittelalter*, Paderborn, 1922, I. p. 212.
4 *Scito teipsum*, 24, col. 669 D.

commends an insufficient form of penance, God himself will exact the surplus owing either in this life or in Purgatory.[1] Again, those who die penitent, but without accomplishing the necessary satisfaction, will be able to do so in Purgatory, thus escaping the pains of Hell.[2]

But, although he insists upon the need for confession, Abailard would not admit that either a bishop or a priest has the power of absolving men from their sins. To the Apostles alone, who were so evidently marked out by such titles as "light of the world" and "salt of the earth" as men of special grace, were the Keys of Heaven and Hell confided,[3] and their particular grace did not descend to their successors. In this way, Abailard definitely rejected the accepted theory of sacerdotal power; but, in so doing, he would have been false to his own conception of the authority of tradition if he had not based his theory upon some quotation from the writers of the church. Discarding the rescript of pope Calixtus, he held to the opinions of Origen and Jerome, both of whom had taught that the Keys had been given to St Peter alone.[4] And, in addition, he quotes from Gregory the Great passages which, though they certainly do not shew that a bishop has no power over Heaven and Hell, none the less assert that, if it is to be valid hereafter, the penance he prescribes must be identical with that demanded by God.[5] From this last quotation especially the reason for Abailard's rejection of the doctrine of the Keys can be plainly seen. It was not that he preferred the teaching of Jerome and Origen to the views of his contemporaries; the opinions of these two Fathers are only cited because they add the weight of some authority to his own doctrine. Abailard could not have subscribed to the usual teaching upon sacerdotal absolution without being disloyal to his own ethical theories. By making intention the standard by which all guilt is judged, he had

---

1 *Scito teipsum*, 25, col. 672 AB.　　　　2 *Ibid.* 24, col. 669 D.
3 *Ibid.* 26, col. 674.
4 Origen, *in Matth.* XII. 14, PG. 13, coll. 1013–16; Jerome, *in Matth.* III. 16, PL. 26, col. 118 B.
5 *Homil. in Evang.* 26. 5–6, PL. 76, coll. 1200–1.

rendered it impossible for a man to gauge with any degree of certainty the sinfulness of a deed and the satisfaction necessary for its atonement. And with his belief that contrition alone removes guilt, the further absolution by a priest becomes unnecessary. Thus, for Abailard confession is not a means whereby absolution is obtained, but a practice by which advice upon the nature of satisfaction necessary for sin is acquired from those whose office it is to care for the souls of the faithful.

Although priests have not the power to absolve men from their sins, Abailard allows that they can free the excommunicated from the bonds which the church has imposed upon them, a power which may only be exercised after sinners have been reconciled to God through penance and confession,[1] and he proceeds to describe the ceremony of reintroduction into the church, the release of Lazarus from the tomb being the origin of the imagery. The person to be readmitted has his feet and hands tied as a sign that the method of his satisfaction for sin has been laid upon him by the prelates of the church and because, as he is not free to go where he would, so he is not at liberty to carry out his own intentions. His face too is covered, for prior to the fulfilment of his penance the devotion of his repentance and the true nature of his sorrow cannot be seen. But the officiating ministers uncover his face to make his devotion plain, and to shew that in readmitting him to the church they recognize as faithful a man who had previously been unknown and had been like a Gentile or a publican. But it must be observed that in describing this ceremony Abailard in no way departed from his view that priests have no power to absolve. All that the ministers concerned can do is to recognize that the excommunicate is released from his sins through his penance and satisfaction;[2] they do not give him absolution by virtue of the Keys, while the church is unloosing a man she has herself bound. And it must further be noticed that according to Abailardian ideas satisfaction is not necessary, once an

1 *Scito teipsum*, 25, col. 669 D.   2 *Sermo* VIII. col. 440 C.

inward act of penance has been made; Abraham was saved
by his faith in God and not by his works.[1]

In his attitude towards confession Abailard was distinctly
reactionary: he disregarded entirely the many attempts which
councils had made to extend the use of the confessional, as
well as the exhortations of previous writers. The church had
long been fighting the vulgar fear of the confessional; yet
Abailard was seeking to give that very apprehension support.
Had his views been accepted, the many abuses in the mediaeval system of penance with its graduated scale of monetary
payments for absolution could never have taken place, and
if he had succeeded in inducing the church to teach that contrition alone obtains absolution for the sinner, the decree of
the fourth Lateran Council (1215) enforcing annual confession would never have been passed. Yet, in estimating
Abailard's historical position, we have to remember that the
doctrine of confession was at the time far from settled.
Certainly, in his denial that priests have the power to absolve
men from their sins he stood alone, but both his contemporaries and his immediate successors debated the questions
whether confession was a necessity and in what way priests
may be said to impart absolution. To say that sins could only
be forgiven through confession naturally appeared impossible, provided that proper contrition took place. Thus,
Gratian preferred to leave to the decision of his readers the
difficult problem whether confession in addition to contrition
was necessary,[2] while Peter Lombard held that contrition by
itself was enough to remove guilt, though he added that the
penitent should also go to confession if time permitted.[3]

The problem, however, concerning the relative actions of
God and the confessor in granting absolution was more difficult to solve. The council of Châlons already referred to had
declared that sins are purged through our confession to God,
while the priest tells men how their guilt is to be removed, a

1 *Epist. ad Romanos*, II. 4, col. 839; *Sermo* VIII. col. 443 D.
2 *Decret.* II. 33, quaest. 3. 88, PL. 187, coll. 1559 ff.
3 *Sentent.* IV. dist. 17. 2.

distinction that had previously been made by Theodulf of Orleans.[1] Gratian again taught that "it is evident that sins are forgiven by the contrition of the heart, and not by verbal confession".[2] Gratian takes the view that auricular confession was merely the rending of our garments and as such the outward sign of our inward repentance.[3] Indeed, no theologian was prepared to state that the actual forgiveness of sin was due to the action of the priest, for guilt can be only remitted by God. Thus, the writer of the *Summa Sententiarum* and Ermengard in his treatise *Against the Waldensians* both assert that God forgives *vivificando*, while the priest absolves men from the debt of future punishment by the satisfaction which he imposes.[4] According to Robert Pullen the priest does not absolve men by releasing them from their sins, but by shewing that they have already been forgiven.[5] The Lombard's conception of penance depends ultimately upon his view that faith, love, and all the virtues are in origin supernatural, being given us by the Holy Spirit;[6] none can therefore either be penitent or come to the confessional without the aid of grace, whether that grace be *operans, praeveniens*, or *cooperans*.[7] And unlike Abailard, but like the writer of the *Summa Sententiarum*, the Lombard declares that fear must be the beginning of all repentance, though he adds that fear must give way to charity.[8] Like his predecessors, the Lombard declares also that it is God alone that forgives sin, for it was Christ that raised Lazarus from the dead. Still, priests have the power of the Keys; Christ gave Lazarus to the disciples to be unloosed. But although a sinner may be

1 Confessio itaque quae Deo fit, purgat peccata: ea vero sacerdoti fit, docet qualiter ipsa purgentur peccata.   Canon 33, Mansi, *loc. cit.*; Theodulf, *Capitulare*, I. 30, PL. 105, col. 200.

2 *Decret.* II. 33, quaest. 3. 30, col. 1528.

3 *Ibid.* 33, col. 1529.

4 *Summa Sentent.* VI. 10, col. 149 A; Ermengard, *c. Waldenses*, 13, *Max. Bibl. Patrum*, XXIV. p. 1611.

5 *Sentent.* v. 13, PL. 184, col. 910 C; Schmoll, p. 61.

6 I. 17. 1; II. 27. 2; see Schmoll, pp. 69 ff.

7 II. 27. 7, 9; IV. 17. 1.

8 IV. 17. 6; *Summa Sentent.* VI. 10, col. 146 D.

freed from his guilt by God, it does not necessarily follow
that he is freed by the church, and this can only be done
through the judgement of her priests. In Levitical law, those
who had been cleansed from leprosy had to shew themselves
to the priests, to men, that is, who did not cleanse them;
Christian priests have a corresponding power, that of shewing that men have been either bound or loosed. Further,
priests have the power of binding and of loosing in that they
can impose or take away penance for sins.[1] Roland also adds
another aspect under which confession may be viewed. By
our misdeeds, he tells us, we not only offend God, but we
cause his church to stumble, and therefore we must render a
double satisfaction, paying our debt to God through the
contrition of our hearts, and, if there is time, to the church
as well by verbal confession and some act of satisfaction.[2]
And so, apart from his denial of the sacerdotal power of the
Keys, Abailard's views upon confession were not so revolu-
tionary in that he denied the necessity of confession; yet his
statement that satisfaction was not necessary and his theory
of intention as the sole criterion of all guilt would have
rendered impossible the later doctrine of confession as
formulated at the fourth Lateran Council.

II

His definition of sin as consent prevented Abailard from
subscribing to the traditional doctrine of Original Sin. He
could not allow that God may be considered as attributing
guilt to those who have actually intended no wrong; the
conception of inherited sin was far from his thought.[3] The
words of the Psalmist: "Behold, I was shapen in iniquity,
and in sin did my mother conceive me", are not interpreted
by him in the traditional manner. There is, he declares, in
them no suggestion that David was born out of wedlock; as
a divine institution marriage, although not the highest form

1 *Sentent.* IV. 17. 3–7.   2 *Sentent.* p. 249.
3 *Epist. ad Romanos,* II. 5, col. 868.

of Christian conduct, cannot be thought of as conferring
guilt, when it is consummated by the begetting of children.
We may not, therefore, take the words just quoted as a proof
that Original Sin is transferred in the act of procreation.[1]
Abailard further refuses to accept the theory of Anselm and
others that through our human nature we have all sinned in
Adam. Yet Abailard cannot be regarded as a Pelagian.
Although he rejected the traditional doctrine of Original Sin,
he did not consider that the Fall of Adam was entirely without
effect upon the human race. He distinguishes between three
ways in which the word *peccatum* is used in the Scriptures;
first, as the guilt of the soul and the contempt of God by
which we are accounted bondsmen before God, secondly the
penalty which we incur through our sin or to which we are
liable through our sin, and thirdly Christ himself is called sin
because he is a hostage for sin. "And so", he says,[2] "when
we say that men are begotten and born with Original Sin and
that this Original Sin is derived from our first parent, it seems
that we ought to think rather of the penalty for sin (*poena
peccati*) than of our guilt of mind and our contempt for God."
Original Sin is the debt by which we are bound and with
which we are born, when we are made liable to the condemnation of eternal punishment on account of the guilt of
our origin, that is, of our first parents from whom our origin
was taken, for unless we are aided by the remedies of the
sacraments, we should be condemned for ever.[3] Adam and
Eve themselves, we are told, were sufficiently punished by
their ejection from Paradise, and therefore since God does

1 Cf. *Scito teipsum*, 3, col. 641 c.
2 Cum itaque dicimus homines cum originali peccato procreari et nasci,
atque hoc ipsum originale peccatum ex primo parente contrahere, magis hoc
ad poenam peccati, cui videlicet poenae obnoxii tenentur, quam ad culpam
animi et contemptum Dei referendum videtur. *Epist. ad Romanos*, II. 5, col.
866 CD.
3 Est ergo originale peccatum cum quo nascimur, ipsum damnationis
debitum quo obligamur, cum obnoxii damnationis aeternae poenae efficimur
propter culpam nostrae originis, id est primorum parentum, a quibus incoepit origo. In illo enim...peccavimus, id est peccati ejus causa aeternae
damnationi ita deputamur, ut nisi divinorum sacramentorum nobis remedia
subveniant, aeternaliter damnemur. *Ibid.* col. 871 AB.

not judge twice for the same offence, no further sentence was passed upon them.[1] But their descendants, the entire human race, with whom God is angry because they were conceived as it were in the sin of carnal concupiscence incurred by their parents as the result of the first transgression, need absolution, and a very easy form of this has been instituted in the sacrament of baptism.[2] Abailard's standpoint, then, is that we are not ourselves guilty by reason of the sin committed by Adam; yet we are adjudged worthy of eternal damnation because of Adam's sin. Men cannot be considered guilty for a sin to the performance of which they have never consented, but they are none the less bound by the penalty of that sin (*poena peccati*). The human race then does not bear the guilt (*culpa*) of Adam's sin, although it is subject to the penalty of that transgression. And, as the wild olive alone can spring from the seed of the wild olive, so out of the human stock there can only be born children who are liable to the effects of this penalty.[3]

Nor was Abailard a Pelagian in his attitude towards the necessity of grace. Again and again he reiterates that men are impotent without the aid of divine grace, and that of ourselves we are unable to gain eternal life. But grace is not given to all men alike and in the same way, for God chooses his elect arbitrarily in accordance with the right he possesses of disposing his creation in whatever manner he may desire.[4] Akin to the power which the potter wields over his clay,[5] God's power over mankind is tyrannical; and so no injury is inflicted upon a man if God refuses him his gift of grace.

1 *Epist. ad Romanos*, II. 5, col. 872 A; cf. Nahum i. 9. The doctrine is Origenistic, and is also to be found in Erigena (*de Div. Nat.* II. 5, col. 532). Abailard quotes neither writer.

2 Filiis autem illorum, videlicet primorum parentum, quibus pariter omnibus etiam pro culpa ipsorum patrum iratus est Deus, tanquam in peccato carnalis concupiscentiae conceptis, quam ipsi videlicet patres ex prima transgressione incurrerunt, singulis propria necessaria est absolutio, quae levissima nobis instituta est in baptismo. *Ibid.* col. 872 B.

3 *Ibid.* col. 872 D; for wild olive cf. Rom. xi. 17, and Augustine, *de Nupt.* II. 34. 58, PL. 44, col. 471.

4 *Epist. ad Romanos*, IV. 9, col. 916.   5 Cf. Rom. ix. 21.

Bound by no obligations until an actual promise has been made, utilizing for good both the wickedness of Judas and the sanctity of Peter, governing the universe with strict rationality, God commits no wrong in thus restricting his gifts. While many were converted and saved through the preaching of Peter, all were turned to salvation by the betrayal of Judas which resulted from God's refusal to impart to him the gift of grace. Yet men cannot even receive grace without the aid of God. We are like sick men to whom a doctor wishes to administer a draught, and who must needs be raised so that they can drink of the healing cup.[1] Thus, men are dependent upon God not only for sufficient grace, but also for his gift of prevenient grace which enables us to receive that which he wishes us to take.

There is, however, one passage which his contemporaries took as evidence that Abailard held Pelagian views. There he says that "it is not necessary for us to beg of God for a new gift of grace for each single good deed we perform".[2] But Abailard does not say that we can act without grace, and he certainly did not intend his statement to mean that free will is sufficient for the performance of a good deed. All he wishes to say is that new grace is not needed for each single good act, and to illustrate his contention he takes an analogy from secular life, based on one of the Gospel parables. A powerful man offers his wealth to some poor men on the condition that they fulfil all his commands; the opportunity is a commercial one, and the merchandise is shared out equally. Fired by his desire of the promised reward, one man sets to and finishes his work, while another, lazy and impatient at the size of his task, is less anxious to carry out his bargain. In the same way, God offers to us the Kingdom of Heaven, but one man, incited by his desire to gain salvation, perseveres in good works, although another grows languid in sloth. To both

1 *Epist. ad Romanos*, IV. 9, col. 917 BC.

2 Dicimus itaque non esse necesse in singulis bonis operibus novam nobis gratiam a Deo impertiri. *Ibid.* col. 917 D.   See also *Disp. altera anonymi abbatis*, III. col. 322.

alike God offers his reward and does whatever is necessary; without the addition of new grace the account and promise of bliss is enough to quicken in each the desire for Heaven. What else, then, is needed save that blessedness to which we are to come, and that the road by which we are to arrive should be shewn and given us?[1] And the same is true of business men who, although they endure so much labour, suffer it all for the sake of that hope which has been theirs since they first began to toil. Yet it is not only to the elect that grace is imparted. Following Catholic tradition, Abailard maintains that even the reprobates, who do not make use of it, receive the gift of divine grace, and that gift is only withheld from those who have been damned from eternity.

III

To understand Abailard's doctrine of the Atonement we must view it in its historical setting, and any discussion of the various doctrines of the Atonement, however brief, must begin with St Paul.

Since Christ was the sin-offering to God for the whole of the human race, St Paul interpreted the Passion as vicarious. In Christ the entire race of mankind was summed up, and by the substitution of his death the sins of all the world were expiated; although he was himself without sin, Jesus was regarded by God as guilty and, accordingly, on him was imposed the punishment which our sins deserved. In saying that we were "bought with a price", St Paul was employing the terminology of contemporary law. As the Greek and Roman slaves obtained their freedom by a monetary payment at their manumission, so by Christ's blood we were freed

---

[1] Aeque tamen Deus utrisque offert illud, et quod est suum efficit, tantumque erga utrumque operatur regni ipsius beatitudinem exponendo et promittendo, quod ad desiderium uniuscujusque accendendum sufficiat, absque nova alia gratia apposita....Ad desiderium itaque nostrum in Deo accendendum et ad regnum coeleste concupiscendum, quam praeire gratiam necesse est nisi ut beatitudo illa ad quam nos invitat, et via qua pervenire possimus, exponatur atque tradatur? *Epist. ad Romanos*, IV. 9, col. 918 CD.

from the thraldom of sin.[1] By Irenaeus (*ob. c.* 202) St Paul's doctrine was developed into the so-called "Ransom Theory". His conception of ἀνακεφαλαίωσις continued the Pauline idea of Christ as summing up in himself the whole human race, but added a new element by teaching that Christ's death was a ransom paid to the devil for the deliverance of man. Accepted by St Augustine, this doctrine of the Atonement held the field for nearly one thousand years. It had previously been somewhat embroidered by Origen, who taught that the Incarnation was intended as a trap by which the devil was to be inveigled into thinking that Jesus was only human. St Augustine himself developed one side of the Pauline theory which had been overlooked—the fact that one result of the Atonement had been that Christ had shewn to men the pattern of the true life.[2]

Anselm of Canterbury, however, inaugurated a far more fundamental advance in the history of the doctrine, and this may be said to have prepared the way for the Abailardian view. Rejecting the idea that Satan possessed any rightful authority over man as the result of the Fall, he rejected also the idea that God was under an obligation to recompense the devil, when by the death of his Son mankind was withdrawn from his rule.[3] Thus, Christ's death was not the payment of a debt owed to the devil. But Anselm did not wholly discard the old view that the Atonement constituted a debt. St Paul's phraseology exerted too strong an influence over his conservative mind, while his studies of law at Padua had taught him something of the Teutonic idea of wergeld or bloodmoney, which led him to retain the old theory of the Atonement under a different form. Christ's death was not regarded as a debt paid to the devil, who had no legal claims to be satisfied, but a debt paid to God, whose majesty had been injured by Adam's sin. This injury, moreover, was of such

1 Cf. A. Deissmann, *Light from the Ancient East*, London, 1910, p. 323.
2 Cf. *de Catech. Rud.* 4. 7–8, PL. 40, col. 314; Seeberg, II. p. 499 and note; Rom. v. 8.
3 *Cur Deus Homo?* I. 7, PL. 158, coll. 367 ff.; also *Medit.* 11, col. 764.

magnitude that no human individual could make sufficient atonement; that could only be performed by some one greater than man, by God in Christ Jesus.[1] Such is the doctrine which is given by Anselm in the *Cur Deus Homo?* In the *Meditations*, however, he alludes to the exemplarist theory which we have found in St Paul and in St Augustine.[2]

Like Anselm, Abailard denied that Satan has any rightful power over mankind, and although he does not refer to the passage in the *Cur Deus Homo?* it is more than likely that he knew the book, for he uses the same arguments. God is the supreme overlord of both the devil and man, and accordingly, all the authority possessed by the devil is held upon the good will of God. And so that authority can be taken away without any injury being done to the devil. But, while St Anselm was concerned solely with the relationship of God and the devil, Abailard introduces the problem of man's relations to Satan. When a servant wishes to desert his master and place himself under the rule of another, he cannot lawfully do so without the consent of his former lord, while, if he disappears without such permission, he can be compelled to return. That, indeed, was the feudal law in so far as a serf was concerned. Again, if one servant persuades a fellow to leave their common master, the first is evidently the more guilty of the two, but he has no real authority over his companion. In like manner, the devil possesses no authority over those whom he has enticed away from God; the mere fact that they have followed him gives him no power over them in law. Indeed, the sole authority possessed by the devil is that given him directly by God when he hands over a man for torture and imprisonment. The devil could have had no just cause for complaint if the Atonement had been effected by some other means than by the death of Christ.[3] But, although Abailard could thus have envisaged the possibility of some different method by which the guilt of the human race could have been remitted, his belief that God can only

1 *Cur Deus Homo?* II. 6, coll. 403–4.
2 12, coll. 771–2.   3 *Epist. ad Romanos*, II. 3, coll. 835.

act in the way he does shews that this possibility was entertained solely for argument's sake. Yet the very fact that
Abailard could have entertained this possibility well illustrates the difference between his outlook and that of St
Anselm. Holding that the debt due to God for man's sin
could alone be paid by someone greater than man, Anselm
was forced to deny that the idea of a different method whereby
the Atonement might have been effected was beyond the
power of man even to contemplate as a hypothesis.[1] Abailard,
however, pushed the doctrine of the work of Christ advanced
by Anselm one step further. While agreeing with his predecessor that no compensation was due to the devil for the
redemption of man, he refused to allow that Christ's death
was absolutely necessary. Calvary could not be regarded as
the payment of a debt due to God for an injury inflicted upon
the divine majesty by the Fall.

Since he did not regard the work of Christ as a ransom
paid either to God or to the devil, Abailard somewhat
naturally fell back upon the exemplarist theories which we
have found in both St Paul and St Augustine, but, unlike
them, he made exemplarism the centre of his doctrine. In
this, he tells us,[2] he was largely influenced by a statement of
Isidore of Seville that the divine Wisdom became man so that
wisdom should lighten the world. As the Word is the divine
Wisdom, Abailard declares, it was natural for him rather than
for either the Father or the Spirit to have become incarnate.
The special properties of the other two Persons would not have
enabled them to teach men the wisdom which they lacked.
So God sent his Son, since it was fitting that, "as it is from
him that men have their being, from him too they should receive the ability to effect whatever they perform".[3] Thus,
the man-ward aspect of Christ's work is made the centre of
Abailard's doctrine of the Atonement. The Cross becomes

1 *Cur Deus Homo?* I. 5, col. 365.
2 Isidore, *Sentent.* I. 14, PL. 83, col. 566 A, quoted *Theol. Christ.* IV. col.
1278 C.
3 *Sermo* VI. col. 423 C, quoting John i. 9.

merely the incentive which induces us to follow in the road
that Jesus trod; it was by shewing us in his person and in his
words the way in which men ought to live that the incarnate
Lord freed us from the penalty of Adam's sin. For Abailard,
Jesus was not the Man of Sorrows carrying the burden of our
guilt or the victim offered up to the Father as a recompense
for our sins, so much as the divine Logos made manifest to
the world, incarnate because he would reveal to mankind the
path of righteousness.

Before commenting further upon his thought, it will be
best to quote two relevant passages from the *Expositio*:

It seems to us that we are justified in the blood of Christ and
reconciled to God in this, that through the singular grace manifested to us in that his Son took our nature and that teaching us
by both word and example he persevered even unto death, Jesus
bound us closer to himself by love, so that, fired by so great a
benefit of divine grace, true charity would no longer be afraid to
endure anything for his sake.[1]

And again:

Every man is made more just, that is more loving towards
God, after the Passion of Christ than he had been before, because
men are incited to love by a benefit actually received more than
by one hoped for. And so our redemption is that great love for us
shewn in the Passion of Christ which not only frees us from the
bondage of sin, but acquires for us the true liberty of the sons of
God, so that we should fulfil all things not so much through fear
as through our love for him who shewed towards us a favour
than which, as he himself says, none greater can be found:
"Greater love hath no man than this, that a man lay down his life
for his friends".[2]

1 Nobis autem videtur, quod in hoc justificati sumus in sanguine Christi,
et Deo reconciliati, quod per hanc singularem gratiam nobis exhibitam, quod
Filius suus nostram susceperit naturam, et in ipsos nos tam verbo quam
exemplo instituendo usque ad mortem perstitit, nos sibi amplius per amorem
astrixit, ut tanto divinae gratiae accensi beneficio, nil jam tolerare ipsum vera
reformidet charitas. *Epist. ad Romanos*, II. 3, col. 836 AB.

2 Justior quoque, id est amplius Dominum diligens, quisque fit post
passionem Christi quam ante, quia amplius in amorem accendit completum
beneficium quam speratum. Redemptio itaque nostra est illa summa in nobis
per passionem Christi dilectio, quae non solum a servitute peccati liberat, sed
veram nobis filiorum Dei libertatem acquirit, ut amore ejus potius quam
timore cuncta impleamus, qui nobis tantam exhibuit gratiam qua major in-
venire ipso attestante non potest (John xv. 13). *Ibid.* col. 836 c.

It will be seen that Abailard regards the work of Christ as inspiring a new motive into our actions. The old Mosaic Law was insufficient for men's salvation, for it was concerned with visible and not with invisible things, with the life of this world as opposed to the life of the Spirit.[1] Certainly, the Law itself did not condemn; like the Gospel, it warns men against specified actions and desires, but, unlike the Gospel, its precepts apply only to man's dealings with his immediate neighbour. Although the Law taught men to love both God and their neighbour, it took the word "neighbour" to mean the members of the Chosen People alone, and thus covetousness is only forbidden where the goods of another Jew are concerned.[2] The basis of the Old Law was fear, and it was through their fear of punishment that men were held in bondage.[3] The Gospel, on the other hand, is universal in its application; we are commanded to treat all men alike.[4] We know already that Abailard considered merit to be attached to the intention alone, and not to the deed performed. While the Decalogue had shewn men what they should and should not do, it had not provided them with the necessary motive which would make their obedience to it meritorious, for if our observance of God's commandments proceeds solely from fear, we cannot be said to gain merit. It was indeed a dispensation of a kindly providence that a people, still totally uncultured and lacking in discipline, always stiff-necked and rebellious, should at least have been given some commandments to teach them obedience,[5] but for man's salvation something more was necessary. The mere performance of some things and the omission of others is not enough; the motive of charity was needed, and this Christ's death supplied. This intimate connexion between Abailard's ethics and his doctrine of the Atonement has not been sufficiently brought out.

1 *Ibid.* IV. 10, col. 923.
2 *Non concupisces*, id est non interdiceret concupiscentiam, licet non generaliter, sed de rebus, ut dictum est, proximi. *Ibid.* III. 7, col. 888 B.
3 *Ibid.* III. 10, col. 902; cf. *Sermo* V. col. 422.
4 *Epist. ad Romanos*, III. 7, coll. 884, 887.   5 *Ibid.* col. 884.

Christ was born under the Law so that he might the more easily free us from our bondage,[1] transferring us thereby from the slavery of the Law to the freedom of the Gospel. Not only did Christ extend the meaning of "our neighbour" by making the term include all men; by his example and by his New Law he fulfilled the Mosaic Code in a far more important way. Christ, the father of the spiritual as Adam was of the carnal, summoned men away from the world to receive the things of God,[2] making us spiritual and no longer the servants of mundane desires.[3] Built upon pity and not, like the laws of princes, upon vindictiveness, his new Gospel holds injustice in check through love and not through fear.[4] The purpose of the Crucifixion, then, was to pour charity into our hearts, and charity is given us by Christ,[5] who makes us thereby sons of God, not his slaves in fear.[6] In this manner a new motive is infused into our actions, which accordingly become meritorious. Christ fulfilled the Law not by abolishing its decrees and substituting a new Gospel, for, as we have seen, Abailard held that the Gospel contained the precepts of the Mosaic Code.[7] By providing a new motive, charity, by which men's loyalty to the Law could become meritorious, Christ enabled them to gain salvation. The Law had only corrected our outward actions; it had not enabled us to acquire merit. Hence, God sends his Spirit to inspire in our hearts that pure love of himself, teaching us to do voluntarily what the Son has taught, and thereby adopting us as his sons.[8]

Still, Abailard did not entirely lose sight of Christ's rôle as a mediator between man and God. His work was indeed more than the example which he gave us through his incarnate life; he gave us also merit from his own merit, and by that we obtain whatever goodness we possess.[9] His justice supplies whatever we lack, and where we are deficient in merit, he gives us of his own, making supplication to the

1 *Sermo* v. col. 422 B. 2 *Epist. ad Romanos*, II. 5, col. 862 D.
3 *Ibid.* III. 8, col. 899 AB. 4 *Sermo* v. col. 422 D.
5 *Epist. ad Romanos*, II. 4, col. 833 A. 6 *Ibid.* I. 1, col. 797 D.
7 *Supra*, p. 71. 8 *Sermo* v. col. 423 D.
9 *Epist. ad Romanos*, II. 5, col. 863 AB.

Father on behalf of those who cleave to him.[1] In this way, we are made co-heirs of God with him. And when we say "Through Jesus Christ our Lord" we recognize that our deeds would be in no way pleasing to the Father save through the Son who has reconciled man with his Creator.[2] But it must be noticed that this reconciliation was not effected through a compensation paid to God for the damage wrought by human sin. Only by following Christ's example do we gain merit for our actions. Thus when Abailard says that Christ freed men from the bondage of guilt (*a servitute peccati*), he did not mean that the death of Christ was vicarious; our reconciliation was spiritual, and not a legal transaction. The Mosaic Code was a temporary measure intended to teach men obedience and to guard them against certain sinful acts. We were reconciled to God through Christ because, by drawing us away from the love of ourselves, he enabled us to fulfil both the Law and the Gospel in that spirit of charity which wins for us approval in the sight of God.

We have already described the three forms of faith which Abailard inherited from St Augustine, and have seen that men are not justified either by a mere belief in the existence of God or in the truth of his promises. Justification comes from our faith in God (*credere in Deum*), which means that we love God and are members of his church, seeking to do his will.[3] The faith, accordingly, by which we are justified is our faith in Christ by which charity is born and infused into our hearts. Only through their faith have the elect of God access to the hope of acquiring that blessedness which is the reward of the sons of God.[4] After the Incarnation those alone who have thus been made sons of God can be justified,[5] although before the Nativity certain who believed in the triune Godhead were saved. And again, it is faith rather than works that wins justification for men.

1 *Ibid.* col. 856 BC.
2 Ac si omne quod agimus recognoscamus Deo Patri minime placiturum, nisi per ipsum mediatorem qui nos ei reconciliavit. *Ibid.* I. 1, col. 798 D.
3 See *supra*, p. 38; *Epist. ad Romanos*, II. 4, col. 840.
4 *Ibid.* II. 5, col. 859 C; cf. Rom. v. 2.   5 *Ibid.* II. 3, col. 833.

But Christ did more than make us the sons of God, freeing us from the bondage of sin; he gave us in addition the sacraments. His substitution of the trinity of faith, charity, and the sacraments for the usual Pauline division of the theological virtues indicates the importance attached by Abailard to sacramental teaching, an importance which is also to be found in the writings of contemporary canonists. Compared with the earlier Burchard of Worms, Ivo of Chartres gives a far more dogmatic treatment of the sacraments,[1] and it may well have been that Abailard's emphasis was derived from his study of Ivo. But beyond this, Abailard's thought does not mark any real advance upon the teaching of his predecessors. He still adhered to the traditional Augustinian definition of a sacrament as "a visible sign of invisible grace", without anticipating the definition, first found in the *Summa Sententiarum* and reproduced by later mediaeval theologians, whereby a sacrament was held to be "a visible sign of invisible grace conferred with it".[2] And it is to be regretted that we do not possess that portion of the *Introductio* which dealt with his sacramental teaching. We do not even know how many sacraments he considered that there were. This is especially unfortunate as it was during the first half of the twelfth century that their number was finally decided upon by the church. In the ninth century Rhabanus Maurus had held that there were but two, Baptism and the Eucharist, Confirmation being included with the first.[3] In one passage Peter Damiani had enumerated three chief sacraments, Baptism, the Eucharist, and Ordination, but in a sermon he declared that their number was twelve.[4] Both Anselm of Laon and William of Champeaux held that there were five, Baptism, the Eucharist, Confession, Marriage, and Unction, and in this enumeration they were followed by the writer of the *Epitome* and of the St Florian *Sentences*. The number given

1 De Ghellinck, *op. cit.* p. 298.
2 *Introd.* I. 2, col. 984 B; cf. Augustine, *de Catech. Rud.* 26. 50, PL. 40, col. 314, and *Summa Sentent.* IV. 1, col. 117 B.
3 *De Cleric. Instit.* I. 28, PL. 107, col. 817 B.
4 *Liber gratissimus*, 6, PL. 145, col. 109, and *Sermo* LXIX. PL. 144, col. 898.

by Hugh of St Victor varies slightly; in one passage he held that their number was seven, though elsewhere he adds the signing of the Cross and the invocation of the Trinity to their number. By including Ordination and Confirmation in the list given by Anselm and William of Champeaux, Hugh, together with Roland Bandinelli and Omnibene, was the first theologian to maintain that seven was the number of the sacraments.[1] As this enumeration was later accepted by the Lombard, it was considered authoritative by all theologians until the time of the Reformation. The fact that the *Epitome* held that their number was seven suggests that its writer was probably following the counting of Abailard.

In his general treatment of the sacraments Abailard felt bound to disprove the teaching of two contemporaries. Peter de Bruys and his followers held that the sacraments were merely figures of a subsequent truth which has since been fulfilled through the advent of Christ. But to this argument Abailard replies that we still observe the sacrament of marriage, the anointing of priests and other rites which were ordained by Melchisedec; to be consistent we should have to abolish these together with any other sacrament which we might consider to have been abrogated by the Incarnation.[2] This course he was unwilling to advocate. Again, the master who, as we shall give evidence to shew, was in all probability Bernard of Chartres, taught that the power of the words of Institution at the Eucharist was such that, whether they were pronounced by a woman, or by a man of non-priestly rank, the consecration must be considered valid.[3] Abailard does not deign to refute so impossible a doctrine. He states, however, quite clearly that the liturgical words of a sacrament are of such force that their efficacy is wholly independent of the moral character of the officiating priest.[4] His statement has a certain historical importance. During the struggle over clerical reform during the eleventh and twelfth centuries

1 Seeberg, III. pp. 270–71; Roland, *Sentenzen*, pp. 267 ff., and Denifle, ALKG. I. p. 467.
2 *Sermo* III. col. 407 BC.
3 *Theol. Christ.* IV. col. 1286 B.
4 *Ibid.* col. 1273 B.

especially, the problem naturally arose whether the sacraments performed by married or simoniacal priests could be
considered valid. Peter Damiani had argued in favour of
their legality despite the uncanonical status of their officiants,
but cardinal Humbert of Silva Candida had held the opposite
view.[1] Damiani's position indeed was the only just one, for
the spiritual welfare of the recipients as well as the legitimacy
of their children depended upon the validity of the sacraments administered by such priests. And so the solution put
forward by Abailard was also that of the church of the time.

As to Baptism, Abailard makes much of the wider scope
and more perfect effect of that sacrament as compared with
circumcision. The latter could only be performed upon a
man, and then upon one part of his body alone, a rite even
then difficult to carry out and terrifying to the Gentiles.
Baptism not only washed the whole man; it sanctified both
men and women, and was a much lighter burden to bear.[2]
Yet Baptism is more than that; it is our marriage with God
when, betrothed to him during the scrutiny of our cate-
chumenate, we are united through Baptism with his body,
the church.[3] The material—the res—of the sacrament is
water, the sign of the cleansing of the soul within when the
body outside is washed.[4] But at this point the question arises
whether those who have not been baptized can be saved.
We have already seen that Abailard considered that some
men who lived before the Incarnation, but yet believed in the
doctrine of the Trinity, are numbered among the blest. He
also held the usual mediaeval doctrine that those who desire
Baptism, but do not live to receive the sacrament, are none
the less justified through their desire.[5] Now there are in St
Bernard's de Baptismo passages which refer to the heretical
views advanced by "a new discoverer of new doctrines".
Vacandard would have us believe that this heretic was

1 See C. Mirbt, Die Publizistik im Zeitalter Gregors VII, 1894, pp. 386 ff.,
424 ff., and L. Saltet, Réordinations, Paris, 1907, passim.
2 Sermo III. col. 404 A.   3 Ibid. col. 404 CD.
4 Introd. I. 1, col. 984 B; cf. Hexaem. col. 736 D.
5 Epist. ad Romanos, II. 3, col. 838.

Abailard, while Deutsch argued that Bernard was criticizing one of Abailard's pupils.[1] Vacandard's thesis is certainly untenable. We are told that this new discoverer taught that none save those who have actually been baptized can be saved, and that the men of old who foreknew the coming of Christ had that knowledge in the same way as we know the events of the past, and that in consequence their knowledge cannot be called justifying faith.[2] Abailard himself taught neither of these doctrines. He did, however, hold a third doctrine with which this heretic is accredited, namely, that sins committed in ignorance do not confer guilt.[3] The *de Baptismo* is really a letter written to Hugh of St Victor in answer to a query, and although Hugh, doubtless, named the heretic complained of, St Bernard does not repeat his name, and no clue as to his identity is afforded us in Hugh's own writings. The letter itself is dated about the year 1125, when both the *Theologia Christiana* and the first portion of the *Introductio*, but not the *Expositio*, had been written. From this it is evident that if Hugh and Bernard were indeed referring to Abailard, their information concerning his views could not have come from his own writings, for none that had then been published contains any reference either to his doctrine of Baptism or to his ethical theories. The source of Hugh's information must, then, have been either a verbal report of Abailard's theology or a rumour concerning his teaching which was in circulation at Paris, and it is easy to understand how his views came to be reported incorrectly. There is, of course, a further possibility that Hugh was referring to some other teacher. But, as the theory concerning sins committed in ignorance is undoubtedly Abailardian and as the title "a new discoverer of new doctrines" so well fits our author, this appears to be unlikely.[4]

1 Vacandard, II. p. 113; Deutsch, pp. 466–72.
2 De Baptismo, 2. 7, PL. 182, col. 1035 CD; 3. 10, col. 1038 B.
3 Ibid. 4. 16, coll. 1041 C–1042 D.
4 The names of Hugh Farsitus and John, archbishop of Seville, have been suggested, but as Hugh is addressed by Bernard as *carissime frater* (*Epp.* 35, 36, coll. 141–2) and as John is praised by Hugh of St Victor for his work among the Mohammedans, the suggestion seems unlikely: *Ep.* 3, PL. 176, col. 1014.

For an account of Abailard's views upon the other sacraments we are almost entirely dependent on the writer of the *Epitome*, and it seems almost certain that his views were identical with those of Abailard. Little is said of Confirmation, save that it is not a sacrament by which sins are forgiven, but the bestowal of a gift of grace given to men through the agency of bishops alone.[1] A good deal of space, however, is devoted to the doctrine of the Eucharist. In the *Theologia Christiana* Abailard himself says that the great controversy concerning this sacrament had not yet reached its end, for he was continually meeting with different doctrines, the growth and dissemination of which it seemed impossible to restrain.[2] He was, of course, referring to the discussion over the meaning of the Real Presence, begun in the three-cornered struggle between Rhabanus Maurus, Radbertus, and Ratramnus in the ninth century and reaching its height in the eleventh when Berengar of Tours declared that the bread and wine were only signs of a spiritual presence of the Body and Blood of Christ. The doctrine of Berengar, attacked by Lanfranc, gave rise to the appearance of many attempts to determine the way in which the bread and wine were changed into the Body and Blood of Christ while yet retaining their visible forms. Against Berengar it was argued that the Body of Christ, although remaining in heaven, could still be present in many places simultaneously, and that in each consecrated Host the whole, unbroken Christ was present. Despite the continuance of the bread and wine in their visible forms, their substance was so completely changed at the consecration that none of it remained in the consecrated Host. Some of Berengar's disciples still taught, however, the theories of impanation and companation: that Christ was personally impanated in the sacrament just as he was personally incarnated in human flesh,[3] thus denying the Real Presence as a belief that

---

1 *Epitome*, 28, col. 1740 BC.   2 IV. col. 1286 B.
3 Ita personaliter impanatum Christum sicut in carne humana personaliter incarnatum deum. Alger, *de Sacramentis corporis et sanguinis*, i. 6, PL. 180, col. 754.

the Body and the bread were bound together.[1] To Rupert of Deutz the two substances, the divine and the earthly, were present together in the sacrament, united in the same way as gold and fire can be joined.[2]

From the *Epitome* it is evident that Abailard believed that after the consecration the bread and wine become the Body and Blood of Christ, the same which he took from the Virgin,[3] and that at the Eucharist the Body is not broken. Certainly, Jesus brake and gave to his disciples, but the word *fregit* must not be taken literally. It implies only that the Lord revealed and made clear to his disciples the meaning of the sacrament, that his Body signifies the church and his Blood the joy which the church has at her redemption.[4] But his account of the mode of transubstantiation is peculiar because, instead of following the usual practice of distinguishing between the forms of the bread and wine which remain unaltered, and their substances which are changed, Abailard bases his idea of transubstantiation upon the theory that in the consecrated elements there exist together two different sets of forms, those of the bread and the wine, and those of the Body and Blood of Christ. And to any critic who might point out that one substance cannot have two different forms, he instances the presence in the incarnate body of Christ of forms which enabled him to be conceived by the Holy Spirit, to enter and depart from a closed womb, to walk upon the water, and to enter the room where his disciples were assembled although the doors were shut against him.[5] Like that of the manna which fell in the wilderness, the nature of Christ's body is beyond human understanding. Still, if we are unwilling to say that the bread and wine are the forms of his Body, we can at least say that the original forms of the elements remain in the air, kept there to hide the Body and the Blood, just in the same way as the human form remains in the air when an angel

1 Cf. Seeberg, III. p. 203.
2 *De Trin. in exod.* II. 10, PL. 167, coll. 617 ff.
3 *Epitome*, 29, col. 1741 A.
4 *Ibid.* col. 1742 CD.
5 *Ibid.* col. 1743 C.

appears in the form of a man.[1] And by his phrase "in the air" Abailard did not mean that the forms exist apart from the changed substance in the consecrated Host; these forms are "in the air" only because they do not inhere in the substance of the Body and the Blood of Christ. They act as a covering to the changed substance of the elements, and they are in substance separate from them. Crudely expressed, it is as if the forms of the bread and wine encircled those of the Body and the Blood. And Abailard maintained that, if mice gnaw at or carry in their mouths the consecrated Host, the original forms remain to correct the negligence of the priest, and thus the sacrament is guarded against defamation.[2] That such unfortunate occurrences frequently happened seems to have been the case, if we may judge from the many references to such accidents in contemporary literature.

[1] Si enim nolumus dicere quod illius corporis sit haec forma, possumus satis dicere quod in aere sit illa forma ad occultationem propter praedictam causam carnis et sanguinis reservata, sicut forma humana in aere est, quando angelus in homine apparet. *Epitome,* 29, col. 1743 D.

[2] De hoc, quod negligentia ministrorum evenire solet, quod scilicet mures videntur rodere et in ore portare corpus illud, quaeri solet. Sed dicimus quod Deus illud non dimittit ibi, ut a tam turpi animali tractetur: sed tamen remanet ibi forma ad negligentiam ministrorum corrigendam. *Ibid.* coll. 1743-4.

Chapter ix

THE COUNCIL OF SENS AND AFTER

I

THE reason for St Bernard's attack upon Abailard at the council of Sens presents a problem of much difficulty. Sometimes it has been held that as a mystic Bernard was actuated by a supposed natural distrust for a scholastic theologian whose approach to theology was so different from his own; other writers have drawn a parallel between the hostility of the two men and the antagonism of the conservative theologian and the modernist at the present time. Neither of these two explanations is, however, satisfactory. In the Middle Ages at least there was no necessary enmity between the mystic and the scholastic philosopher. If his metaphysical writings have earned for St Anselm the title of the Father of Scholasticism, it must not be forgotten that these very books are steeped in the mysticism of Plato, while his devotional works—such as his *Meditations* and *Homilies*—are thoroughly mystical in character. Even so intellectualist a thinker as Aquinas was not untouched by mysticism, a fact which is evident from his *Catena Aurea* and from his hymns for the feast of Corpus Christi. Mysticism and scholasticism are, then, not mutually exclusive terms.

In its technical meaning, Modernism implies a re-evaluation of traditional dogma in the light of contemporary philosophical knowledge. Abailard, as I have endeavoured to shew, did not seek to recast the doctrines which he accepted upon the authority of the church. Far from wishing either to question or to alter their content, he made it his aim to interpret, explain, and defend the authenticity of the Creeds. In the twelfth century, indeed, when all learning was in the hands of the church, there existed no body of secular philosophy, the tenets of which were antagonistic to the accepted truths of Christian revelation. Although there were many heretics, no thinker at the time possessed the critical ability which would have enabled him to question the fundamental truths of Christian philosophy, had he so wished. Nor was it his dislike of learning that induced St Bernard to take up the cudgels against Abailard. To be sure, we find the worthy abbot inveighing against some of his monkish friends who devoted their time and energy to secular studies, but his criticism was due to his firm belief that a monastery was not the proper place for the study of worldly scholarship. In his eyes, a monastic house could only be called a school if it was always remembered that within its precincts men studied the wisdom (*sapientia*) of God, and not the science (*scientia*) of the world. And such wisdom was not to be discovered in the pages of a Boethius or a Porphyry; it could only be acquired through prayer and meditation. Yet St Bernard was not without sympathy for the scholars of his day, and in the fortunes of some of them he took a lively interest, trying to find for them the necessary preferment which would aid them in their studies.[1] But his concern for men like John of Salisbury and Robert Pullen did not prevent him from warning other students against the trammels of worldly ambition, which could so easily entrap them if they paid too great attention to the rewards of scholarship. Preaching before the students of Paris, he exhorted them to flee to cities of refuge where they could do penance for their past sins, where they would be able to obtain grace for their present deeds, and where they could await with confidence the glory that is to come.[2] No avowed enemy of learning as such, Bernard was fully aware of its dangers both to the monk and to the secular priest.

Once the Saint had read the various theological opinions of Abailard which were brought to his notice, it was in-

1 Cf. his letters on the behalf of John of Salisbury, Robert Pullen, and Peter the Lombard, *Epp.* ccclxi, ccv, cccx.
2 *De Conversione ad Clericos*, 21, col. 855 B.

evitable that he should have been both astonished and out-
raged by their character. Despite the beauty of his own
religious experience and the knowledge which he gained
from his contacts with so many men of different types, the
abbot was very narrow in his outlook and incapable of
sympathizing with those who did not see eye to eye with
himself. St Bernard can hardly be blamed for this narrowness
of outlook; it was characteristic of his time, and was largely
responsible for his own success. It was his pertinacity and
his firm belief in the righteousness of his own cause that
enabled him to effect so much, although he was often faced
with such great difficulties. Zealous always to defend the
church and her doctrine, he regarded those who appeared to
be her enemies as men who must be stamped out, if they
could not first be persuaded to abandon their teaching.
A typical reformer with all the reformer's eager narrowness,
he viewed with the greatest apprehension the dangers which
seemed to threaten the church from within and from without,
and this apprehension brought him to demand the use of the
heaviest artillery.

Although mysticism and scholasticism were not necessarily
antagonistic, St Bernard's mysticism shaped his thought in
such a way that he could not appreciate either the aim or the
method of his opponent. The fundamental distinction between their attitudes towards the nature of credal assent has
already been described; the intellectualism of the one was
totally different from the voluntarism of the other. The Saint
did not approach the problems of theology through dialectic
as did Abailard. Basing his theology upon a deep experience
aided by a mystical, ethical method of exegesis,[1] he did not
feel the need of proofs to convince either himself or his
hearers of the reasonableness of the doctrines that were taught
by the church. The coexistence of unity and plurality within
the Godhead was "a great mystery, worthy of all veneration,
which was not keenly to be scrutinized. To examine it closely

1 Ries, *op. cit.* p. 16.

is ", he declares,[1] "rashness, to believe it piety, to know it life and life eternal". Ascetic practices, meditation, and a mystical union with the Bride of the Song of Songs were the means by which Bernard sought to know the mysteries of God. With these preoccupations he could only regard Abailard's attempt to apply logic to theology as an attempt to make all dogma a matter of human opinion. Not only was it sinful, but it was also impossible for man to discuss the truth of doctrines which are immutable in God and far removed from the proper field of human enquiry. Obedient acceptance of the truths of revelation—obedience such as that evidenced by countless martyrs who had chosen to die for their faith— was the correct duty of every Christian man. Anything that might appear even a vague attempt to make belief dependent upon the results of human reasoning was to be scouted, while to investigate the truths of God by the agency of dialectic appeared to St Bernard little short of blasphemy.

Certain of Abailard's particular tenets were especially strange to a man of St Bernard's way of thinking. His own Christology was centred upon the personal Jesus who had suffered on Calvary, and accordingly he could not sympathize with the "nihilistic" tendencies which he found in Abailard, or with his almost exclusive emphasis upon the incarnation of the eternal Word. Although he allowed that without baptism salvation was possible for men, St Bernard held that revelation had been limited to the people of Israel. Thus he was unable to subscribe to any theory which claimed that revealing grace had given some knowledge of Christian doctrines to the philosophers of Greece and Rome. And it was inevitable that he should have been astounded by the exemplarist theory of the Atonement with its apparent derogation from the work of Christ. A theology which seemed to teach that Jesus became incarnate only to teach mankind the Christian life was unsufficing to a man gifted with his

1 Sacramentum hoc magnum est, et quidem venerandum, non scrutandum. ...Scrutari hoc temeritas est, credere pietas est; nosse vita, et vita aeterna est. *De Consid.* v. 7. 18, col. 799 C.

immense devotional genius. Although Bernard held no Calvinist theories concerning the freedom of the will, he was yet a Puritan in his unbending attitude towards every kind of sin. The Fall was a cataclysmic event which had plunged the entire world into the deepest darkness, and from its effects mankind could be rescued only through the suffering of Jesus and through the gift of divine grace. A writer who denied that the guilt of Adam's sin was inherited by man, and who proceeded to declare that a new gift of grace was not needed for each single good deed, appeared to St Bernard as a Pelagian. The doctrine, expressed in the *Scito teipsum*, that intention alone constituted guilt seemed to stultify a large proportion of Christian ethics. To its abbot, Clairvaux was a rigorous school where the athletes of Christ were to train themselves against every impulse of the flesh and against all the suggestions of the devil. By insisting that sins committed in ignorance did not confer guilt, and by teaching that misdeeds may only be judged by the actual intention of the perpetrator, was not Abailard advocating a far less severe system of ethics than that which was warranted by the necessarily high standard of Christian conduct? His denial that priests have the power to absolve men from their sins appeared as an attack on that very ecclesiastical authority which St Bernard was so anxious to defend.

When St Bernard first came to know of Abailard and his teaching is not evident from the facts at our disposal. As Abailard was a well-known figure throughout France and St Bernard himself was in close touch with the events outside his cloister, it seems unlikely that he was unacquainted with Abailard's story long before the council of Sens. We are told that St Bernard was ordained priest in 1115 by no less a personage than William of Champeaux.[1] It is possible that that bishop may have told him of the difficulties which he had experienced at the hands of Abailard during his professorial career at Paris. Both men, we have seen, were present together at Morigny in 1131. Even if St Bernard was

1 *Vita Prima*, I. 7. 31, PL. 185, col. 245.

not then familiar with Abailard's story, he would surely have enquired about the abbot of St Gildas who seemed to be in favour with some members of the papal entourage. Later, on a visit to the Paraclete, the abbot of Clairvaux had criticized an interpretation of the phrase, *panis supersubstantialis*, in the Lord's Prayer, as a reference to the Eucharist, and had received from Abailard a letter defending the exegesis of the nuns. The earlier apprehension which Abailard had felt at Quincey, although unfounded, seems at least to suggest that Bernard knew of Abailard and his theological activity before the latter was elected to St Gildas. Since the chronicler of Morigny does not mention any noticeable estrangement between the two men during their stay at his abbey, and as Abailard in defending the exegesis of the nuns does not refer to any difference of opinion between St Bernard and himself, it seems safe to conclude that Bernard's hostility towards Abailard and his views dates from a period shortly before the meeting at Sens.

In his *Life of St Bernard* Alan states that Abailard was delated to the abbot of Clairvaux,[1] but he does not give the name of the informant. We possess, however, a letter written to St Bernard in which his friend, William of St Thierry, denounces the opinions that he found in the *Theologia*, a book which he happened to read by chance.[2] He had only read, he says,[3] two books of the *Theologia*, although he knew that others existed, among them the *Sic et Non* and the *Scito teipsum*. If he read these other treatises, they would, he felt sure, be found to contain doctrines which were equally outrageous. Among the opinions criticized by William are those of the Atonement and the Eucharist as well as Abailard's denial of the traditional conception of Original Sin. As these doctrines are not discussed in the now extant portion of the *Introductio*—that is, in the first two books and part of the

1 *Vita Secunda*, 26. 71, PL. 185, col. 513 D.
2 Casu nuper incidi in lectionem cujusdam libelli hominis illius cui titulatus erat, Theologia Petri Abaelardi. Bernard, *Ep.* CCCXXVI. PL. 182, col. 531 C.
3 *Ibid.* coll. 531 D, 532 D–533 A.

third—it must be supposed that William had read a possible fourth book of the treatise as well as a complete copy of the third. The other doctrines for which Abailard is criticized are to be found in the second book of the *Introductio*. There is no reason to suppose that the *Epitome* was the source of William's knowledge; since that treatise is not divided into books, it would be impossible to account for the divisions of which William speaks. But not only was William astonished by the novelty of the views expressed; since Abailard's writings were being carried across the seas and over the Alps where they were even said to carry weight amongst the members of the Roman Curia,[1] he was anxious that the teaching of the church should be defended. Now that nearly all the great professors of theology were dead, Abailard, an enemy from within, was attacking the empty republic of the church, seizing for himself the sole magistracy in it. By applying to theology the same methods which he was accustomed to use in dialectic, he was a critic of the faith, not a disciple, a corrector and not an imitator.[2] And so, as he read, William noted down passages which especially aroused his indignation, putting these together in the form of his *Disputatio adversus Abaelardum*.[3] Apart from his close friendship with the abbot, there were few men more able to help him in his aim to prosecute Abailard than St Bernard, who was in many ways the most influential ecclesiastic of the time and was regarded with great respect in those very lands across the Alps, where the writings of Abailard were being studied. He sent, accordingly, a copy of the *Disputatio* to St Bernard with a covering letter in which he explained the reason for his action. The treatise was also sent to Geoffrey of Lèves, bishop of Chartres, who was both a friend of St Bernard and,

1 *Ibid.* col. 531 B.

2 Emortuis quippe ex Ecclesia omnibus paene doctrinae ecclesiasticae magistris, quasi in vacuam rempublicam Ecclesiae domesticus irruens inimicus, singulare sibi in ea magisterium arripuit: agens in Scriptura divina quod agere solebat in dialectica...censor fidei, non discipulus; emendator, non imitator. *Ibid.* 2, col. 532 A. The reference is to the death of Anselm of Laon and of William of Champeaux.

3 PL. 180, coll. 249 ff.

what was perhaps more important, papal legate in France at the time.[1]

To William St Bernard replied that his action was necessary as well as just.[2] He recognized the need for further action, but before anything could be done it would be best for them to meet and discuss the whole question. As the season during which he wrote was one in which their prayers should not be disturbed in any way, Bernard added that their meeting could not take place until after Easter.[3] Unfortunately, we possess no evidence to shew if and when the friends ever conferred together prior to the subsequent meeting at Sens when their proceedings against Abailard were opened. Nor were St Bernard and William of St Thierry the only men who desired the condemnation of Abailard. Writing some time before the council of Sens, of which he makes no mention, Hugh Metellus besought Innocent II to condemn both Abailard and his theology. He was, Hugh declared,[4] a second Phaeton who had mounted the chariot of the true Sun as its driver— into the chariot, that is, of the four Gospels—in order to illumine the world; he had not, however, proceeded on the right course and had ruined himself together with a large part of the world by the fire of his own pride.

According to Geoffrey, one of the contemporary biographers of St Bernard, the abbot of Clairvaux had an interview with Abailard, in which he attempted to persuade him —apparently without success—to alter his views.[5] The historicity of this private meeting is also borne out by a passage in the report of the proceedings at the council of Sens.[6] This

1 Geoffrey was appointed to the so-called Aquitainian legation with oversight over the arch-dioceses of Bourges, Bordeaux, Tours, and Dol in 1130. Cf. Deutsch, *Abälards Verurtheilung*, Berlin, 1880, p. 10.

2 See *Ep.* CCCXXVII. col. 533 A.

3 Idipsum tamen ante Pascha fieri posse non arbitror, ne, quod praesens tempus indicit, studium orationis impediatur. *Ibid.* col. 533 B.

4 Ecce alter Phaeton qui quadrigam veri solis, quadrigam quattuor Evangeliorum, ad illuminandum mundum impetuosus et praesumptuosus auriga ascendit, sed non recto tramite processit, secum multam partem terrae igne superbiae perdidit. *Ep.* IV. Hugo, *Sacrae Antiquitatis Monumenta*, 1731, p. 331.

5 *Vita Bern.* VI. 5. 13, col. 311.

6 *Ep.* CCCXXXVII. 2, col. 541 A.

report further states that Bernard encouraged many of Abailard's students to repudiate his books, which were filled with poison, and to be on their guard against doctrines which were injurious to the Catholic faith.[1] Now we know that at the invitation of the bishop St Bernard visited Paris to address the students assembled there, and we possess his sermon, the *de Conversione ad Clericos*. It is true that this sermon does not refer to any particular heretical doctrine; fully aware of his own inability to argue with scholars who had been trained in dialectic, Bernard may have been unwilling to attack publicly a man against whom he might have been unable to defend himself successfully. Again, he may have preferred to confine himself to a general denunciation of heretical doctrines without mentioning any names, a policy which was more consistent with the character of a sermon. The statement, however, in the report addressed to the pope is clear evidence that Bernard attacked Abailard and his theology. Now we know that Abailard was probably in Paris from 1139 until his appearance at Sens. The visit paid by St Bernard to the Parisian schools is dated 1140,[2] and it is natural to think that his interview with Abailard took place at this time. In his letters St Bernard makes it clear that he knew something of Abailard's mode of life during this period, for he speaks of the French bee buzzing to the bee from Italy,[3] thus indicating that he was familiar with the acquaintance of Abailard and Arnold of Brescia.

The actual summoning of the assembly at Sens was not, however, due to any action on the part of St Bernard. The criticisms which the Saint levelled against his theology strengthened Abailard in his earlier belief that the abbot was working to effect his ruin. True to his character as a dialec-

---

1 Plures autem scholarium adhortatus est ut et libros venenis plenos repudiarent et rejicerent, et a doctrina quae fidem laedebat catholicam, caverent et abstinerent. *Ibid.* col. 541 B.

2 Vacandard, II. p. 115.

3 *Ep.* CLXXXIX. 3, col. 355 B. Bernard was evidently thinking of "the Lord shall hiss for the fly..." in Isaiah vii. 18. Cf. also *Ep.* CCCXXX. col. 353 C.

tician, he was apparently anxious to hold a public disputation in which he could prove and defend the catholicity of his theological position. Dialectical argument was the method whereby Abailard held that heretics were to be persuaded of their errors; the same method was to be employed to silence his own detractors. But, to judge from a letter of Abailard's which has recently been discovered, it was his students who petitioned Henry le Sanglier, archbishop of Sens, to arrange for a public disputation between Abailard and the abbot of Clairvaux.[1] That they should have addressed themselves to the archbishop, who was a close friend of St Bernard, is at first somewhat surprising, and various explanations have' been put forward. We have noticed that a canonry at Sens was associated with Abailard's name, and it is possible that he was then holding his benefice; but, as he was probably residing at Paris, this preferment would not have placed him under the jurisdiction of the archbishop. The noteworthy absence of Stephen, bishop of Paris, suggests a far more likely reason for the students' application to Henry. It is possible that Stephen was absent, and thus it would have been correct for an appeal to have been lodged with the metropolitan of the province. The newly discovered letter from which I have just quoted gives what was certainly the real reason for their choice. Reference is there made to the hostile attitude which Stephen adopted towards Abailard,[2] and it is plain that the students held that an appeal to the bishop would have been useless. Stephen's hostility had doubtless been shewn by his invitation to St Bernard to preach before the Parisian students.

Now it happened that the archbishop was planning a display of relics in his church on the octave of Whitsun. To this he had invited the bishops of his own province and those of Rheims, together with a large concourse of distinguished men,

1 Heidelberg Cod. 359. 8, folio 15 v. The letter (ff. 14 v.–15 v.) has been found by Dr R. Klibansky and will be published by him. The University librarian has kindly supplied me with photographs.
2 *Ibid.*

including the king.[1] This projected assembly seemed opportune for the disputation demanded. A trial of strength between St Bernard and the most renowned logician of all
France would provide an additional attraction to the meeting.
Informed of the archbishop's decision, Abailard addressed
the Heidelberg letter to some of his students, begging them
to come to Sens and aid him in his defence. Such a disputation was the very last thing that St Bernard desired. He did
not feel that he possessed the necessary equipment to withstand the dialectical ingenuity of his opponent. Only when
he heard that Abailard was summoning his students to his
aid did he consent to come. Burning with the fire of the
Holy Spirit and fearing that his absence would make possible
the utterance of profane and foolish opinions which would
seem authoritative both to their defenders and to men of insufficient understanding, he came to Sens.[2]

It is most unfortunate that the letters dealing with the
events of the assembly do not mention the year in which the
exposition of relics took place. The older view, supported by
Robert of Auxerre, held that the assembly met in 1140.[3] The
relics would then have been exposed on Sunday, June 2nd,
and Abailard would have been heard on the following day.
Deutsch, however, put forward evidence by which he attempted to shew that the assembly did not come together

1 Jacques de Vitry (ob. 1240) states that Louis had forbidden Abailard to
teach in his land. Whereupon Abailard took a small boat and taught his
"disciples" who stood on the river bank. When he was summoned before the
king, he replied that he had not taught on the land, but on the water. The king
then acknowledged that he had been beaten. See J. Greven, Die Exempla aus
den Sermones feriales et communes des J. von Vitry, Heidelberg, 1914, p. 36. The
story is certainly apocryphal and certain scriptural parallels seem to be suggested, but it illustrates the fame of Abailard's dialectical power.

2 Sed quia Magister Petrus interim suos nihilominus coepit undequaque
convocare discipulos, et obsecrare ut ad futuram inter se dominumque
abbatem Clarae-Vallensem disputationem una cum illo sententiam simul et
scientiam defensuri venerint, et hoc dominum Clarae-Vallensem minime
lateret; veritus ipse ne propter occasionem absentiae suae tot profanae, non
sententiae sed insaniae, tam apud minus intelligentes, quam earumdem defen-
sores majore dignae viderentur auctoritate. Ep. cccxxxvii. 2, col. 541 CD.

3 Chron. MGH.SS. xxvi. p. 235; cf. Revelatio Sancti Eleutherii, Acta Sanctorum, Feb. iii. p. 196.

until May 25th, 1141. His argument is based upon the date
which he found it necessary to assign to the consecration of
Samson as archbishop of Rheims. Samson, we know,[1] was
present at Sens, where he is alluded to as archbishop. Now
his predecessor, Rainald of Martigné, died on January 13th,
1139, and, we are informed, there was a vacancy in the arch-
bishopric for two years. Samson's consecration would then
have to be dated 1141. This, however, is not conclusive
evidence. It is quite possible that the consecration could have
taken place in 1140, the chronicler reckoning as two years
the remainder of 1139 after the death of Rainald and the part
of 1140 prior to the consecration of Samson. More weighty
evidence is provided by two documents belonging to the city
of Rheims. These make it clear that Samson could not have
been consecrated before August 1st, 1140, for they equate the
seventh year of his episcopate with the tenth and eleventh
years of the reign of Louis VII. That king did not come to the
throne until August 1st, 1137, and so the eleventh year of his
reign did not commence until August 1st, 1147. Thus, we
are forced to date the consecration of Samson some time after
August 1st, 1140, and, since Samson is mentioned as the
archbishop of Rheims, the assembly cannot have met until
1141.[2] Again, we are told that Alvisus, bishop of Arras, was
at Sens. On the Wednesday of Whitsun week, 1140, he was
present at the monastery of Marchiennes for the translation
of St Rictrude.[3] As Marchiennes is over thirty miles from
Sens, Deutsch considered it unlikely, though not impossible,
for Alvisus to have arrived at the cathedral city in time.[4]
Lastly, Deutsch refers to a letter written to Peter the Venerable by Hatto of Tours in which the bishop speaks of the
peace in France after the king's return from his campaign,

1 Bernard, *ibid.* and *Revelatio, loc. cit.*
2 Deutsch, *Verurtheilung*, pp. 50–54, quoting P. Varin, *Archives administra-
tives de la ville de Rheims*, I. 1, p. 296.
3 *Miracula S. Rictrudis*, II. 4. 45, *Acta Sanctorum*, May, III. Alvisus was
bishop from 1131 to 1148; he had previously been abbot of the Benedictine
house of Avesnes, founded in 1128.
4 Deutsch, *Verurtheilung*, p. 53.

adding that Nicholas—presumably the messenger sent to
Rome by St Bernard with the reports of the proceedings
against Abailard—was with him as he wrote.[1] Deutsch dates
this letter September, 1141, thinking that the campaign referred to was the siege of Toulouse undertaken by the king
in the summer of 1141.

The year 1141, however, seems an impossible one for the
meeting of the assembly, despite the evidence produced by
Deutsch. According to Ordericus Vitalis,[2] the campaign
against Toulouse was begun on the Feast of St John Baptist
(June 24th), 1141. Even in the twelfth century the summoning
and equipment of a large army must have necessitated much
organization; it is therefore difficult to understand how Louis
could have spared the time to be present at Sens, which, if it
had happened in 1141, could have occurred only a calendar
month before his departure for the south. The evidence provided by the itinerary of bishop Alvisus is of little account.
Even allowing for the bad state of the roads, the bishop
could, as Deutsch himself allows, have accomplished so short
a journey in the time, had his presence at Sens been required.
Further, there is nothing to shew that Hatto's letter to Peter
the Venerable was written in the same year as the assembly at
Sens. Nicholas was a close friend of the abbot of Cluny and,
though he could easily have returned from Rome by harvest-
time, no matter in which year the assembly took place, we
cannot conclude that the letter was sent when Nicholas was
staying with Hatto on his return from Italy. The bishop of
Tours would naturally have mentioned his presence if
Nicholas had been at Tours at any time when he happened
to be writing to Cluny. And, though it seems certain that the
campaign referred to was indeed the one directed against
Toulouse, Nicholas might well have visited Hatto in 1141—
on other business.

St Bernard was determined to effect the condemnation of
Abailard at all costs, and he was apparently not over-

1 Peter the Venerable, *Ep.* lib. IV. 2, PL. 189, coll. 303-4.
2 *Hist. Eccles.* XIII. 2, PL. 188, col. 981 B.

scrupulous about the means to be employed. Abailard's refusal to emend his theological views warranted drastic action in the interests of the church. No risks were to be run; his condemnation must be ensured. And so, on the night preceding the meeting which was to hear Abailard, St Bernard called the bishops together and read to them the charges which he intended to prefer against the philosopher of Le Pallet. These charges were different from those drawn up by William of St Thierry both in the number and the order of the *capitula*. While William, as we have said, derived his list from the *Introductio* only, the charges read at Sens and afterwards sent to the pope came from the *Scito teipsum* and the *Epitome* as well.[1] We have no information as to who composed the list brought forward by St Bernard. The historicity of this meeting has been questioned by Wilhelm Meyer on the ground that the use of such methods was incompatible with St Bernard's noble character,[2] but the evidence at our command does not permit us to accept his view. The bishops themselves admit that they came together on the day previous to the council and condemned the theological opinions of Abailard,[3] while two contemporary writers, John of Salisbury and Berengar, refer to the meeting. John of Salisbury declares that Bernard employed against Gilbert Porrée the same methods which he had used against Abailard. He tells us that at the council of Rheims (1148) the Saint secretly arranged a meeting prior to the opening of the council, and that there it had been agreed that Gilbert should be condemned, the cardinals who were in charge of the council protesting afterwards to Eugenius III against the unconstitutional behaviour of St Bernard.[4] The tractate which the

1 The charges are best given in W. Meyer, "Die Anklagesätze des hl. Bernhards gegen Abaelard", in *Göttingen Nachrichten*, 1898, pp. 432 ff. Cf. Haec capitula partim in libro Theologiae, partim in libro Sententiarum magistri Petri, partim in libro cujus titulus est Scito teipsum reperta sunt. *Ibid.* p. 432.

2 *Ibid.* p. 410.

3 Pridie ante factam ad vos appellationem damnavimus. Bernard, *Ep.* CCCXXXVII. 4, col. 542 C.

4 *Hist. Pontif.* 9, pp. 20–21; the letter is given in full by Otto of Freising, *Gesta Fred.* I. 60, pp. 85–6.

monk, Berengar, wrote in defence of Abailard, is a piece of party-diatribe, almost worthless as evidence, yet he refers to this meeting of the bishops on the night before the council of Sens was opened. When the errors of Abailard were read, some of the audience were so sleepy and heavy with wine that in their attempt to pronounce *Damnamus*, they only succeeded, Berengar tells us,[1] in mumbling *Namus*. The details of the meeting must certainly be dismissed as libellous, but the account of the meeting of the bishops and of their condemnation of Abailard must be regarded as founded on fact. And so we may take it that on the night preceding the council some at least of the bishops assembled and agreed to censure Abailard.

The plan to which the bishops, under the instigation of St Bernard, had consented was, however, stultified by the action of Abailard himself. When the abbot of Clairvaux propounded the *Theologia*, calling upon Abailard either to deny his authorship or, if he accepted the book as his, to prove or to correct the views it contained, Abailard seemed to hesitate and to be unwilling to answer. He then appealed from the assembly to the pope. Much was made by the bishops in their report of the free hearing in a safe place before unbiased judges which was accorded to Abailard, and they were evidently much surprised and not a little annoyed when he made his appeal and left the assembly.[2] But in so doing, it is clear that he made no open attack upon the integrity of the assembly.[3] Later, he refused to accept as his a book called the *Sentences* from which, as we have seen, St Bernard had drawn some of his charges.[4] This book was almost certainly the *Epitome*

1 PL. 178, col. 1858 CD.

2 Dominus abbas cum librum Theologiae magistri Petri proferret in medium, et quae adnotavit, absurda, imo haeretica plane capitula de libro eodem proponeret, ut ea magister Petrus vel a se scripta negaret, vel si sua fateretur, aut probaret aut corrigeret, visus diffidere magister Petrus Abaelardus et subterfugere, respondere noluit, et quamvis libera sibi daretur audientia tutumque locum et aequos haberet judices, ad vestram tamen, sanctissime Pater, appellans praesentiam cum suis a conventu discessit. *Ep.* CCCXXXVII. 3, col. 542 AB.   3 See Bernard, *Epp.* CXCI, CLXXXVII.

4 *Responsio*, PL. 180, col. 332 B.

written by one of his students. But during the council he does not seem to have preferred any complaint against his treatment, nor does he appear to have made any comment upon the nature of the heretical doctrines which he was supposed to have held. Apparently the whole of his defence was contained in the *Apologia* addressed to St Bernard before the assembly met. There can be no doubt, however, that he was sorely disappointed by the turn that events had taken, and he was apprehensive about the result. He had understood that the meeting was to be a public disputation in which he was to defend himself against the imputations cast upon his doctrines. Instead, he found himself confronted with an assembly which had all the outward appearance of an ecclesiastical council, summoned to try a case of heresy in which he was to play the part of the defendant. Possibly he may have had some information concerning the events on the previous evening, but of this there is no evidence, and he makes no reference to the decision of the bishops. But, with a great deal of truth, he could have claimed that the archbishop had not been straightforward. Standing before the assembly, he must have remembered his treatment at the council of Soissons when the mob had been stirred up against him by Alberic and Lotulf. At Rome he had friends—doubtless some of his former pupils—and in that city he would at least be ensured an unprejudiced hearing.

Although such an appeal seemed to them uncanonical, the bishops had no other alternative than that of deferring to the Holy See and of suspending their own sentence.[1] Accordingly, they sent to Innocent II a report of their transactions, being careful to point out the widespread evil influence of Abailard's theology. Nor did they fail to add that they had themselves agreed to condemn him as a heretic.[2] At the same time St Bernard also wrote letters demanding that a sentence of excommunication should be passed. One of these letters he addressed to the pope himself, while others were sent to some

1 *Ep.* cccxxxvii. 4, col. 542 B.
2 *Ep.* cccxxx. col. 535.

of the cardinals with whom he was, doubtless, acquainted. Among these were Stephen of Praeneste, a Cistercian;[1] Guido of Castello, the future pope Calixtus II, who had once been a pupil under Abailard;[2] and Ivo, cardinal of St Laurence, who is roundly scolded for the popularity with which the books of Abailard were received at Rome.[3] All these letters were apparently despatched to Rome by Nicholas, St Bernard's secretary. Innocent II answered the appeal of the bishops by confirming the sentence they had agreed upon and placing Abailard under a ban of excommunication,[4] and his books were burnt at St Peter's in Rome.[5]

Leaving Sens, Abailard set out for Italy to lay his case before the pope. On the way he turned aside to visit Cluny, the abbot of which, Peter the Venerable, happened at the time to be on unfriendly terms with St Bernard. The cause of their friction was a difference of opinion between the two congregations of Cluny and Clairvaux upon the way in which the Rule of St Benedict should be observed. The Cluniacs, a rich congregation who were known for their love of scholarship, their beautiful churches and their comparatively easy mode of life, regarded the poverty and the artistic Puritanism of the Cistercians as pharisaical. St Bernard had already addressed to William of St Thierry an apology for the severity of his congregation and an attack upon what he held to be Cluniac ease. Whether Abailard knew of this estrangement between the two congregations in the Benedictine fold is not known. He certainly could not have gone to a more sympathetic adviser than Peter the Venerable, who counselled him to prosecute his appeal, telling him that Apostolic justice never failed.[6] While Abailard was at Cluny, the abbot

1 *Ep.* cccxxxi. col. 536; cf. *Vita Prima*, ii. 8. 49, PL. 185, col. 297 B.
2 *Ep.* cxcii. col. 358.   3 *Ep.* cxciii. col. 359.
4 See Jaffé-Löwenfeld, *Regesta*, No. 5767, and Otto of Freising, *Gesta Fred.* i. 50, pp. 72-3. The bull is dated July 21st and Jaffé has followed Deutsch in adding the year. It must be assumed that the bull was issued in the same year as the assembly met, and this would have given Nicholas six weeks—ample time—in which to reach Rome.
5 Gaufred, *de Condemn. Gilb. Porret.* 14, PL. 185, col. 596 A.
6 *Ep.* lib. iv. 4, PL. 189, col. 305 C.

of Cîteaux arrived. Admonishing him to retract and expunge from his books anything that he might have written or said which was offensive to Catholic ears, Peter advised Abailard to return with the abbot of Cîteaux, presumably to make his peace with St Bernard. Abailard wisely acted upon this advice, and through the mediation of the Cistercian abbot he made his peace with St Bernard, and then returned to Cluny. The abbot and the monks there counselled him to forsake the tumults of the lecture-halls, and he himself chose a "perpetual mansion" in their abbey. On account of his age and the weak state of his health, thinking it suitable to his profession as a monk, the chapter consented to his request. Peter the Venerable thereupon wrote to the pope,[1] asking him to allow Abailard to remain at Cluny and enclosing a confession of faith which Abailard had drawn up.[2] Abailard was thus reconciled with St Bernard, while the old conflict between the Cluniacs and the Cistercians was ended. And in either 1142 or 1143 we find Peter the Venerable sending to St Bernard his book against the followers of Peter de Bruys, accompanied by a letter couched in the most glowing terms of appreciation.[3]

At Cluny Abailard's humble devotion astounded the abbot and his monks; his health and the difficulties which he had experienced at St Gildas had evidently softened his character and, a sick man, already sixty years of age, he was totally different from the turbulent professor who had caused such great trouble both at St Denys and at St Médard. Content with the plainest clothing and the simplest food, taking only what was needful, he spent his time at Cluny in reading and prayer. Only when the brothers themselves initiated a discussion upon matters of theology did he break his silence.[4] The monks, indeed, found him to be a righteous man who feared God and kept himself from evil. Nor did he give up

1 *Ep.* lib. IV. 4, PL. 189, coll. 305-6.
2 PL. 178, coll. 105-8.   3 *Ep.* lib. IV. 17, coll. 321 ff.
4 Peter the Venerable, *Ep.* lib. IV. 21, PL. 189, coll. 350-51; *Vita altera, ibid.* col. 54.

entirely his literary work, for it was at Cluny that he wrote his *Apologia*, his *Monitum* to Astralabe, and his Dialogue between a Philosopher, a Christian, and a Jew, the last being intended as his chief book upon ethics. But his health did not improve and, thinking that a better climate would be more suitable, Peter the Venerable sent him to Châlons-sur-Saône, to a daughter-house of Cluny dedicated to St Marcellus. There Abailard died on April 21st, 1142. Following a practice which certainly dates back to the time of Gregory the Great, Peter absolved the dead man from his sins, sending the charter of absolution to Héloise at her request. The worthy abbot also promised to procure some prebend for the young Astralabe.[1] For Abailard Peter the Venerable composed an epitaph which, as it bears witness to the regard in which the philosopher was held at Cluny, may well be quoted here:

Gallorum Socrates, Plato maximus Hesperiarum,
Noster Aristoteles, logicis, quicunque fuerunt,
Aut par, aut melior: studiorum cognitus orbi
Princeps; ingenio varius, subtilis, et acer;
Omnia vi superans rationis, et arte loquendi
Abaelardus erat; sed tunc magis omnia vicit,
Cum Cluniacensem monachum moremque professus,
Ad Christi veram transivit philosophiam.
In qua longaevae bene complens ultima vitae,
Philosophis quandoque bonis se connumerandum
Spem dedit, undenas Maio revocante Kalendas.[2]

True to his own profession, Peter neglects any mention of Abailard's residence either at St Denys or at St Gildas; he could not withstand the temptation to refer to the superiority of his own Cluniac congregation.

II

How far the condemnation of Abailard first by the bishops assembled at Sens and then by the pope may be regarded as just is a difficult matter to decide. Abailard himself never seems to have questioned the authority of the meeting, nor

1 *Epp.* lib. VI. 21 and 22, coll. 427–8, 429.
2 PL. 178, col. 103; PL. 189, coll. 329–32.

does he appear to have doubted the propriety of his sentence, once it had been promulgated and ratified at Rome. He made no attempt to prove the soundness of his theology as he had wished to do in a disputation between himself and St Bernard. Instead, he retracted those opinions to which exception had been taken, and retired to the secluded peace of Cluny. His ill-health had clearly deprived him of his old love for public disputation, while his age and his approaching end made him apprehensive of the final result if he remained hostile and un-reconciled to the expressed authority of the church. This fear was surely responsible for his declaration that he did not wish to be a philosopher and to be cut off from Christ and St Paul.[1] His submission to the decree of the pope, his reconciliation with St Bernard, his obvious desire not to discuss problems of theology with the monks of Cluny, and his letter to Héloise, all indicate a very fundamental change. Far from desiring to continue the defence which he had so long been making against his various critics, he now accepted as final the sentence passed upon his writings and wished only to remain in peace with the church. At St Médard Gosvin had called him "that rhinoceros", but to the brethren at Cluny Abailard seemed a peaceful, quiet old man, wholly lacking that self-assertiveness which had formerly characterized his attitude to ecclesiastical authority.

Berengar, however, continued his defence of his former master for some little time. In his scurrilous apology, written with a pompous show of classical and patristic allusion, he argued that the condemnation was unjust, since, owing to the secret assembly of the bishops on the previous night, Abailard had not been afforded a hearing. Against the influence of St Bernard with the bishops and with the pope he had no chance of defending himself. Not content with this attack upon the council, Berengar proceeded to deliver a violent and entirely unjustifiable onslaught upon St Bernard's sermons on the Song of Songs, and, disappointed at the ill-success of this pamphlet, he issued another, which has not

1 *Ep.* xvii. col. 357 c.

survived. As we might expect from the libellous character of the treatise we possess, neither pamphlet had the desired effect. Even the monks of the Grande Chartreuse were aroused from their self-imposed silence to attack the monk who dared to criticize the abbot of Clairvaux. The letter in which Berengar answered the Carthusians is extant, but its flattery of their Rule, coupled with the assertion that they had fallen from their original purity, only infuriated the monks the more against him,[1] and he was forced to leave his native Poitiers for the district of the Cevennes. Terrified by the antagonism of the Grande Chartreuse, he felt it necessary to appeal for protection to the bishop of Mende.[2] The cardinal sub-deacon, Hyacinth, also threatened to defend Abailard before the Curia at Rome, but we have no record of his attempt and nothing came of it.[3] Apart from Berengar's diatribes and the threats of Hyacinth, no voice seems to have been raised in his defence until Robert of Melun attempted to shew that his ascription of the three attributes of Power, Wisdom, and Goodness to the three Persons was justified both by ecclesiastical authority and by theological considerations. His pupils scattered directly Abailard left the assembly and, so far as we know, did not attempt to rehabilitate the good character of their master.

It is quite clear that St Bernard and William of St Thierry had two objects in view when they sought to procure the condemnation of Abailard. They wished to stop his activities as a professor and to prevent the study of his books. To them Abailard appeared as a man who wished to make the articles of the Creeds dependent upon human reasoning, regarding opinion as the criterion of belief and subjecting traditional theology to the solvent of logical analysis. That they erred in their estimation of his objects and attainments is certain, but there was much truth in their claim that his theology must be censured. Abailard, indeed, had no real appreciation of the

1 PL. 178, coll. 1873-4.
2 *Ibid.* coll. 1875-6; cf. *Hist. litt.* XII. p. 251.
3 Bernard, *Ep.* CLXXXIX. 5, col. 357.A; Vacandard, II. p. 158.

historic experience of the church. He was indeed learned in what may be called patristic case-law, and his knowledge of this is well illustrated by the many quotations from the Fathers given in the *Sic et Non*, but he had no full conception of Christian theology as a unified whole. His writing lacks that tone of peace and solidarity which is so characteristic of St Anselm of Canterbury. Though there is naturally some interdependence of thought in each of his two big theological books, Abailard seems to have regarded each doctrine as a proposition—akin to those of logic—separate and complete in itself. In Anselm, on the other hand, there is no straining after the impossible, no interpretation of a doctrine which jars because it is out of harmony with all that we may or can experience. St Bernard, as we know, built his theology upon mystical intuition and vision, seeking to interpret the teaching of authority through the experience which he had himself felt, and to a large extent the greatness of his thought is due to his intuitive sense of harmony with the experience of the historic church. A man of tremendous religious gifts, he could appreciate the religious significance of the credal formulae drawn up by the Fathers. The school of St Victor, again, although its members relied to a great extent upon dialectic, based their theology on the facts of experience, whether that experience was their own or that of the entire church. Eminently conservative in their outlook, they held fast to the belief that all theological activity must proceed from a thorough and intimate knowledge of the whole stand-point of any patristic writer. That is the reason why in Hugh of St Victor—as indeed in Anselm of Canterbury—we meet with a sympathetic presentation of the theology of St Augustine, although no mention of his name and but little quotation from his writings are made. With a very great deal of truth, St Bernard could have argued—and he must have realized—that the mere application of the methods of dialectic to the problems of theology, no matter with what con-servative aim, must by itself lead to theological bankruptcy, unless it was balanced by some such knowledge of the experience and religious feeling of the historic church. Did Abailard not appear to Bernard as dangerous to the well-being of theology as he had himself considered Cornificius destructive to the best interests of logic? A man to whom the welfare of the church was always exceedingly precious, St Bernard felt himself bound to take action against Abailard with a view to preventing the influence of his theology. Every means therefore seemed justifiable, even if his policy of persuading the bishops to agree to a condemnation before the case was heard may appear unjust. To him, at least, Abailard's heretical views as shewn by his writings were sufficient to warrant his condemnation; his guilt, unless he retracted his opinions or denied his authorship, could not be gainsaid. A debate in which he was to play David to Abailard's Goliath was certainly not what St Bernard desired, for he considered himself unequal to a contest with the most renowned dialectician in all Europe. And public disputations did not fit in with his conception either of theological method or of ecclesiastical authority. Whether St Bernard most feared the influence of the theological doctrines put forward by Abailard, such as those of the Trinity or of Christology, or whether his dread of his opponent's dialectical method drove him to the attack, is an interesting problem upon which we have little evidence. The criticism brought against Abailard by other writers—such as Walter of Mortagne—suggests that they at least were chiefly afraid of the unhappy results which might follow from any such application of the method of the logicians to the problems of theology. To a large extent their apprehension was supported by the unorthodox character of his opinions. This fear, evidently, was shared by St Bernard, who made much of the unsuitability of Abailard's dialectical method; and from the prominence accorded to his criticism of Abailard's methodology we may take it that the sentence delivered at Sens was as much due to a dispute over the proper character of scholastic method as to the consequences of Abailard's dialectic—the unorthodoxy of his views.

In their attempt to stultify the influence exerted by Abailard

St Bernard and William of St Thierry were largely successful, and they did much to check the possible excesses to which his theology might lead. Abailard cannot now be said to have been so important in the history of scholastic method as critics once thought. The two views that he was the originator of the scholastic disputation so typical of the mediaeval schools,[1] and that the *Sic et Non* method was his own invention must be discarded, and with them the idea that he had no disciples who reiterated at least some of his characteristic opinions. Disputation is the method whereby arguments *pro* and *contra* were put forward by opposing sides, logic being employed to prove one set and refute the other.[2] The nature of this procedure can well be illustrated by reference to the pages of the two great *Summae* of Aquinas. The practice of holding disputations is much older than the time of Abailard. It certainly dates back to Greek philosophy, to Aristotle in particular, and it was employed by Christian theologians in the East as early as the sixth and seventh centuries.[3] Evidence of its use in the West before the time of Abailard is also forthcoming. At Munich Dr Grabmann has discovered a MS. dating from the eleventh century in which the merits of such disputations are praised,[4] while at the end of his *de Grammatico* Anselm of Canterbury speaks of its practice.[5] Abailard, too, states that he held a disputation with William of Champeaux over the question of the nature of universals.[6] But, as John of Salisbury intimately connects the holding of stereotyped, regular and formal disputations with the advent of the New Logic,[7] it would appear that such a formal method was unknown before his time. Indeed, this novel form of disputation seems to have been one of the chief results of the access to fresh portions of the Aristotelian *Organon* then made

---

1 Denifle, ALKG. i. p. 745.
2 Cf. John of Salisbury, *Metal.* ii. 4, col. 860 c.
3 In what Grabmann calls the *Aporienliteratur*, in writers such as Alexander of Aphrodisias and Dexippus, i. pp. 101 ff.
4 ii. p. 16, citing Munich MS. Clm. 14401, ff. 154 r.–196 r.
5 21, PL. 158, col. 582 A.   6 *Hist. Calam.* 2, col. 116 A.
7 *Metal.* iii. 10, col. 910 c.

available to the Christian scholars of the West. And that this new method of disputation was known during the lifetime of John is evident, for we are told that both Robert of Melun and Maurice of Sully made use of it in their theology. So recognized, indeed, did the new method become in their hands that John of Cornwall could make a clear distinction between *disputatio* and the old method, the *lectio*.[1]

Our conclusion must therefore be that the *Sic et Non* exerted no really novel influence upon the development of the scholastic method of disputation. Indeed, we should have hardly expected the case to have been otherwise. As we know, the book is simply a collection of opposing biblical and patristic statements, and in it no attempt is made to effect a *Concordia discordantium*. Although in his discussion of the Atonement Abailard gives a *solutio* to a problem which he has stated in the form of a *quaestio*, the characteristics of the later formal disputation are entirely lacking. And, despite the fact that Roland adopted a somewhat more formal method, our conclusion is true of those writers who followed Abailard in his theology. These writers sometimes marshal their arguments *pro* and *contra*, but they lack the stereotyped formality which is first to be found in books written by Parisian masters in the mid-twelfth century. Nor, as we have argued, is Abailard to be regarded as the founder of the *Sic et Non* method which, in its more developed form, was accepted by successive theologians throughout the later Middle Ages. The method itself was derived from the efforts of earlier canonists to reduce their authorities to some order, as may be seen from the aspirations and writings of lawyers from Hincmar to Bernold of Constance. Hence I doubt whether Abailard influenced Gratian in the composition of his *Decretal* as much as scholars in the past have asserted. They considered that the method of Gratian's book was borrowed from the *Sic et Non*, probably through the agency of Roland Bandinelli, who taught theology at Bologna at the time when the *Decretal* was written. The writings of the canonists of the early twelfth

1 *Eulogium ad Alexandrum III*, PL. 199, col. 1055 A.

century have not been fully studied, but it appears certain that a closer examination of their character will shew that Gratian was using a method which had been known during the previous hundred years. In his *Liber de Misericordia*, written before the year 1121, Alger of Liège employed the same method, and from the many citations made by Gratian, it is clear that that work was used in the task of compiling the *Decretal*.[1]

The influence of Abailard upon his successors is to be traced in a new concern with patristic and scriptural quotation more than in their acceptance of the various doctrines which he taught. The wealth of patristic learning apparent in the *Sentences* of Anselm of Laon must not be forgotten, but in those writers who were directly influenced by Abailard an even greater and certainly more general preoccupation with the value of quoting the opinions of authority is to be discerned. Citations from authority were given either to add weight to some conclusion which the writer desired to draw or to support the tenability of a position he desired to uphold. This preoccupation is not met with in the books of men like Hugh of St Victor who, though they were thoroughly conversant with the opinions held by Abailard, were never members of his school. It is, however, evident in the *Summa Sententiarum*, a treatise often erroneously attributed to Hugh,[2] which bears the clear marks of an Abailardian influence. The same preoccupation is also patent in the *Sentences* of Peter the Lombard who, we know, was taught by Abailard. Their method is wholly different from that of earlier theologians such as Anselm of Canterbury. It was certainly not their

1 See G. Le Bras, "Le Liber de misericordia et justitia d'Alger de Liège", *Nouvelle Revue historique de droit français et étranger*, XLV. 1921, pp. 116–17; J. B. Sägmüller, *Lehrbuch des kath. Kirchenrechts*, 1. 4th ed. Freiburg, 1926, p. 232.

2 The authorship of the treatise has given rise to much discussion. See P. Chossat, *La Somme de Sentences*, Louvain, 1923. In most MSS. the author is given as Hugh, and Chossat suggests Hugh of Mortagne. Richard of Poitou (*Chron.* MGH.SS. XXVI. p. 81) does not mention the *Summa* in his list of Hugh of St Victor's writings. The wide differences of thought and method in the *Summa* and the authentic *de Sacramentis* seem to militate against a common authorship. See C. Bouuart, *Revue de l'histoire eccl.* X. 1909, pp. 710–19.

ignorance of patristic literature that was responsible for the paucity of their quotations; rather, spurning the need of support from authority in the form of citation, they considered it sufficient for their own opinions to stand by themselves.

But in spite of his condemnation Abailard was not entirely without influence upon later theology. Subsequent writers, indeed, rejected many of his characteristic theories—for instance, his denial of the traditional doctrine of Original Sin[1] and of the complete omnipotence of God[2]—but the very fact of their criticism made Abailard negatively influential in the development of mediaeval theology. However unacceptable his own theories may have been, he at least raised many problems which theologians at some time or other would have had to meet. His doctrine of the Atonement did not survive, although, possibly as the result of his teaching, both the Lombard and Thomas Aquinas emphasized the humility of Christ shewn by his Incarnation as opposed to the pride of Adam.[3] His ethics seem to have exerted no influence, and would at any rate have been superseded when the *Nicomachaean Ethics* were translated. Except for his probable influence upon the Lombard, his Christological theories also vanished. The mantle of Abailard, however, fell upon one interesting set of twelfth-century theologians, upon the writers of the *Epitome* and the so-called St Florian *Sentences*, and on both Omnibene and Roland Bandinelli, later pope Alexander III. Not all of these four writers accepted the teaching of Abailard with the same loyalty. As we might well expect from a future pope, Roland rejected those doctrines which appeared to him doubtful, while there is evidence to shew that Omnibene knew of Roland's work and incorporated many of his criticisms.[4]

1 Hugh of St Victor, *de Sacrament*. I. 7. 28, col. 298; *Summa Sentent*. III. 11, col. 106; Peter Lombard, II. dist. 30. 5.
2 Hugh, I. 2. 22, coll. 214–15; *Summa Sentent*. I. 14, coll. 68–79; Lombard, I. distt. 43–4. Cf. Aquinas, *Summa Theol*. I. quaest. 25, art. 5, and *c. Gentiles*, II. 3.   3 *Sentent*. dist. 18. 5; *Summa Theol*. III. quaest. 1. ad 4.
4 Gietl, p. liii.

All these four writers took over from Abailard his division of the three theological virtues into faith, charity, and the sacraments,[1] as well as his analogy of the copper seal, employing it, as Abailard had done, to illustrate the Generation of the Son and the Double Procession of the Holy Spirit.[2] Only two writers, however—those of the *Epitome* and the *Sentences* of St Florian—followed him in his definition of faith as *existimatio*.[3] These two authors also reproduced Abailard's account of the doctrine of the Trinity with its emphasis upon the several attributes of Power, Wisdom, and Goodness,[4] together with his denial of the full omnipotence of God.[5] With Omnibene they held to his theory of Original Sin as guilt alone inherited from the sin of Adam,[6] and to his exemplarist doctrine of the Atonement.[7] Roland, as I have had occasion to note during my description of Abailard's theology, refused to accept most of the characteristic doctrines contained in the *Introductio*. His study of Abailard had, however, an unfortunate influence upon his Christology. With the very unsatisfactory way in which Abailard treated of the hypostatic Union of the two natures before him, he felt himself unable to draw the "nihilistic" conclusions found in Peter Lombard. Consequently, he was forced to reject the Abailardian theories that the divine and human natures were parts of Christ,[8] and that divinity was separated from the body of Jesus at the moment of his death.[9] While allowing, as against Abailard, that Jesus is a third Person in the Trinity, Roland had no real understanding of what the phrase, *Christus est tertia persona in Trinitate*, meant, nor did he fully know what was implied by the hypostatic Union.[10] Like

1 *Epitome*, 1, col. 1695 A; St Florian, 1, ed. Ostlender, p. 1; Roland, p. 1; Omnibene, f. 151, in Denifle, ALKG. 1. p. 461.
2 *Epitome*, 12, col. 1715 C; St Florian, 10, p. 5; Omnibene, f. 150, p. 460; Roland, p. 28.
3 *Epitome*, 2, col. 1697; St Florian, 1, p. 1.
4 *Epitome*, 5, coll. 1699 ff.; St Florian, 7, pp. 3-4.
5 *Epitome*, 20, coll. 1724 ff.; St Florian, 22, pp. 9 ff.
6 *Epitome*, 33, coll. 1752 ff.; St Florian, 54, p. 26; Omnibene, f. 181, p. 461.
7 *Epitome*, 23, col. 1730; St Florian, 30, p. 14; Omnibene, f. 185, p. 461.
8 P. 174.   9 P. 192.   10 P. 175; cf. Gietl, pp. xxx–xxxiii.

Peter Lombard and Aquinas, Roland pointed to the lesson in humility given by the earthly life of Christ but, unlike them, he accepted the exemplarist theory of the Atonement.[1]

Abailard then founded no lasting school of theology at Paris. Whether or not Abailard actually taught within the precincts of Ste Geneviève is unknown, but once he had left the city none of his pupils carried on his school. The abbey of Ste Geneviève was reformed in 1147 by some Cluniacs, and their place was subsequently taken by canons from St Victor. An end was then made to the teaching of the Arts within the monastery, and a private school of theology was set up, and at this the Augustinian canons alone attended.[2] Judging from the letter of Fulk de Deuil, Abailard must have greatly enhanced the renown of the Parisian schools by the numbers of students which he drew from every part of Western Europe. Thus he contributed to the future fame of the University which was to receive its charter from Philip Augustus in the opening years of the thirteenth century.

1 P. 158.
2 Denifle, Die Universitäten, 1. p. 656.

CONCLUSION

To the modern reader Abailard may seem far too intellectualist in his theology. Certainly, he would have had no sympathy for the subjectivism of the present day, nor for the modern attempt to re-discover from the Gospels the full picture of the historical Jesus. In face of the criticism of mystical theologians, such as St Bernard and William of St Thierry, he held that logic could rightfully be applied to matters of faith. By his use of logic, the theologian was to explain the doctrines of the church as well as to reconcile the discordant statements in the pages of ecclesiastical authority. To be sure, he recognized that all human knowledge is necessarily finite. Man has not the power to comprehend the secrets of God. But, by the use of analogies and by demonstrating the falsity of heretical teaching, logic can shew men the compelling reasonableness of orthodox theology.

Abailard's intellectualism is to be explained by two factors : his training in dialectic before he turned to the study of theology, and his concern with the various heretical theologians of his day. It was inevitable that a man who had studied and taught with such success in the schools of Paris should have been attracted to the philosophical and dogmatic side of theology. He was clearly unaffected by the mysticism of St Augustine. All through his life, he appears to have been a nervous, highly-strung man but, unlike the bishop of Hippo, he did not seek to find his rest in God alone. His nature was too combative to allow him to retire into solitude and to seek peace in a life of contemplation. The lecture-halls of Paris, not the seclusion of St Denys—if we can indeed call so worldly an abbey secluded—were always summoning him. Even after he had gone out into the wilderness by the Arduzon, he was very much gratified when his former students followed him. Discussions between rival schools of logic delighted him, and his victories gave him obvious pleasure. It was only natural for him to regard theology as composed of doctrines similar to those of dialectic. Theological problems called for elucidation, and this was to be effected in precisely the same way as difficulties in logic were solved. Boethius had recognized that in some cases the enquirer must be content to doubt, for to make a decision would be dangerous. In theology, doubt too must find its place, for it is by doubting that we come to the truth. Abailard, as we know, scorned the apparatus of the gloss; unaided reason and critical ability were to be sufficient for the exegete. Pre-Christian philosophers had arrived at a knowledge of the Trinity by the aid of their reason without the help of revelation. Christian theology was a rational system, the tenets of which lay within the scope of human discursive thought; the reasonableness of its doctrines could be made plain by the use of dialectic, just as the problems of philosophy were explained by logic. In his philosophical writings, Abailard holds that all knowledge must begin with the study of words, the meaning of which was to be discovered by logical analysis. The texts of the Bible and the Fathers were to be subjected to the same process, since their meaning could not be learnt through a study of the various glosses, but through a minute, dialectical investigation into the words employed. Hence, we find Abailard founding his explanation of the reasonableness of the orthodox doctrine of the Trinity upon a careful enquiry into the meaning of identity and dissimilarity.

To a large extent, Abailard's intellectualism was also due to his concern with the heretical views of Roscelin and Gilbert Porrée. He was, we must remember, engaged in the training of students who might perhaps have to withstand the teaching of these unorthodox professors, and he therefore considered it important that his students should be able to understand the reasons by which their own beliefs could be defended. Living at a time when so much heresy existed, when new sects were springing up in the south of France, it was the duty of professors and students alike to train themselves in such a way as would enable them to convince the heretic of his errors. The mere *ipse dixit* of canonical authority was insufficient. So far as it was humanly possible, the teaching of the church must be explained to those who refused allegiance. Further, some heretics had themselves made use of logic, and as this had been largely responsible for their mistaken views, they must be confuted by the aid of the weapons which they had themselves employed. Such methods, as I have already said, were diametrically opposed to those used by St Bernard. That Saint won many men for the church through the irresistible power of his rhetoric, while he silenced others through conciliar action, at Sens and Rheims. He made his appeal to ecclesiastical authority vested in the papacy and the episcopate. But as a dialectician and an intellectualist, Abailard sought to refute the heterodox by shewing to them the superior truth of the official teaching of the church. It was so easy to compel men to believe without insuring that they possessed a proper understanding of the content of their faith. The man, indeed, who believes quickly will soon diminish. Faith is more than the acceptance by the will of articles which are neither discussed nor understood; it is that which we hold firmly in our minds. The task of the apologist is at once to disprove the tenets of the unorthodox and to make sure that his convert understands, in so far as men can understand, the faith of the Creeds. In addition, God must be served by the mind as well as by the lips.

But, in thus stressing the intellectualist character of Abailard's theology, one element in his thought must not be overlooked. He was a great ethical thinker, and his preoccupation with ethics is basic to his doctrinal views. Here, I am not so much referring to his actual ethical teaching as to the effect which it had upon his Christology. Certainly, his statement that a venial sin, when committed intentionally, becomes mortal, made his moral philosophy more rigid than that of the rigorous St Bernard. His analysis of human

motives, which led him to formulate the theory that intention
alone should be our criterion of guilt, would by itself demand
for Abailard a high place among ethical writers. But the
point I wish to make is that his ethical theories shaped the
nature of some of his most characteristic doctrines. I have
already argued that his doctrine of the Atonement is intimately connected with his conception of sin, a connexion
which, as it seems to me, has not sufficiently been recognized.
It is true, of course, that his intellectualist, almost Gnostic,
outlook, led Abailard to regard Christ mainly as the Word
made flesh, and not, as was the way of the Benedictine mystics,
as the Man of Sorrows. These mystics delighted to allegorize
each scene in the Gospels; Abailard concentrated his attention on the teaching of Christ. To him, Jesus was not the
Suffering Servant so much as the Master who taught the new
Way of life; his disciples were lovers of wisdom. Reason indeed had discovered much concerning the true mode of life,
a fact which is clear, since the Gospel teaching is but a
fulfilment of the teaching of Natural Law. Much, too, had
been provided by the gift of the Mosaic Code. But still more
was needed, if men were to serve God in the proper way.
A new motive was necessary, for of old fear, not love, had
actuated men. The Incarnation, then, was ethical in character;
the sacramental aspect of the Cross is minimized; its legalistic
character rejected in favour of exemplarism. Christ came to
teach, to act as an example to the whole human race. Certainly,
as we know, the atoning work of Christ in bringing men into
closer relationship with God is not abandoned. Abailard
speaks of Christ as our Advocate with the Father. But it is
abundantly clear that to Abailard the chief purpose of the
Incarnation was ethical; the provision of a new motive in
charity, whereby men may acquire full merit for their deeds.
The institution of the sacraments was a further means to this
end. And, although Abailard was driven by the sheer force
of his logic to formulate his doctrine of the omnipotence of
God, his interest in ethics seems to me also responsible for
the strange character of his thought. His concern with God

as the *Summum Bonum*, who can only do what is absolutely good, prevented him from seeing whither he was being led by the exigencies of his dialectic.

I have said enough to shew that Abailard was no rationalist in the Voltairian sense of that word. Like all the great scholastic thinkers, he was, however, a rationalist in that he considered human reason competent to arrive at some knowledge of Reality. Both this type of rationalism and intellectualism itself are somewhat out of fashion to-day. Neo-Thomists are certainly trying to spread the Aquinean doctrine of intellectual assent to matters of faith, and are attempting to destroy the criticism of Kant. Aquinas has many followers too outside the Roman fold. But the majority of men distrust "Reason's glimmering ray" in matters of religion, and prefer to rely chiefly upon the data of experience and historical fact. Yet, in judging Abailard's aims and method, we must allow for the great value of his apologetic programme. Differences of thought in matters of dogma can only be discussed and rectified by reasoned argument. The majority of heretics with whom he came into contact, men like Roscelin and Gilbert Porrée, were academic, and they had to be refuted by the methods of the schools. But in his attempt to explain to his students the reasonableness of the Creeds, Abailard, as I have tried to shew, placed too much confidence in the power of reason. It was not that he wished to make reason the criterion of belief, nor was intellectualism itself at fault. Abailard must not be criticized for lacking what none of his contemporaries could then possess: a knowledge of modern historical criticism. Every mediaeval writer employed biblical and patristic statements without the slightest regard for their contexts, often using them in the opposite way from that in which they were originally intended. But other writers based their theological investigations upon the data of experience, whether of the historic church or of their own acquisition, as well as upon the results of their logic. Anselm of Canterbury knew his St Augustine, and, influenced by that Father, he realized the religious significance of all dogma. Their mysticism gave to the theology of the Victorines a quality of human value and solidity. For both Anselm and Hugh of St Victor doctrine was, consciously or unconsciously, expressive of religious feeling. Abailard's preoccupation with logic made him negligent of these matters. His sermons are certainly full of religious sentiment, and he was well read in patristic "case-law". But his training as a dialectician brought him, as we have seen, to regard each doctrine separately, neglecting its religious signification and concentrating upon its intrinsic truth. Thus, impelled by his intellectualism, he failed to understand that an undue emphasis upon the rôle of Christ as the Teacher of mankind deprived the Cross of a great deal of its religious appeal. Discarding the traditional conception of Original Sin, he did not realize how much he belittled the grandeur of Christ's redeeming work and the relative insufficiency of man. His dialectical approach to the problems of theology demanded more than a brilliant ability in logic. Logic might indeed provide the method, but personal experience and a deeper knowledge of the experience of the historic church than that possessed by Abailard were also required. Further, Abailard, ever careful to insure the soundness of his logic, was apt to be careless when it came to theological precision. Headstrong and fully convinced of the correctness of his views, he failed to realize that very often his theology was open to criticism because it was carelessly expressed. This is very evident in the case of his exposition of the dogma of the Trinity. There he frequently made statements, apparently without intention, which were patent of some heretical construction. Again, a more careful self-examination might have shewn him that his use of the traditional attribution of Power, Wisdom, and Goodness to the three Persons needed more precise treatment.

It is indeed unfortunate that we possess so little contemporary information about Abailard's character. From our description of his life and thought, however, much can be added to what I have already quoted from writers who knew him personally. It is evident that he was fully aware of his own intellectual powers and contemptuous of those who opposed him. Nothing seems to have given him greater pleasure than the numbers of students who thronged about him at Melun and Paris, or who followed him in his retreat at Quincey. His self-assurance, indeed, led men like Joscelin to think quite wrongly that he was a charlatan. This self-assurance grew as he was subjected first to the examination at Soissons, and then to the constant, though unfounded, dread that St Bernard and Norbert were working to effect his ruin. For those who were his opponents in the schools, he had the greatest contempt. He had no praise for William of Champeaux, to whose lectures upon logic he must have been greatly indebted. Once he had gathered his audience of admiring students, he set up a rival school. To be sure, he began his teaching career at Melun, not at Paris where William was still lecturing, but the moment war broke out between the two men, Abailard was determined to fight to the finish. His quick assertiveness made him impatient of the wordy scholarship of Anselm, and he did not shrink from criticizing a man who was held in the highest esteem by most of his contemporaries. The attack of St Bernard upon his theological orthodoxy he treated with scorn; was not the abbot an ignoramus in matters of logic? The monks of St Denys found him a difficult companion, while prior Gosvin had none too easy a task in controlling the "rhinoceros" committed to his charge. Evidently, it might seem, the adulation which Abailard received in the schools of Paris, where students, according to Fulk, came from all over Western Europe to attend his lectures, made it hard for him to bear the reverse of good fortune.

But, in appraising Abailard's character, we have to remember the difficulties which always appeared to stand in his way. If he was harsh in his condemnation of William of Champeaux, could he not with some truth trace his subsequent misfortunes to the animosity of his former master? William was clearly jealous of his student's intellectual powers, and, naturally enough, he did not relish the victory

Abailard had gained over him in forcing him to change his views concerning the nature of universals. Yet, was there not sufficient space for them both to teach in northern France? Abailard, it is true, was unhappy in the number of foes which he made. His disdain for Anselm roused the school of Laon against him. But all through his life Abailard felt that he had to be on the defensive, and that fact increased his self-assertiveness as well as his caustic hostility towards those who attacked his theology. His experiences at Laon were a repetition of those he had encountered at William's school; Alberic and Lotulf prosecuted him at Soissons. After his retirement to Quincey, where he hoped for peace, he thought that St Bernard and Norbert were plotting against him. In composing his theological treatises, he held it necessary to forestall their criticism of his dialectical method. At St Gildas he was harassed by a crowd of undisciplined monks who even threatened to murder him. Certainly, he cannot be regarded as a man who found it easy to endure another's rule. Independent, anxious to win his spurs, he longed to control his own school. Life at St Denys was difficult, in exile from his students and under durance, but after his escape to Quincey he seemed in reach of peace, and he became more contented as his former pupils flocked around him. But there was always the fear of danger, and from this his departure for Brittany did not free him. Small wonder then that he did not spare his enemies, when he came to write his *Historia Calamitatum*, and his *Apologia* to St Bernard.

To Lucia he seems to have been a devoted son, speaking affectionately of her in his autobiography and visiting her before she took the veil. It may be that I am right in supposing that she influenced Abailard to study theology. His first encounter with Héloise must probably be regarded as the deed of a passionate man brought on by close intimacy. When their son had been born, he refused to allow himself to be dissuaded by her avowal that she did not wish to hinder his clerical preferment, and he insisted on their marriage. It is difficult to picture her, for she takes a secondary part in the

Historia; nor is it easy to estimate her influence upon his career. We know that she was a clever woman, well read in the classical literature known at the time, and, from her letters and queries addressed to Abailard, it is plain that she was interested in patristic problems and biblical difficulties. At Paris she was well known both for her learning and for her physical charms. Despite their separation, the one to St Denys, the other to Argenteuil, Abailard was always concerned for her interests. From his description of the condition of her nunnery, it would appear that in a house, apparently noted for its lack of discipline, Héloise was the leader of a party which aimed at order. She was certainly able to attract to her person a group of devoted sisters. Once she had been installed at the Paraclete, it was to Abailard that Héloise looked for advice upon matters of monastic government. She continued her studies, writing to Abailard for information upon obscurities in the Bible, including the difficult problem of the creation story. It seems highly probable that after the transference of the Paraclete to Héloise, and especially after Abailard's departure from St Gildas, they not only corresponded freely, but in all likelihood saw a good deal of each other.

Abailard's own monastic career throws an interesting light upon his character. His critics poured scorn upon his behaviour at St Denys, and St Bernard, who hated the *gyrovagus* or wandering monk, ridiculed him for leaving his monastery. Yet, in his letter to Héloise, Abailard shews that he was keenly interested in monastic conditions and problems. Part of his unpopularity with Adam and his monks was due to his attack upon the lax state of their house. At St Gildas, he did his best to bring his unruly, immoral monks to some kind of discipline. Situated on the western coast of Brittany, that monastery had not been influenced by the reforming movements which had already done so much to improve monastic conditions. If the brethren thought that their new abbot would pay no attention to their irregularities, they were sorely disappointed. Abailard, an ethical writer, proved a strict

ruler who wished to enforce discipline in a house where, even
in a barbarous land, the behaviour of the monks must have
been a scandal.

In spite of the condemnation of Sens and his failure to
build up anything like a lasting school of theology, Abailard's
career was not entirely fruitless. The drama of Sens was the
last act in the struggle between dialectician and anti-dialec-
tician. The application of logic to theology was never again
called into question. The *Sic et Non* method was not his own
invention, but through his immediate pupils, especially
through Peter the Lombard, that method was popularized by
the fashion which he set of quoting numerous authorities to
support his arguments. As we know, in a more developed
form the method which he used became the recognized
method of the schools. Men learnt more of the limitations
of logic and of the necessary boundaries between reason and
revelation, and thus safeguarded themselves the more against
rash statements and unsatisfactory conclusions.

APPENDIX I

THE CHRONOLOGY OF ABAILARD'S WRITINGS

THE first collected edition of Abailard's writings was published in 1616 at Paris by André Duchesne and François d'Amboise, but it contained only a few of his theological works: the *Expositio ad Romanos*, the *Introductio*, and the *Historia Calamitatum*. Later, however, various single treatises found their way into different collections of mediaeval texts. Thus, Martène and Durand published the *Theologia Christiana* in their *Thesaurus Anecdotorum*,[1] while the *Scito teipsum* was printed by Bernard Pez.[2] The first modern edition of his writings came from Victor Cousin who published in 1836 the *Dialectica* and an incomplete text of the *Sic et Non*,[3] following this with a two-volumed edition of Abailard's letters, sermons, and theological works.[4] A full text of the *Sic et Non* was not forthcoming until 1851, when it was edited by Henke and Lindenkohl of Marburg. The Abbé Migne printed the texts of Duchesne and Pez in his *Patrology* together with the Marburg edition of the *Sic et Non*, but he did not reprint the logical treatises. An edition of the *Epitome* was published by Rheinwald,[5] and this was subsequently reprinted by Migne. Rheinwald also edited the unfinished *Dialogus*,[6] his text being later conjecturally emended by Victor Cousin. Another volume was added to the Abailardian corpus by the discovery at Erlangen by Remigius Stölzle of the *Tractatus de Unitate et Trinitate Divina*,[7] while Hauréau was able to provide a fuller text of the poem which Abailard addressed to his son Astralabe.[8] Quite recently, Dr Bernhard Geyer found in the Ambrosian Library another set of Abailard's books upon logic, and these he published under the title *Logica 'Ingredientibus'*.[9] A very important portion of the Apology which Abailard sent to St Bernard, presumably before the council at Sens, has also been discovered lately and has been

---

1 v. pp. 1156–1359.
2 *Thesaurus anecd. novissimus*, III. 2, pp. 626 ff.
3 *Ouvrages inédits d'Abélard*, Paris, 1836.
4 *Opera*, Paris, 1849, 1859.   5 Berlin, 1835.
6 Berlin, 1831.   7 Freiburg, 1891.
8 *Notices et Extraits de quelques manuscrits latins de la Bibliothèque nationale*, XXXIV. 2, 1895, pp. 153–97.
9 BGPM. XXI. 1919–27.

made accessible.[1] One treatise however, the *Nostrorum petitioni*, a tractate upon logic, still awaits an editor.[2]

The task of dating these different books is a somewhat complicated matter. The able criticism of G. Robert has indeed made it possible for us to fix the chronology of Abailard's theological writings with a certain amount of accuracy,[3] but at present only approximate dates can be given for the composition of his books upon logic. While both internal and external evidence enables us to date his theological writings, no such evidence is available when we come to his philosophical treatises.

Since the date of the *Dialectica* largely depends upon that of the *Theologia Christiana*, it will be more convenient to deal with the chronology of Abailard's theological books first. Here our initial problem must be to discover which of his treatises was the one condemned to be burnt at Soissons. Cousin once held that the book in question had been lost,[4] but when he came to edit Abailard's theological writings, he argued that it was the *Introductio* that had been condemned.[5] The criticism of Goldhorn, however, was able to shew that in date the *Introductio* was later than the *Theologia Christiana*,[6] and that it could not have been the treatise which Alberic and Lotulf had attacked in 1121. It is now abundantly evident that the *Introductio* is a more developed edition of the *Theologia Christiana*, containing material—notably the comparison of the Trinity to a copper seal—which led to Abailard's final condemnation at Sens. Now the name, *Introductio*, has no MS. authority. It was plainly given to the book by its first editors because its preface states that it was written in response to the demand of his students for an introduction to the Scriptures,[7] and, as the treatise condemned at Soissons had the same object, it was natural to infer that the two books were identical. But such an argument can no longer be accepted. From many references in the *Expositio ad Romanos* we know that Abailard wrote a book entitled the *Theologia*,[8] and, as these correspond with statements found in the *Introductio*, and not with passages in the *Theologia Christiana*, we must conclude that the original name of the *Introductio* was the *Theologia*. And this is supported by a de-

---

1 "Ein neuaufgefundenes Bruchstück der Apologia Abaelards", ed. Paul Ruf and Martin Grabmann, *Sitzungsberichte der Bayerischen Akademie der Wissenschaften*, Phil.-hist. Abt. 1930, Heft 5.

2 *Logica*, p. x; Lunel MS. no. 2.

3 See his *Les écoles et l'enseignement de la théologie pendant la première moitié du XIIe siècle*, Paris, 1909.

4 *Ouvrages inédits*, p. cxcvi; his theory was accepted by Deutsch, pp. v and 265.   5 *Opera Abaelardi*, ii. pp. 1 ff.

6 *Zeitschrift für hist. Theologie*, xxxvi. 1866, pp. 161–229.

7 *Introd.* col. 979 A.   8 See *infra*, p. 266.

claration of William of St Thierry that he had read the *Theologia* of Peter Abailard.[1]

His argument led Goldhorn to assume that it was the *Theologia Christiana* that was condemned at Soissons, but when he discovered the *de Unitate*, Stölzle maintained that he had found the missing treatise, the existence of which Cousin had once posited. But the proofs which he put forward in support of his contention are not entirely conclusive. There can indeed be no doubt that the *de Unitate* was prior in composition to the *Theologia Christiana*; a passage in this latter book indicates that Abailard had already written a defence of his theological opinions.[2] Further, while the *de Unitate* contains the substance of the *Theologia Christiana*, it has not, in so far as the MS., which may possibly be defective, shews, any portion corresponding to the fifth book of the *Theologia*, a fact which strongly suggests that the *Theologia Christiana* was an elaboration of the earlier work. To suppose that the *de Unitate* was written by some unknown epitomist appears unwarranted. Many of its statements are to be found repeated in the *Theologia Christiana* in a modified form, and it is clear that the reason for this was the removal of objections and not their correction,[3] while some passages of more questionable orthodoxy were entirely expunged in the later recension. Thus, the *Theologia Christiana* shews clearly that Abailard watered down his comparison of the Platonic World-Soul with the Christian doctrine of the Spirit,[4] obviously because some criticism had been passed upon it, when the *de Unitate* was published. Again, the highly objectionable statement in the *de Unitate*, "Ex eo quod Pater est, hoc solum exigit ut sit potens vel etiam omnipotens", was deleted, although the surrounding passages were reproduced.[5] It is impossible to hold that such alterations would have been the work of an epitomist.

But although it is evident that the *de Unitate* was the earliest of Abailard's three theological books, we cannot accept as entirely conclusive the theory of Stölzle that it was the treatise that was burnt at Soissons. To be sure, Abailard himself says that the condemned book was *de unitate et trinitate divina*,[6] but it is quite impossible to say whether he was actually giving the title of the treatise or merely referring to the subject-matter with which it

1 *Ep.* cccxxvi. PL. 182, col. 531 c.

2 Superest ut hostilis malitiae jacula pluribus retundamus rationibus...ne, quod ad fidei nostrae defensionem sincera conscripsimus intentione, inde eorum invida sive erronea criminatione vilescat fidelibus. *Theol. Christ.* ii. col. 1171 c, which seems to refer to the account of Soissons given in *Hist. Calam.* 9, col. 152 A.

3 Cf. CQR. xli. 1895, p. 143.

4 *De Unitate*, i. 5, pp. 9–10; *Theol. Christ.* i. 5, col. 1147 B.

5 *De Unitate*, ii. 4, p. 62.   6 *Hist. Calam.* 9, col. 140 A.

dealt. St Bernard, for instance, wrote to Innocent II that Abailard was the author of a book *de sua Trinitate*, "about his own Trinity",[1] a statement which clearly describes the content of the treatise and not the title itself. It is more than probable that Abailard intended the passage in the *Historia*, to which reference has just been made, to mean that the book under criticism was merely about the doctrine of the Trinity. In addition, the title which Stölzle has given his text is not authorized by the MS. In the Erlangen codex the book is entered as "Petri Adbaiolardi capitula librorum de trinitate", an entry which is but the mediaeval equivalent of the modern "Contents of the books of Abailard concerning the Trinity",[2] the book's title being *Libri de Trinitate*. Any idea of a title-page was quite foreign to the Middle Ages, and it is only through the presence of either an *Incipit* or a colophon that the title of a mediaeval book can be known. In the MS. under discussion neither exists. And so there is no necessary connexion between the passage in the *Historia* describing the subject-matter of the condemned treatise and the text printed by Stölzle. Nor does any evidence which can be gleaned from its contents enable us to identify the date when the *de Unitate* was composed. All we know indeed is that at Soissons Abailard was charged with holding that the Father alone of the three Persons was omnipotent,[3] and the omission of the words, "Ex eo quod Pater est...", might well suggest that this was the passage to which his enemies took exception. But in the *Theologia Christiana* there are many passages which might equally have been responsible for the condemnation of Abailard.[4] Both Otto of Freising and the *Historia* state that the charge preferred was one of Sabellianism;[5] but unfortunately the phrase quoted by Otto cannot be discovered in any of Abailard's books. Stölzle attempted to identify Otto's passage with one in the *de Unitate*, but it is by no means certain whether his identification can be accepted as sound.[6] While, however, there is thus no actual proof that the treatise, printed as the *de Unitate*, was indeed the book subjected to an examination at Soissons, there yet remains a very strong likelihood that the Stölzle's treatise was the book that was censured.

1 *Ep.* CXCI. PL. 182, col. 357 C.

2 Cf. CQR. *loc. cit.* p. 134.

3 Quidam...submurmuravit, quod in libro scriptum deprehenderat, solum Deum Patrem omnipotentem esse. *Hist. Calam.* 10, col. 150 A.

4 E.g. *Theol. Christ.* I. 2, col. 1224 A.

5 Sicut eadem oratio est praepositio, assumptio et conclusio, ita eadem essentia est Pater et Filius et Spiritus sanctus. *Gesta Fred. ed. cit.* I. 49, p. 69; *Hist. Calam.* 9, coll. 147–8.

6 Pp. 74 ff.; see Stölzle, pp. xxiv, 79; CQR. *loc. cit.* p. 135.

But, before we can proceed further, another claim advanced by Stölzle in connexion with the *de Unitate* must be considered. From a letter written by Roscelin to Abailard it is clear that Abailard had already written three letters of protest against the theology of his former master,[1] and, Stölzle maintained, the *de Unitate* itself was the third of these letters which drew from Roscelin the spirited answer we have just mentioned. This answer may be roughly dated. As it taxes Abailard with the disgrace of his affair with Héloise and refers to Fulbert's attack on him and his subsequent retirement to St Denys, it must have been written after 1118.[2] To establish his argument Stölzle pointed to the use of the second person in two passages and to the use of the phrase, "an astute dialectician", also in the second person, in a third.[3] It is, however, quite impossible to regard the *de Unitate* as a letter, and thus the argument put forward by Stölzle is in the main untenable. Yet it may well contain an element of truth, for we know that Abailard had already written against the Trinitarian doctrines held by Roscelin,[4] and thus it is quite possible that the *de Unitate* may have been modelled on the letter to which Roscelin objected,[5] or, better, that the letter in question was an abstract of that treatise. Accepting then the strong probability that the *de Unitate* was the book produced at Soissons, we must conclude that its composition dates from the period 1118–19, when he entered St Denys, to 1121, the year in which the council was summoned. Its possible connexion with the letter written by Roscelin *circa* 1118, and the fact that some little time would be required for the spread of his theological ideas, incline us to date the composition of the *de Unitate* somewhere in the middle of the period stated, that is, in 1120.[6]

Since it was written first, the date of the *Theologia Christiana* necessarily depends upon that of the *Introductio*, and it is with that book that we must now deal. The year in which at least part of the *Introductio* was written can only be ascertained through allusions to contemporary teachers made in the second book of the treatise. There a certain Tanquelm is mentioned, and it appears that he was but recently dead.[7] Tanquelm is known to have visited Rome in 1112 on business connected with the diocese of Utrecht, and some three years later, that is, about 1115, he was

1 Tu duobus primis mandatis subito iracundiae furore calcatis ad tertium inordinate transvolasti. *Ep.* xv. PL. 178, col. 359 A.
2 *Ibid.* coll. 386 BC, 370.
3 Responde tu mihi, astute dialectice, II. 3, p. 48; cf. II. 4, p. 59, III. 1, p. 87; Stölzle, p. xxvi.
4 *Ep.* xv. coll. 361 ff.   5 So CQR. *loc. cit.* p. 138.
6 This date is also accepted by Robert, p. 196.
7 II. 4, col. 1056 A.

killed by a blow on the head delivered by an avenging priest.[1]
Peter de Bruys is also mentioned, and again, since the same word
nuper is used, it is possible that Peter too had died before the
publication of the second book of the *Introductio*. Peter's dates,
however, are difficult to determine, and our only sources of information are the *adversus Petrobrusianos* of Peter the Venerable
and a letter which Peter wrote in either 1142 or 1143, shortly after
his return from Spain. In this letter the abbot of Cluny tells St
Bernard that he had sent him a book against the followers of de
Bruys composed some four or five years previously.[2] Now if
Peter de Bruys had been alive when the *adversus Petrobrusianos* was
written—and its composition could not have been before 1137—
we should have to date the second book of the *Introductio* after
that year. But this date is unsuitable; all Abailard's other theological works, with the exception of the *Sic et Non* and the *Theologia Christiana*, were obviously written after the second book of
the *Introductio* had been published, and the period 1137-42 is too
short a period for their composition. It is, however, quite unnecessary to suppose that Peter de Bruys was dead when Abailard
wrote the passage describing his heretical views. In the *adversus
Petrobrusianos* Peter the Venerable states that the heretic began to
disseminate his theories about twenty years before his own
treatise was written,[3] and this would give us the years 1117-20 as
the beginning of the career of de Bruys as a heretical teacher. It
will be noticed that these dates are very close to the year of
Tanquelm's death in 1115. Even if the word *nuper* used in connexion with Tanquelm refers to his death, it does not necessarily
follow that it refers also to the death of Peter de Bruys; it may
well indicate the beginning of the latter's career as a heretical
preacher. We can therefore take the years 1117-20 as the earliest
possible date for the composition of *Introductio*, book II.

But, in view of the date which we have assigned to the *de
Unitate*, these years seem too early; the *Introductio*, as we have said,
was the later of the two books. Another passage in the second
book of the *Introductio* provides us with a much nearer clue as to
the date of its composition. Immediately after his reference to
Peter de Bruys, Abailard states that, as he wrote, four masters
were "holding chairs of pestilence" around him, in France—that

---

1 See A. S. Turberville, *Heresy and the Mediaeval Inquisition*, London, 1920,
p. 14.

2 Misissem et ego nostram eruditae dilectioni vestrae, quam contra
haereticorum Provincialium quaedam capitula ante quattuor vel quinque
annos scripsi. *Ep.* lib. IV. 17, PL. 189, coll. 343-4.

3 Et quia prima erronei dogmatis semina a Petro de Bruis per viginti fere
annos sata et aucta. Prolog. col. 722 A.

is, in the Île de France—in Burgundy, at Angers, and at Bourges,[1] and it is possible to identify these masters. The one who was teaching in France must have been the Alberic of Rheims whom we have already encountered as an enemy of Abailard at Laon and Soissons.[2] In the corresponding portion of the *Theologia Christiana* Abailard attributes to him the doctrines held by Gilbert Porrée, the justice of this being confirmed by John of Salisbury.[3] The identity of the master teaching in Burgundy depends upon the identity we give to the brothers added to the list in the *Theologia Christiana*, but omitted in the *Introductio*, for we are told that the Burgundian professor was a compatriot of the other two.[4] Goldhorn supposed that these two brothers were Anselm and Ralph of Laon,[5] but, apart from geographical considerations, we know that Anselm died in 1117, whereas it is clear that both the brothers were alive at the time when the *Introductio* was published. It was suggested by Clerval that they were Bernard of Chartres and Thierry. Bernard died some time before 1130, perhaps as early as 1125, while Thierry, who was archdeacon of Chartres, was present at the council of Rheims in 1148 and seems to have died between 1150 and 1155, when a new archdeacon was appointed.[6] It seems certain that Clerval's suggestion must be accepted.

Now Roscelin himself has been regarded as the master who taught in Burgundy, but there is no evidence to shew that he was ever a professor in that part of France. Clerval again put forward the theory that the master in question was possibly Éon de l'Étoile, a strange heretic who identified himself punningly with Christ, of whom it is said in the grace at exorcism "per eum qui venturus est".[7] Although Éon enjoyed considerable reputation on account of the audacity of his claims, he does not seem to have been of sufficient academic importance to warrant Abailard's attack upon his theological teaching. With better reason Deutsch held that the Burgundian was no other than Gilbert Porrée, but Gilbert was born at Poitiers and, after teaching at Chartres, he

1 Sed nec magistros divinorum librorum, qui nunc maxime circa nos pestilentiae cathedras tenent, praetereundos arbitramur, quorum unus in Francia, alter in Burgundia, tertius in pago Andegavensi, quartus in Bituricensi. Col. 1056 BC.

2 Cf. Robert, p. 198.   3 IV. col. 1285 B, and *Hist. Pontif.* p. 20.
4 *Theol. Christ.* IV. col. 1286 B.   5 *Art. cit.* p. 202.
6 Poole, EHR. XXXV. 1920, p. 327, and *Illustrations*, p. 101 note, gives Bernard's death as before 1130. Robert thinks 1125 possible. For Thierry, see Clerval, p. 169.

7 Robert, p. 159. For Éon see William of Newburgh, *Hist. rerum Anglicarum*, ed. R. Hewlett, RS. I. 19, pp. 60–64, and Sigebert of Gembloux, *Chronic.* MGH.SS. VI. p. 389.

became bishop of his native city.[1] It appears certain, however, that this master was Gilbert the Universal, a Breton by birth, who is found among the clergy of Auxerre with the title of *magister* from 1110 to 1127, when he became bishop of London.[2] His learning was well known[3] and, like Alberic, he was a disciple of Gilbert Porrée.[4] The third master mentioned, at Angers, was beyond question a scholar named Ulger. Born probably in Anjou and certainly educated at Angers, his good character had obtained for him a canonry in the city and the position of *scholasticus*. After being archdeacon of Outre Loire (in either 1113 or 1119), he was consecrated bishop of Angers on September 20th, 1125.[5] He was known as a trusted partizan of the Empress Mathilda,[6] and he surpassed, we are told,[7] the other French bishops of the time in age and learning as well as in his uprightness and kindliness. The fourth master mentioned was Joscelin, who taught at Bourges until 1125, when he became bishop of Soissons. Joscelin had been present at the disputes between Abailard and William of Champeaux and, although he apparently held the same theory upon the nature of universals as did our author,[8] we have already seen that he regarded Abailard as a charlatan.[9] A close counsellor of both Louis VI and Louis VII, he was also a friend of Suger and a frequent correspondent with St Bernard. He died in 1151.

From these short descriptions of their careers it will be seen that all four masters were men of academic distinction. A contemporary, reading Abailard's pages, would have immediately known to whom he was referring. Assuming then—and it seems that we must—that all four were actually teaching when Abailard wrote, the latest date which we can assign to the composition of *Introductio*, book II would be 1125, when both Ulger and Joscelin were consecrated to their respective bishoprics. Now we know that between 1122 and 1125 Abailard was first at Quincey and then at the Paraclete. As both these places lie within a rough circle drawn through Rheims, Auxerre, Bourges, and Angers, geographical evidence bears out the truth of Robert's identification.

1 Clerval, p. 169.

2 Robert, p. 202; *Hist. litt. de la France*, XI. p. 236. He was consecrated in January, 1128.

3 See Bernard, *Ep.* XXIV. col. 128.

4 John of Salisbury, *Hist. Pontif.* 8, p. 20.

5 *Hist. litt.* XII. pp. 302 ff.; Ulger died on October 17th, 1148.

6 *Hist. Pontif.* 41, p. 85.

7 *Ibid.* pp. 86–7; Bernard, *Epp.* CC, CCCXL.

8 Cf. Est et alius qui cum Gausleno Suessioni episcopo universalitatem rebus in unum collectis attribuit et eamdem singulis demit. *Metal.* II. 17, col. 876 A.

9 See *supra*, p. 6.

And, since the *Theologia Christiana* contains a corresponding reference to these four masters,[1] the composition of that treatise must be dated before the year 1125, though it was certainly written after 1121, the date of the council of Soissons. And if we were correct in our statement that the *Theologia Christiana* at one point echoes the criticism aroused by the publication of the *de Unitate*,[2] we should be inclined to place its date as early after 1121 as would be consistent with the actual time required for its composition. With his love for the arena of theological controversy Abailard would hardly have waited long before answering his critics. But, as we shall see, the *Sic et Non* was clearly written some time between 1122 and 1123; we are thus compelled to assign the composition of the *Theologia Christiana*, book IV to the years 1123–4. Most likely the fifth book was written at the same time, for its matter was incorporated into the later *Introductio*.

The *Expositio ad Romanos* supplies us with sure evidence that the *Introductio* was written and published in at least two sections. Denifle indeed tried to shew that its present division into books and chapters was not intended by Abailard,[3] but in various passages our author refers to the divisions of his treatise, and these are often cited by their number. Further, Walter of Mortagne had clearly read only the first book of the *Introductio*.[4] This book must therefore have been accessible in a separate form. Now, in certain passages in the *Expositio* the reader is referred to Abailard's book on the Trinity which has already been published, and he will find there an elaboration of some points which are not fully discussed in the Commentary.[5] A study of these references shews that the first and second books alone of the *Introductio* are meant. In the *Expositio* again there also occur references to the *Theologia* which is yet to be published,[6] and these passages are to be found in the third book of the *Introductio*. The inference is obvious. The first two books of the *Introductio* were written and published together, and then Abailard began the *Expositio*. His references to the third book would lead us to conclude that that book was issued immediately after the publication of the Commentary, perhaps almost at the same time. The exact dates of the remaining portions of the *Introductio* cannot be determined, for they are no longer extant. That their composition was at least contemplated is evident, as the prologue outlines the contents of the book, which was to include a discussion of the sacraments, and this is not given in the

1 IV. col. 1285.   2 See *supra*, p. 260.
3 ALKG. I. pp. 240 note 1, 600 note.
4 Cf. *Ep.* ed. Ostlender, p. 35.
5 See coll. 802 D, 804 A, 805 A, 858 D.
6 Coll. 808 D, 836 D, 930 B, 943 D.

portion which now exists. And from the *Epitome* it is also clear
that, at least in his lectures, Abailard must have outlined his sacramental views, and as the writer usually follows closely the wording
of the *Introductio*, it appears certain that a final book or books of
that treatise must have once existed. It is quite possible that
these were written at a much later period.[1]

Since its method is employed in the *Theologia Christiana* and in
the *Expositio*, and as it contains no reference to these or to his
other later writings, it is safe to assume that the *Sic et Non* is one
of Abailard's earliest books. Had it been written after these other
treatises, we should have expected some such references, especially as it contains the discordant statements of authority upon
problems which are discussed at length in both the *Theologia
Christiana* and the *Introductio*. And that the *Sic et Non* is later than
the *de Unitate* also seems certain; the latter book makes no use of
the vast amount of patristic learning stored within the pages of
the *Sic et Non*. We should then date the book between 1122 and
1123, that is, between the council of Soissons and the publication
of the *Theologia Christiana*. No mention of its existence was apparently made at the council itself.

The date of the *Scito teipsum* again depends upon internal evidence, but this is only sufficient to allow us to date the book in
relation to his other writings, for there is nothing to shew when
it was actually written. It is plain that the *Scito teipsum* was composed after the third book of the *Introductio* and after the publication of the *Expositio*. The reader is advised to seek in the third
book of the *Theologia* for further elucidation upon the question of
possible forgiveness for sins committed against the Holy Spirit,
while in the *Expositio* certain problems are left over to receive
further discussion in the *Ethics*.[2] From a fragment published by
Cousin[3] a second book of the *Scito teipsum* appears to have been
intended, and thus on the very probable assumption that *Introductio*, book III was written a good while after the publication of
the second book of that treatise, we might suppose that the *Scito
teipsum* was one of Abailard's last literary essays.

The introductory address of the Philosopher provides us with
a clue as to the period during which Abailard wrote the *Dialogus*.
There he is addressed as a master who is counted superior to all

1 As William of St Thierry apparently had read the third book of the
Introductio (see *supra*, p. 224), it is quite probable that it was written in 1137
after Abailard's return to Paris, its publication being partly responsible for
the antagonism of the bishop of that city.

2 Tertio Theologiae nostro libro absolvimus, *Scito teipsum*, 23, col. 668 B,
and nostrae id Ethicae discussioni reservemus, *Epist. ad Romanos*, II. 4, col.
842 A. Cf. also v. 13, col. 951 A; v. 14, col. 959 D.

3 *Opp.* II. p. 642.

his contemporaries, and we are told that he is the author of "that wonderful work, the *Theologia*".[1] Such praise could only have been accorded him some time after his return to Paris in about 1136; it seems unlikely that the Philosopher would have been made to speak in this way if Abailard had been either at the Paraclete or at St Gildas. In his reply, Abailard recognizes that the Philosopher is trying to soothe him by referring to his success as a theologian and as a teacher;[2] such praise would have been out of place unless his reputation had been called into question. These considerations point to the fact that the *Dialogus* was written after the council of Sens, when Abailard was in retirement at Cluny. The quietness of the book's tone, the absence of any bitter recrimination against his enemies, and the omission of any attempt to disprove the theories of thinkers with whom he did not agree, all appear to reflect the calm resignation with which he accepted his final sentence. The lateness of its date would then account for the unfinished state of the book as well as for the ripe character of its contents.

We turn now to the problem of the authorship of the *Epitome* or *Sentences*, a book which has been often attributed to Abailard. St Bernard certainly considered that he wrote the treatise, but the passage he quotes—dealing with the doctrine of the Atonement—cannot be found in the *Epitome*, nor for that matter in the *Expositio* where the nature of Christ's redeeming work is discussed. Writing after the council, Abailard himself denied his authorship.[3] Deutsch maintained that the book came from Abailard's pen despite his denial, and as his reason he pointed to the use of the first person in a chapter where the *Expositio* is mentioned.[4] There is, however, a very marked stylistic difference between the *Epitome* and the other books which were unquestionably written by Abailard, and in consequence it has been suggested that it might have been taken down by a student during Abailard's lectures, this fact being responsible for the more lively style in which the *Epitome* is written.[5] But, as Deutsch rightly remarks, this would not explain the presence of long extracts from the *Introductio* which have been copied out word for word. Though this might perhaps not have been an impossible feat of penmanship, it is difficult to account for their choice, unless the scribe had been able to

1 Col. 1631 CD.

2 Ac deinde, tanquam adulationis oleum vendens, et caput meum hoc unguento demulcens statim intulit. Col. 1613 C.

3 *Tractatus de error. Abaelardi*, 5. 11, PL. 182, col. 1062 D. Cum nunquam aliquis liber, qui Sententiarum dicatur, a me scriptus reperiatur. *Responsio*, PL. 180, col. 332 B.

4 Deutsch, pp. 453 ff.; *Epitome*, 34, col. 1756 A.

5 Gieseler, *Studien und Kritiken*, 1837, pp. 366 ff.; Deutsch, pp. 455–6.

meditate at leisure over the text of Abailard's book. In addition, the *Epitome* contains some slight differences of thought which suggest that the book was more than a report of Abailard's lectures.[1] That the book was the work of a student seems therefore abundantly evident. Now Denifle has shewn that the *Epitome* is one of three such abstracts of the opinions held by our author,[2] all of which were written by persons who had access to the *Introductio* in manuscript. Thus, the change in style is explicable, while the inclusion of the first person in the passage noticed by Deutsch must be accounted for either by supposing that the author subconsciously assumed the personality of Abailard as he went over the text, or by the fact that he was actually reproducing some portion of the original which lay before him, but which is no longer extant. Further, Ostlender, who is preparing a new edition of the work, has been able to shew that the *Epitome* was written by one Hermann.[3]

The authenticity of Abailard's letters has often been questioned, both because we possess no contemporary MSS. and because there is a certain similarity between the style of Abailard and that of Héloise which is held to be suspicious. The non-existence of any contemporary MS. is difficult to explain, though the history of MSS. often presents some strange tales, and, since an early thirteenth-century copy of a new letter has just been discovered, it is more than likely that further MSS. may be found hidden away in the various European libraries. The similarity of the two styles is hardly good evidence; Héloise had been educated by Abailard, and she would have naturally wished to model her Latin on his. The first letter—the *Historia Calamitatum*—is so well authenticated by other independent sources that it cannot be regarded as a forgery; that the eighth, giving a scheme for monastic government, should have been included by a later forger in a series of love-letters seems to be extremely strange, unless it was actually by Abailard. Besides, the letter just mentioned contains a recommendation that the sisters at the Paraclete should learn Greek and Hebrew, and this recommendation is echoed in the *Sermons*.[4] The mention of his flight from St Gildas in the *Historia Calamitatum* and the lack of any reference to his return to Paris allow us to date the letter between the years 1131 and 1135. The letter itself is addressed *ad Amicum*, but its contents shew that it was not intended for any single correspondent. The detached

---

1 Deutsch's opinion (p. 56) that these differences were due to Abailard's change of thought seems unwarrantable.
2 ALKG. I. p. 587; cf. the *Sentences* of St Florian and of Omnibene.
3 Geyer-Ueberweg, p. 225.
4 *Ep.* IX. coll. 325 ff.; *Sermo* XVIII. coll. 511–12.

nature of the style, especially when his first meeting with Héloise
is described, is evidence that it was meant as a pamphlet written
to prepare the way for his return to the schools of Paris. The other
letters cannot be dated with any assured precision, although as in
one instance reference is made to his difficulties just before his
departure from St Gildas, and as they are mainly concerned with
the problems which faced Héloise when she was abbess of the
Paraclete, they appear to have been written after the period 1131–
32. The last letter, containing Abailard's declaration that he did
not wish to remain loyal to Aristotle if that loyalty meant separation from Christ, was certainly penned after the council of
Sens.

Nor can any date be assigned to the hymns. As they were intended for the use of the nuns at the Paraclete, it would seem that
they were put together as a collection after that house had been
granted to Héloise. There are, however, indications that some of
them may have actually been composed earlier, for, as we have
seen,[1] they shew the influence of his love-affair at Paris. The use of
liturgical hymns was then a new and growing fashion which was
not altogether well received.[2] According to Abailard, St Bernard
and his party were opposed to the novelty, being content to use
only one hymn, the *Aeterne rerum Conditor* of St Ambrose. He
sought to defend the practice of adding new hymns to the liturgy
by pointing to the difference of liturgical customs then prevalent; only at the Lateran, we are told,[3] was the old use strictly
kept. And so Abailard made it his aim to compose a set of
hymns which would prove suitable for every season of the
church's year.

It is possible that one or two of the songs printed by Schmeller
in his edition of the *Carmina Burana*[4] may have come from Abailard's pen. No. 131, *Hebet sidus laeti visus*, contains a reference to
the "daughter of Helios":

> In amoris haec chorea
> Cunctis praenitet
> Cujus nomen a Phoebaea
> Luce renitet....

But it is evident that the author of the poem is attending to
the moon and not to Phoebus, and consequently, if the poem

[1] See *supra*, p. 11.
[2] Cf. P. Batiffol, *History of the Roman Breviary*, trans. A. M. Y. Baylay,
London, 1912, p. 136.
[3] *Ep.* x. coll. 339–40.
[4] Stuttgart, 1847. See also F. A. Wright and T. A. Sinclair, *A History of
Later Latin Literature*, London, 1931, pp. 326–7.

is French in origin, to a lady named Diane.¹ Again, six lines
in one of his hymns² seem to be reflected in *Carmen* No. 176:

> Instrumenta
> Sunt his tua
> Per quos mira peragis,
> Et humana
> Moves corda
> Signis et prodigiis.

The evidence of his authorship is, however, not conclusive. It
is quite possible that this *Carmen* was written as a parody of
Abailard's work.

We come lastly to the question of the dates which are to be
assigned to his various writings upon logic. As we have said,
these cannot be fixed with any real degree of certainty. Robert,
who did not know of the existence of the *Logica 'Ingredientibus'*,
held that the *Dialectica* was composed before the council at
Soissons,³ but his theory is not entirely acceptable. A passage in
the *Theologia Christiana* refers the reader for a further discussion of
a problem of logic to a passage in the *Dialectica*.⁴ From this we
may assume that the *Dialectica*—or at least part of it—was written
before 1125. His interest in theological matters, together with the
numerous theological and ethical writings which he produced
after 1121, certainly gives support to Robert's suggestion, and we
know that during his earlier years he was famous as a dialectician.
Since Abailard quotes in the *Dialectica* from an unknown translation of the *Prior Analytics*, there is, however, a slight possibility
that that portion of the book may have been written after the year
1128 when another version of Aristotle's treatise was made by
James of Venice.⁵ It appears certain that the so-called *Logica
'Ingredientibus'* was prior in date to the *Dialectica*. Although the two
books deal with the same subject, the first makes no mention of
the second, and, as the *Logica* is the more elementary of the two,
it is natural to think that it was written first.

1 Cf. *Times Literary Supplement*, Oct. 1st, 1931, p. 748.
2 No. 83, col. 1811.   3 Pp. 189–90.
4 Pp. 305, 307.
5 See B. Geyer, "Die alten Lateinischen Uebersetzungen der Arist. Analytik", in *Phil. Jahrbuch*, xxx. 1917, p. 38 note 1, and *infra*, Appendix II.

APPENDIX II

THE ARISTOTELIAN TRANSLATIONS KNOWN TO ABAILARD

THE subject of the translations of the *Organon* made during the twelfth century is one which is at present engaging the attention of mediaeval scholars.[1] It is not necessary for us to go fully into the problem; all that is needed is to determine what translations of Aristotle's logical writings were available for Abailard. We know for certain that Boethius translated the *Categories* and the Περὶ Ἑρμηνείας, writing one commentary upon the first and two upon the second, and that his translations were universally used by students in Abailard's day. In addition, translations of the two books of the *Analytics*, of the *Topics*, and of the *Sophistici Elenchi* have been traditionally ascribed to Boethius. Dr Grabmann, arguing that the style of these later translations is markedly inferior to that of his other writings, maintains that these were not the work of Boethius, but of James of Venice.[2] His argument, however, is not fully conclusive. The Latinity of the translations which are indisputably Boethian is no better than that of the translations which Grabmann would have us eject from the Boethian corpus,[3] while we are informed by Boethius himself that he translated the two books of the *Analytics*.[4]

A chronicler—Robert de Monte—tells us that James of Venice translated the *Topics*, the *Analytics*, and the *Sophistici Elenchi* in the year 1128.[5] Since the passage containing this information is written by a later hand, it is possible that the translations were made at a date somewhat after the one specified. Robert or his

---

1 For the problem of Aristotelian translations in the twelfth century, see among others, Grabmann, I. pp. 149–63, II. pp. 64–81; C. H. Haskins, *Studies in Mediaeval Science*, Harvard, 2nd ed. 1924, pp. 223–41; A. Hofmeister, *Studien über Otto von Freising, Neues Archiv*, XXXVII. 1912, pp. 654–81; the prolegomena to C. C. J. Webb's edition of the *Policraticus*, Oxford, 1909, pp. xxxiii ff.

2 I. p. 150; II. p. 71.
3 Cf. Haskins, *op. cit.* pp. 232–3.
4 Cf. PL. 64, coll. 1051, 1052, 1173, 1184, 1193, 1216.
5 Jacobus clericus de Venicia transtulit de Graeco in Latinum quosdam libros Aristotilis et commentatus est, scilicet Topica, Analyticos priores et posteriores et Elenchos, quamvis antiquior translatio super eosdem libros haberetur. *Chron. sub anno* 1128, MGH.SS. VI. p. 489. James afterwards went to Constantinople on an embassy with Anselm of Havelburg in 1135–6; see D'Achéry, *Spic.* XIII. pp. 126 ff., and Anselm's *Dialogus*, PL. 188, col. 1140 B.

emendator adds the significant fact that translations of these three books were already available. By whom these other translations were made the chronicler does not say; it seems, however, highly probable that Robert was referring to the translations of Boethius. Professor Haskins concludes that the reception of the New Logic, consequent upon fresh translations of the *Organon*, ought to be dated in the earlier rather than in the later portion of the period 1121–58.[1] But the earliest book in which the new Aristotelian translations can be traced is probably the still unpublished *Heptateuchon* of Thierry of Chartres, which was written in 1140. The theory that Adam of Petit Pont used the new translations in his *Ars Disserendi* (1132) can no longer be held.[2] It will be evident then that at the time when he wrote his treatises upon logic, Abailard could not have known the translations of James of Venice.

Abailard says that the men of his day were only familiar with the *Categories* and the *de Interpretatione*.[3] It is, however, evident that he knew more of Aristotle's writings than those which he mentions. A passage in his gloss upon the *de Interpretatione* makes it clear that at one time he had read the *Sophistici Elenchi*, although he gives us to understand that that treatise was not well known.[4] It is here that we encounter a difficulty of some magnitude; we cannot identify with any degree of certainty the translation which he used. The quotations which he gives in the passage cited, and elsewhere, are not verbally identical with the Boethian translation as given by Migne. That another translation of the *Elenchi* was then current seems highly improbable. I can only suggest that the many variants known to exist in the MSS. of Boethius are the cause of the textual differences between Abailard's citations and the text of Boethius in the uncritical edition of Migne, and by the additional fact that in the passage to which we refer Abailard appears to have been quoting from memory. References to the two books of the *Analytics* also occur in Abailard's gloss on Porphyry,[5] but they are not in themselves sufficient to allow us to conclude that he was familiar with the entire texts of these books. But in the *Dialectica* there are actually two quotations from the

1 *Op. cit.* pp. 228–9. 1158 is the date of John of Salisbury's *Metalogicus*, which freely uses the New Logic.

2 Hofmeister, *op. cit.* p. 665; Clerval, *Écoles*, p. 224, calls Thierry probably the first vulgarizer of the new translations. For Adam, see B. Geyer, *Philosophisches Jahrbuch*, xxx. 1917, pp. 29–30.

3 Aristotelis enim duos (*scil.* codices) tantum, Praedicamentorum scilicet et Peri ermenia libros usus Latinorum cognovit. *Dialect.* p. 228.

4 Memini tamen quendam libellum vidisse et diligenter relegisse, qui sub nomine Aristotelis de sophisticis elenchis intitulatus erat. *Logica*, p. 400.

5 *Logica*, p. 2.

Prior Analytics, one giving in full Aristotle's definition of a syllogism,[1] while a passage in the gloss on the *de Interpretatione* again shews that Abailard was acquainted with the contents of the book.[2] The quotations, however, given in the *Dialectica* do not come from the translation of Boethius, but, as Geyer points out, from two different versions which were made from the original Greek independently of each other.[3] From Boethius Abailard was also aware that Andronicus had queried the authenticity of the *de Interpretatione* as an Aristotelian work,[4] and from the same source he learnt something of the criticism of Herminus and Alexander of Aphrodisias.

Prantl has argued that Abailard only knew of the *Prior Analytics* through hearsay, but this seems improbable as a theory. From his quotations from the book and his knowledge of its contents it is safe to assume that, despite his reticence, Abailard really had first-hand acquaintance with the treatise.[5] This knowledge of both the *Prior* and the *Posterior Analytics* may have been derived from some MS. of the Boethian translation to which at present we have no access. The date of the *Logica* and the texts of the quotations it contains will not allow us to suppose that Abailard used the translation of James of Venice.[6] It is more probable that Abailard was dependent upon some other version or versions than those of Boethius, and the fact that other translations of the *Posterior Analytics* were in existence has been proved by Professor Haskins. Dr Haskins has discovered at Toledo a MS. containing a triple translation of the *Posterior Analytics,* the Boethian version, a version clearly made from the Arabic translation, and a third, which, on account of the difficulty of access to the library, he was unable to identify.[7] One difficulty, however, presents itself in this connexion; John of Salisbury states that in his time the *Posterior Analytics* was hardly used.[8] But this does not preclude the possibility that more than one translation was available in France for those who wished to study it.

Abailard knew neither the *Metaphysics* nor the *Physics* of Aristotle, both of which, as he says,[9] were not yet translated. He

1 *Dialectica,* p. 305; cf. also p. 307.
2 *Logica,* p. 394, where reference is erroneously made to the *Posterior Analytics.*
3 Geyer, *op. cit.* p. 35.
4 *Logica,* p. 3; see Boethius, Περὶ Ἑρμ., ed. Meiser, II. p. 11.
5 Prantl, *Geschichte der Logik,* II. p. 103. See Hofmeister, *op. cit.* p. 664, and Geyer, p. 37.
6 Geyer, pp. 38–9.
7 Toledo MS. 17–14; Haskins, *Studies,* pp. 228–9.
8 *Metal.* IV. 6, col. 919 D.   9 *Dialectica,* p. 200.

knew of their existence, however, from references in Boethius.[1]
From Chalcidius he learnt that Aristotle held that the soul was
the form of the body,[2] but he was totally ignorant of the real
significance of this doctrine. In the *Dialectica* he denies that he
possessed any knowledge of Aristotle's teaching upon psychology.[3] Both in his own commentary and elsewhere, Abailard
utilized Boethius' translation of the *Isagoge* of Porphyry and his
commentary upon that book. The commentary which Boethius
made upon the *Topics* of Cicero was also known to him. For his
knowledge of grammar Abailard was dependent upon the
writings of Priscian, who is often cited.

1 *Logica*, p. 316; Boethius, Περὶ Ἑρμ., *ed. cit.* ii. p. 28.
2 Chalcidius, *Platonis Timaeus*, ed. Wrobel, p. 262, quoted *Logica*, p. 212.
3 *Dialectica*, p. 206.

SHORT BIBLIOGRAPHY

ABAILARD. *Ouvrages inédits*, ed. V. Cousin, Paris, 1836.
—— *Petri Abaelardi Opera*, ed. Cousin, Paris, 1849, 1859.
—— *Opera Omnia*, PL. 178.
—— *Dialogus*, ed. Henke and Lindenkohl, Marburg, 1851.
—— *De Unitate et Trinitate Divina*, ed. R. Stölzle, Freiburg, 1891.
—— *Die philosophischen Schriften Peter Abaelards*, ed. B. Geyer, 1919–27 (BGPM. XXI. 1–3).
—— "Ein neuaufgefundenes Bruchstück der Apologia Abaelards", ed. P. Ruf and M. Grabmann (*Sitzungsberichte der Bayerischen Akademie der Wissenschaften*, Phil.-hist. Abt. 1930, Heft 5).
ADELARD OF BATH. *De Eodem et Diverso*, ed. H. Willner, 1903 (BGPM. IV. 1).
ANSELM, ST. *Exameron*, ed. C. Schenkl, 1897 (CSEL. XXXII).
—— *Opera Omnia*, PL. 158–9.
ANSELM OF LAON. *Systematische Sentenzen*, ed. P. Bliemetzrieder, 1919 (BGPM. XVIII. 2–3).
BALTZER, O. *Beiträge zur Geschichte des christolog. Dogmas im XI und XII Jahrh.*, Leipzig, 1902.
BEDE. *Opera Omnia*, PL. 90–95.
BERNARD, ST. *Opera Omnia*, PL. 182–5.
BERNARD SYLVESTER. *De Mundi Universitate*, ed. C. S. Baruch and J. Wrobel, Innsbruck, 1876.
BETT, H. *Johannes Scotus Erigena*, Cambridge, 1925.
BOETHIUS. *Opera Omnia*, PL. 63–4.
—— *In Isagogen Porphyrii Commenta*, ed. S. Brandt, 1906 (CSEL. XXXVIII).
—— *Commentarii in librum Aristotelis*, περὶ ἑρμηνείας, ed. C. Meiser, Leipzig, 1877, 1880.
DU BOULAY (BULAEUS). *Historia universitatis Parisiensis*, Paris, 1665–73.
Chronica Mauriniacensis. Ed. L. Mirot, Paris, 1909.
CLERVAL, A. *Les Écoles de Chartres au Moyen-Âge*, Paris, 1895.
DENIFLE, H. S. *Die Entstehung der Universitäten des Mittelalters bis 1400*, Berlin, 1885.
—— "Die Sentenzen Abaelards und die Bearbeitungen seiner Theologie", ALKG. I. Berlin, 1885.
DENIFLE, H. S. and CHATELAIN, E. *Chartularium Universitatis Parisiensis*, I. Paris, 1889.
DEUTSCH, S. M. *Die Synode von Sens 1141 und die Verurtheilung Abaelards*, Berlin, 1880.
—— *Peter Abälard, ein kritischer Theologe*, Leipzig, 1883.
DITTRICH, O. *Geschichte der Ethik*, III. 1926.
FOURNIER, P. *Études sur Joachim de Flore*, Paris, 1909.
GANDULPH. *Gandulphi Bononiensis Sententiarum libri* IV, ed. J. de Walter, Vienna, 1924.
GERHOH OF REICHERSBERG. *Liber de Novitatibus*, MGH. *Libelli de Lite*, III.
GEYER, B. *Die Stellung Abaelards in der Universalienfrage*, BGPM. Supplementband, I. 1913.
—— "Die alten Lateinischen Uebersetzungen der Aristotelischen Analytik", *Philosophisches Jahrbuch*, XXX. 1917.

GHELLINCK, J. DE. *Le Mouvement théologique du XIIe siècle*, Paris, 1914.
GRABMANN, M. *Die Geschichte der scholastischen Methode*, Freiburg, 1909, 1911.
—— *Mittelalterliches Geistesleben*, Munich, 1926.
HASKINS, C. H. *Studies in the History of Mediaeval Science*, 2nd ed. Harvard, 1927.
—— *The Renaissance of the Twelfth Century*, Harvard, 1927.
HAURÉAU, B. *Histoire de la philosophie scolastique*, Paris, 1872.
—— *Notices et Extraits de quelques manuscrits latins de la Bibliothèque nationale*, Paris, 1880 ff.
HEITZ, TH. *Essai historique sur les Rapports entre la Philosophie et la Foi*, Paris, 1909.
HOFMEISTER, A. "Studien über Otto von Freising", *Neues Archiv*, XXXVII. 1912.
HUGH OF ST VICTOR. *Opera Omnia*, PL. 175–7.
JEROME. *Opera Omnia*, PL. 22–31.
JOHN OF CORNWALL. *Eulogium ad Alexandrum III*, PL. 199.
JOHN OF SALISBURY. *Opera Omnia*, PL. 199.
—— *Policraticus*, ed. C. C. J. Webb, Oxford, 1909.
—— *Metalogicon*, ed. Webb, Oxford, 1929.
—— *Historia Pontificalis*, ed. R. L. Poole, Oxford, 1927.
JOHN SCOTUS ERIGENA. *Omnia Opera*, PL. 122.
KAISER, E. *Pierre Abélard, critique*, Thesis, Freiburg, 1901.
LOOFS, F. *Dogmengeschichte*, 4th ed. Leipzig, 1904.
MIGNON, A. *Les Origines de la Scolastique et Hugues de Saint-Victor*, Paris, 1895.
OTTO OF FREISING. *Gesta Frederici*, ed. de Simson, Hannover, 1912.
PAULUS, N. *Geschichte des Ablasses im Mittelalter*, I. Paderborn, 1922.
PICAVET, F. *Roscelin, philosophe et théologien*, Paris, 1902.
POOLE, R. L. *Illustrations of the History of Mediaeval Thought and Learning*, 2nd ed. London, 1920.
PRANTL, K. *Geschichte der Logik im Abendlande*, Leipzig, 1885.
RADULFUS ARDENS. *Opera Omnia*, PL. 155.
RÉMUSAT, C. DE. *Abélard*, Paris, 1845.
RHABANUS MAURUS. *Opera Omnia*, PL. 107–12.
RIES, J. *Das geistliche Leben in seinen Entwicklungsstufen nach der Lehre des hl. Bernard*, Freiburg, 1906.
ROBERT, G. *Les écoles et l'enseignement de la théologie pendant la première moitié du XIIe siècle*, Paris, 1909.
ROLAND. *Sentenzen*, ed. A. M. Gietl, Freiburg, 1901.
SCHRÖRS, H. *Hinkmar, Erzbischof von Reims*, Freiburg, 1884.
SEEBERG, R. *Dogmengeschichte*, III. Leipzig, 1913.
Sententiae Divinitatis. Ed. B. Geyer, 1909 (BGPM. VII. 2–3).
Sententiae Florianenses. Ed. H. Ostlender, Bonn, 1929 (*Florilegium Patristicum*, fasc. XIX).
SUGER. *Vita Ludovici*, ed. A. Molinier, Paris, 1887.
UEBERWEG, F. *Grundriss der Geschichte der Philosophie, die patristische und scholastische Philosophie*, ed. B. Geyer, Berlin, 1928.
VACANDARD, E. *Vie de St Bernard*, Paris, 1920.
WEBB, C. C. J. *Studies in the History of Natural Theology*, Oxford, 1915.
WILLIAM OF CONCHES. *De Philosophia Mundi*, PL. 172, coll. 39–102.
WILLIAM OF ST THIERRY. *Opera Omnia*, PL. 180.
WITELO. *Opera*, ed. C. Baeumker, 1908 (BGPM. III. 2).

INDEX

(a) NAMES AND PLACES

Adam of Bremen, 64
Adam of Petit Pont, 94, 106
Adam, abbot of St Denys, 13, 19
Agobard, 49 n.
Alan of Clairvaux, 224
Alan of Lille, 191
Alberic of Rheims, 9, 15, 150, 234, 259, 265
Albert the Great, 147 n.
Alcuin, 35 n.
Alexander of Aphrodisias, 274
Alger of Liège, 216 n., 244
Alvisus, bishop of Arras, 230, 231
Ambrose, St, 132, 133, 134 n., 138 n., 139
Ambrosiaster, the, 113
Anaxagoras, 116
Andronicus, 274
Anseau de Garlande, 20
Anselm, abbot of Bury, 169 n.
Anselm of Canterbury, St, xv, 53, 60, 97, 113, 118, 133 n., 169 n., 181, 182, 193, 194 n., 201, 205, 206, 219, 240, 242, 244, 252, 253
Anselm of Havelburg, 272 n.
Anselm of Laon, 8, 15, 51, 56, 74, 86, 212, 225 n., 244, 255, 264
Aratus, 64
Aristotle, 28, 180, 241, 271, 272 ff.
Arnold of Brescia, 26, 227
Astralabe, 12, 237, 258
Augustine, St, xii, 38, 45, 69, 72, 73, 79, 113, 114, 115 n., 118, 122 n., 125, 127 n., 131 n., 132, 133, 136, 137 n., 139, 141 n., 143 n., 144 n., 145, 149, 150, 153, 161 n., 164, 172, 180, 181, 182, 188, 190, 191 n., 202 n., 205, 207, 212 n., 240, 248, 252

Baeumker, C., 113 n.
Baltzer, O., 172 n.
Basil, St, 135 n.
Batiffol, P., 270 n.

Bede, 18, 132, 134 n., 135 n., 136 n., 137 n., 138, 140 n., 141 n., 142 n.
Berengar (Abailard's father), 1, 6
Berengar of Poitiers, 232, 233, 238 ff.
Berengar of Tours, xiv, 51, 216
Bernard of Chartres, 64, 66 n.
Bernard of Clairvaux, St, 13, 20, 21, 30, 35, 46, 63, 120 n., 155, 157, 159 ff., 166, 168, 169 n., 181, 193, 194 n., 214 ff., 216 n., 219, 221 ff., 230 n., 232 ff., 240, 248, 250, 254 ff., 258, 261, 265, 270
Bernard Sylvester, 66, 97
Bernold of Constance, 87, 243, 264
Bett, H., 50 n., 51 n.
Boethius, xii, 50, 83, 89 n., 92 n., 96 n., 103, 108, 109, 110, 111, 119 n., 124, 146, 151 n., 169, 180, 220, 249, 272, 274, 275 n.
du Boulay, 10 n., 16 n.
Bouuart, C., 244 n.
Burchard of Worms, 212

Calixtus I, pope, 196
Calixtus II, pope, 235
Cambridge Songs, xiii
Carmina Burana, 270
Casey, R. P., 169 n.
Chalcidius, 28, 66 n., 116 n., 275
Charlemagne, xiii, 64
Chartreuse, the Grande, 239
Chossat, P., 244 n.
Cicero, xiii, 64 n., 66 n., 69, 88, 109, 110, 113 n., 116, 128 n., 275
Claudianus Mamertus, 65
Clement of Alexandria, 69
Clerval, A., 16 n., 107 n., 264
Conon of Praeneste, 15, 16
Cornificius, 55, 56
Council of Arras (1025), 192
    of Châlons (813), 191, 198
    of Lateran (1179), 174
    of Lateran (1215), 198
    of Paris (829), 191

Council of Rheims (1148), 232
    of Rouen (1048), 195
    of Sens (1140), 228 ff.
    of Soissons (1121), 15, 16, 17
Cyril of Alexandria, 174

Deissmann, 205 n.
Denifle, H., 16 n., 51 n., 77 n., 174 n.,
    242 n., 247 n., 266, 269
Denys, St, 18
Denys, abbey of St, 13, 236, 237, 256
Deutsch, S. M., 29, 30 n., 39 n., 42 n.,
    82, 229, 230, 231, 259 n., 264,
    268
Disputatio anonymi abbatis, 155 n.,
    161 n., 203 n.
Donatus, 56
Dorner, J. A., 174 n.
Duchesne, A., 258

Eadmer, 4 n.
Eckbert, 192 n.
Elipandus, bishop of Toledo, xiv
Éon l'Étoile, 264
Epistle of Barnabas, 62
Epitome, the, 126 n., 129, 161, 175,
    176 n., 177 n., 212, 217, 233,
    245, 246
Ermengard, 199
Eugenius III, pope, 232
Eusebius, 14 n., 18 n., 78

Felix, bishop of Urgel, xiv
Florian, *Sentences* of St, 129, 161, 212,
    245, 246
Fournier, P., 63 n., 77 n.
Fulbert, bishop of Chartres, xiv
Fulbert of Notre-Dame, 11, 13, 262
Fulk of Deuil, 14, 247

Gandulph, 120 n., 132 n.
Gaufred, 235 n.
Geoffrey of Auxerre, 148 n.
Geoffrey of Clairvaux, 226
Geoffrey Col de Cerf, 17
Geoffrey of Lèves, bishop of Chartres,
    16, 225
Gerbert of Aurillac, 85
Gerhoh of Reichersberg, 173
Gervaise of Canterbury, 26 n.
Geyer, B., 97 n., 102 n., 103 n., 104 n.,
    166 n., 258, 269 n., 271 n., 273 n.

de Ghellinck, 27 n., 49, 212 n.
Gieseler, H., 268 n.
Gilbert Porrée, 107, 108, 146, 147 ff.,
    150, 153, 232, 249, 264, 265
Gilbert the Universal, bishop of Lon-
    don, 265
Gildas, abbey of St, 22, 23, 189, 236,
    237, 256, 269
Godell, William, 21 n.
Goldhorn, J. D. H., 259, 264
Gosvin, prior of St Médard, 6, 17
Gottschalk, 155
Grabmann, M., 36 n., 71 n., 82 n.,
    87, 97 n., 156, 242, 259 n., 272 n.
Gratian, 199, 243, 252
Gregory I, pope, 51 ff., 181, 190,
    191 n., 196
Gregory of Tours, 78
Gualo, 56
Guido of Castello (Calixtus II), 235

Haskins, C. H., 63 n., 272 n., 273, 274
Hatto, bishop of Tours, 20, 230, 231
Hauréau, B., 258
Haymo, 78, 79
Heitz, Th., 36 n.
Héloise, 11, 12, 13, 23, 132, 141, 237,
    255, 256, 261, 269, 271
Henry le Sanglier, archbishop of
    Sens, 228
Hermann, 269
Hermes Trismegistus, 65
Herminus, 274
Hilary of Poitiers, 176
Hildegarde, St, 140 n.
Hilduin, 18
Hincmar, archbishop of Rheims, 155,
    243
Hofmeister, A., 25, 272 n., 273 n.
Hugh Farsitus, 215 n.
Hugh Metellus, 226
Hugh of Mortagne, 224 n.
Hugh of St Victor, 49 n., 129, 131 n.,
    132 n., 161, 174 n., 177, 213,
    215, 240, 244, 245 n., 253
Hugonin, A., 14 n.
Humbert of Silva Candida, cardinal,
    214
Hyacinth, cardinal, 239

Innocent II, pope, 24, 25, 226, 234,
    235, 261

Irenaeus, 205
Isidore of Seville, 71, 193, 207 n.
Ivo, bishop of Chartres, 77 n., 85, 212
Ivo, cardinal of St Laurence, 235

Jacques of Vitry, 229 n.
James of Venice, 271, 272, 274
Jerome, St, 12 n., 18 n., 29, 30, 45, 72 n., 78, 132, 135 n., 196
Joachim da Fiore, 63
John Chrysostom, St, 162
John of Cornwall, 173, 243
John Damascene, 174
John Duns Scotus, 104
John of Salisbury, 8, 26, 51, 94 n., 106 ff., 113, 148 n., 220 n., 232, 243, 264, 275
John Scotus Erigena, 50, 113, 118, 202 n.
John of Seville, 215 n.
Joscelin, bishop of Soissons, 6, 127 ff., 254, 265
Josephus, 137 n.
Justin Martyr, 73

Kaiser, E., 66 n., 81 n.
Klibansky, R., 228 n.

Lanfranc, archbishop of Canterbury, 216
Lea, H. C., 190 n.
Le Bras, G., 244 n.
Leclercq-Hefele, 192 n.
Loofs, F., 39 n.
Lotulf of Lombardy, 9, 15, 234, 255, 259
Louis VI, 20, 265
Louis VII, 230, 231, 265
Lucan, 8
Lucia, 1, 6, 7

Macrobius, 28, 58, 66, 67, 105
Manegold of Lautenbach, 64, 66 n.
Marchiennes, 230
Maurice of Sully, 243
Médard, abbey of St, 17, 236, 238
Mende, bishop of, 239
Meyer, Wilhelm, 232
Michaud, E., 4 n., 7 n.
Mirbt, C., 214 n.
Morigny, 25

Nicholas, 231, 235, 255
Norbert of Prémontré, St, 21, 46, 47, 254

Omnibene, 86, 126 n., 194 n., 213, 245, 246
Ordericus Vitalis, 231
Origen, 14, 45, 77, 122, 196
Ostlender, H., 269
Otto, bishop of Freising, 1, 2, 8 n., 9 n., 10 n., 26, 106, 148 n., 166, 232 n., 235 n., 261
Ovid, 6

Paraclete, oratory of the, 21
Paulus, N., 195 n.
Peter de Bruys, 32, 213, 236, 262
Peter Damiani, 63, 120, 124, 214
Peter the Lombard, 113, 129, 130 n., 173, 174, 175, 194 n., 198, 199, 244 ff., 248, 256
Peter the Venerable, 230, 231, 235 ff., 263
Philip Augustus, 247
Picavet, F., 2 n., 4, 10 n.
Plato, 28, 61, 65 ff., 115, 116, 134, 139, 219
Poole, R. Lane, 1 n., 3 n., 10, 260, 261, 264 n.
Porphyry, xiii, 88, 151 n., 220, 275
Prantl, C., 90 n.
Priscian, 96 n., 97, 105

Quincey, 20, 22

Radbertus, xiv, 216
Radulfus Ardens, 190 n., 191 n.
Rainald of Martigné, archbishop of Rheims, 230
Ralph of Laon, 8, 56, 264
Rand, E. K., 63 n.
Ratramnus, xiv, 216
Rémusat, C., 10 n., 19 n.
Reuter, H., 82
Revelatio S. Eleutherii, 229 n., 230 n.
Richard of Hexham, 10 n.
Richard of Poitou, 1 n., 244 n.
Rictrude, abbey of St, 230
Ries, J., 35 n., 221 n.
Rhabanus Maurus, xiv, 64, 86, 113, 140 n., 191 n., 212, 216
Robert of Auxerre, 21 n., 229

Robert of Melun, 162, 163, 239, 243
Robert de Monte, 3 n., 262, 273
Robert Pullen, 220
Robert, G., 259, 262 n., 265, 271
Roland Bandinelli (pope Alexander III), 40, 86, 120 n., 126 n., 130 n., 131 n., 161 n., 174, 194 n., 200, 213 n., 243, 245 ff.
Roscelin of Compiègne, xi, xv, 2 ff., 15, 32, 45 ff., 90, 103, 113, 146, 148, 166, 249, 252, 254, 264
Rupert of Deutz, 217

Sägmüller, J. B., 224 n.
Saltet, L., 214 n.
Salvian, 66 n.
Sandys, J. E., 63 n.
Schrörs, H., 85 n.
Schmoll, P. P., 190 n., 193 n., 194 n., 199 n.
Seeberg, R., 50 n., 108 n., 147 n., 205 n., 213 n., 217 n.
Sententiae Divinitatis, 192 n.
Sibyl, the, 68
Sigebert of Gembloux, 264 n.
Stephen de Garlande, 20
Stephen, bishop of Paris, 228
Stephen, cardinal of Praeneste, 235
Stölzle, R., 258, 260, 261, 262
Suger, abbot of St Denys, 13, 19, 20, 23
Summa Sententiarum, 35 n., 126 n., 194 n., 199

Tanquelm, 32, 262, 263

Theobald, count of Champagne, 19
Theodulf of Orleans, 199
Theophrastus, 12 n.
Thierry of Chartres, 2, 264, 273
Thomas Aquinas, St, xvi, 38 n., 39, 60, 75, 103, 105 n., 162 n., 192 n., 219, 245, 252

Ulger, bishop of Angers, 265

Vacandard, E., 14 n., 227 n.
Valerius Maximus, 70
Victor, abbey of St, 4
Virgil, xiii, 61, 64, 68

Waddell, Helen, 11 n.
Walter of Mortagne, 37, 57 n., 94, 106, 157, 241, 266
Watkins, O. D., 190 n.
Webb, C. C. J., 27 n., 35 n., 272 n.
Wibert, 56
William of Champeaux, 3, 5, 7, 93, 106, 212, 223, 225 n., 242, 254
William of Conches, 113 n., 134, 135 n., 161
William de Garlande, 20
William of Malmesbury, xv n.
William of Nangey, 21 n.
William of Newburgh, 264 n.
William of St Thierry, 27, 155, 156, 157, 162, 167, 170 n., 224, 225, 239, 241, 248, 265, 267 n.
de Wulf, M., 14 n., 96 n., 226 n.

Ziegler, Th., 184 n.

(b) SUBJECTS

Abailard's writings, 26, 258
Arianism, brought against Abailard, 185
Astrology, 139
Atonement, 204, 222

Baptism, 216
Bible, the, mistakes in, 42; authority of, 43

Canon Law, 85, 243
'Catholic', meaning of, 40
Celibacy, 186

Christ, as the Λόγος, 48, 168; as quaedam potentia, 157; Eternal Generation, 163; Birth, 170; the Two Natures, 171; his power of sinning and volition, 175; as Mediator between God and man, 210
Classics, propriety of reading the, 63
Confession, 190, 193 ff.
Confirmation, 216

Dialectic, improper use of, 54; correct rôle, 59, 83

Disputation, 242

Eucharist, the, 213, 216

Faith, assent, 32; intellectualism, 35; voluntarism, 35; understanding of faith, 36; faith as *existimatio*, 38
Foreknowledge of God, 121

God, proofs of existence, 114; unity, 117; being shewn by analogies, 119; omnipotence, 120; limited activity, 122, 127; his government of the world, 125; immutability, 126; will, 127
Grace, 202

Ideas of God, the, 105, 133
Imagination (φαντασία), 97
Immaculate Conception, the, 169
Indifferentism, 5, 93

Justification by faith, 39, 211

Native forms (*formae nativae*), 107
Natural Law, 71
Nominalism, 90, 105
Nominalistic theology, 146, 166
Notae, 111
Notiones, 110

Old Testament, Trinitarian teaching in, 62
Original guilt, 211
Original Sin, 181, 200 ff.

Patripassianism, 152
Penance, 190, 193 ff.
Predestination, 121
Psychology, 97
Punishment, theory of, 189 ff.

Realism, 95
Reason, necessary for faith, 45; use justified, 48; in Gregory the Great, 51 ff.

Sabellianism, 15, 152, 165
Sacraments, 212 ff.
Sin, character of, 180; venial sin, 188
Spirit, Procession of the Holy, 164
Status, in Walter of Mortagne, 94; in Abailard, 101, 104
Stoicism, 50, 73, 109

Trinity, doctrine of the, 145 ff.

Understanding, the (διάνοια), 97

Voluntarism, 35
Vox, 99, 111

World-Soul (νοῦς), 66